Luke, the Jew

Peter van 't Riet

LUKE, THE JEW

Introduction to the Jewish Character
of the Gospel of Luke and the Acts of the Apostles

Folianti

Original title in Dutch: Lukas, de Jood
© Folianti, Zwolle, The Netherlands 2009 (3d revised printed edition)

Translated into English by Dick Broeren Sr
© Folianti, Zwolle, 2012 (E-book edition)

© Folianti, Kampen, 2018 (Paperback edition)
ISBN/EAN: 978-90-76783-45-1

NUR-code: 703 (Bible Sciences)

All rights reserved. Nothing in this publication is allowed to be multiplied, stored in an automated database and/or published, in any form, or in any way, neither electronically, nor mechanically, by press, photocopies, microfilm, records or in what way ever, without preliminary and written permission given by the publisher.

Content

PREFACE	9
To the English paperback edition	9
1. LUKE, THE BELOVED PHYSICIAN?	**11**
The Luke-tradition	11
2. DO YOU KNOW GREEK?	**16**
The language of Luke	16
2.1 Hebrew and Aramaic as languages of Judaism	16
2.2 Greek, the language of the Diaspora	19
2.3 The Semitic character of the Greek of the Jews	25
2.4 The language of Luke	28
2.5 The public he wrote for	33
2.6 Conclusions	34
3. AND THEY WORKED TOGETHER	**35**
The use of technical terms by Luke	35
3.1 Medical terms	35
3.2 Nautical terms	37
3.3 Legal terms	39
3.4 Political terms	40
3.5 Conclusions	45
4. AND IT BEGAN WITH MOSES AND WITH ALL THE PROPHETS	**46**
The midrash-character of the gospels	46
4.1 The origin of the gospels	46
4.2 John the Baptist	50
4.3 John the Baptist according to Matthew	51
4.4 The other vision of Luke	53
4.5 John the Baptist according to Luke	55

Content

    4.6 The Song of Mary ..., or of Elizabeth? 57
    4.7 The gospels as midrash 60
        a. Tanakh as a starting-point 61
        b. The transformation of history 63
        c. The didactic-polemic character of midrash 65
        d. Difference of opinion 66

5. AMONG OURSELVES **68**
    Author, adressee and purpose 68
    5.1 The prefaces 68
        a. Among us: Christians? 70
        b. Among us, the Apostles? 71
        c. Among us, disciples? 72
        d. Among us, eye-witnesses and servants of the word? 72
    5.2 The we-stories 79
    5.3 Most excellent Theophilus 82
    5.4 The purpose of the Gospel of Luke and the Acts 84

6. IN THE ENTIRE JEWISH LAND **86**
    Jesus' stay in Galilea-Judea 86
    6.1 Geography and composition 86
    6.2 The comparison with Mark 88
    6.3 Extra information about geographical sites 91
    6.4 The lake and the sea 94
    6.5 Extension from Galilee to Galilee-Judea 96
    6.6 Removal of gentile regions 99
    6.7 The land of the Gerasenes 101
    6.8 Mentioning Galilean places 105
        a. Nazareth 105
        b. Capernaum 108
        c. Nain 111
        d. Bethsaida 114

Content

7. THE THINGS THAT MAKE FOR YOUR PEACE 117
    Jesus' travel to and stay in Jerusalem 117
    7.1 The travel story (Luke 9,51 – 19,28) 117
        a. The map of Luke's gospel 117
        b. The Deuteronomic background of the travel-story 124
        c. The character of Jesus' actions 128
    7.2 Jerusalem 134
    7.3 Emmaus 140

8. HE DECIDED TO RETURN THROUGH MACEDONIA 143
    The geography of the Acts of the Apostles 143
    8.1 The map of the Acts 144
    8.2 Antioch in Syria 146
    8.3 Macedonia 149
    8.4 The itinerary of Paul in the second half of the Acts ... 152
    8.5 Paul's travelling company 153
    8.6 Rome 156

9. ZEALOUS TOWARD GOD AS YOU ALL ARE TODAY 159
    Factions in Judaism 159
    9.1 The Pharisees 160
        a. The Pharisees in Luke in comparison with Mark and Matthew
        160
        b. The character of the Pharisaic movement 164
        c. The evangelists' attitude towards the Pharisees 168
        d. Luke and the School of Hillel 169
        e. The conflict with the strictest Pharisees 173
        f. Summary and conclusion 175
    9.2 The Sadducees and the chief priests 176
    9.3 The Zealots 188
        a. The Zealots are only mentioned sporadically 189
        b. Analogies and differences between Luke and the Zealots 193
        c. The polemic against the Zealots 198

Content

10. FOR THE HOPE OF ISRAEL 206
    ISRAEL AND THE NATIONS 206
    10.1 THE JEWS.. 206
    10.2 THE GENTILES 210
    10.3 THE ROMANS 213

NOTES 218
LITERATURE 229
ABOUT THE AUTHOR 233

Preface
To the English paperback edition

The first Dutch edition of this book appeared in 1984. Reprints appeared in 1997 and 2009. I wrote this book to show that the gospel of Luke and the Acts of the Apostles should and could be read in a way completely different from the way it was read and is still being read in Christianity. The fact is that as soon as we're going to read these books as Jewish texts by a Jewish author for a Jewish audience we'll understand them better than read as Christian texts, written by a non-Jewish Christian author for a Christian audience. The theme of this book is: For centuries Luke was thought of as a Greek and I will make it perfectly clear that he's a Jew rooted in the Judaism of his days. This idea, of course, didn't come out of the blue in 1984. After the World War II an increasing number of Jewish scholars took up the study of the New Testament: Joseph Klausner, Schalom Ben Chorin, David Flusser, Pinchas Lapide, Samuel Sandmel, Geza Vermes, Paul Winter and many others. This book is built on their publications.

The book is especially meant for houses of study, discussion groups and courses on the Jewish character of the Gospels. But it can also be used as a textbook by those interested and – as a stimulant – by theologians and bible-scholars alike to explain the books of Luke differently. Many recent publications on the work of Luke show undeniably that the theme of this book is still topical – even after 30 years! For yet many exegetes still take the unproven assumption that Luke was a non-Jewish author for granted. Consequently my ideas aren't a matter of course in this respect. They are based on a method of bible-reading the results of which differ greatly from the results of the accepted theology.

Moreover, this book assumes that it's read with 'the Bible open'. That's the reason why you'll find only a few quotations of passages from the Bible and those few are usually from the New King James

Preface

Version (NKJV). Sometimes we'll refer to the King James Version (KJV) and in other cases we've added a few corrections of our own.

This book offers you both an exegesis and a lot of background information on the Judaism of the first-century: historical, political, linguistic and social information. The chapters 1, 2, 3, 9 and 10 are mainly informative. In chapter 4 you'll find a discussion about the exegetical method of the midrash and the chapters 5, 6, 7 and 8 stress the exegesis in general. But, of course, exegesis and background information can never be separated completely: otherwise exegesis would become trivial and information pointless.

The English translations of this book as an e-book (2012) and as a paperback (2018) are based on the 3rd revised Dutch edition of 2009. Concerning contents it remained largely unchanged compared with the editions of 1984 and 1997. However, we made a great many textual corrections and tried to modernize the style of the language a little where necessary. We also added some new information for the sake of our line of reasoning. When bible passages played an important part in the argument, more quotations have been added. Those who want to know more about the scholarly sources of the relevant subjects may use the notes and glosses in the back of the book. The notes that give extra information on the current text can be found as footnotes at the bottom of the pages.

With this English translation a wider public could become acquainted with the content of this work, as I am convinced that it is still as topical as almost 30 years ago.

October 2018   Peter van 't Riet

1. Luke, the beloved physician?
The Luke-tradition

A Jewish introduction to the Gospel of Luke and the Acts of the Apostles will certainly have to dedicate some words to the ideas which have existed in the church for centuries about the author of these books. The more so as these notions don't point into the direction of Judaism at all. An old tradition ascribes both books to Luke who would have been a follower, co-worker and physician of Paul. However, there are no clues of this 'Luke-tradition' in the Gospel of Luke and the Acts themselves. Luke can't be found in the Acts, nor a physician among Paul's followers. What we do know about this Luke is from Paul's letter to Philemon (id. 24) and from two Deutero-Paulinic letters[a, 1] (Colossians 4,14 and 2 Timothy 4,11). On the strength of Colossians 4,10-11 it is supposed that he wasn't a Jew but a Greek. The World English Bible translates:

> "Aristarchus ... greets you, and Mark ... and Jesus who is called Justus. These are my **only fellow-workers** for the Kingdom of God **who are of the circumcision**, men who have been a comfort to me."

The words in bold type suggest that Luke who is mentioned some verses later (in verse 14), wasn't a Jew. However, in the original text the words "the only fellow-workers" don't precede the words "who are of the circumcision", but follow on them. The King James Bible (KJV) translates more accurately:

---

[a] The Bible science of today holds only the letters to the Romans, 1 and 2 Corinthians, 1 Thessalonians, Philippians, Galatians and Philemon as true letters of Paul. The other, Deutero-Paulinic letters are written by later followers of Paul (see endnote).

The Luke-tradition

"Aristarchus ... saluteth you, and Marcus ... and Jesus, which is called Justus, who are **of the circumcision. These only** are my fellow-workers unto the kingdom of God, which have been a comfort unto me".

It's clear that the words 'these only' don't refer to those who are 'of the circumcision', but to the 'fellow-workers' or to those 'which have been a comfort unto me'. At best it can be concluded that Luke wasn't a fellow-worker of Paul for the kingdom of God, òr he hadn't been a comfort unto Paul. The conclusion that Luke wasn't circumcised, and consequently wasn't a Jew, can't be drawn from this text! But the so-called Luke-tradition is further weakened by the fact that the letter to the Colossians was not written by Paul himself but by one of his later followers.

Besides, there is a time-gap of almost half a century between the real letters of Paul (ca 50 CE) and the origin of the Gospel of Luke and the Acts (ca 90 CE). Important for us is the question where this Luke-tradition originates from. It can't be denied that it's a time-honoured tradition. For centuries it was handed down unanimously, and if we try to trace its origin we arrive at the end of the second century CE. The church-father Irenaeus is the first who mentions Luke as the author.[2] Irenaeus lived from 130 to 202 CE. Two other writings could be considered to belong to the oldest sources of the Luke-tradition. The first one is the *Codex Muratori*, a kind of canon of gospels and letters, compiled in Rome in about 200 CE.[3] The second one is the Anti-Marcion-prologue to the gospel of Luke written between 160 and 180 CE at the earliest.[4]

The context in which these three traditions ascribe the authorship of the third gospel and the Acts to Luke is an apologetic one. That means that the authorship of Luke played a part in the discussions with heretical movements.[5] A not unimportant fact for our subject, because it was just at the end of the second century CE that the third gospel must have been discussed about. Those were the days when Marcion (85 – 144 CE) and his followers shook the church to its foundations. He proclaimed an absolute contrast between the merciless God of Tanakh (the Hebrew Bible) and the loving God of the gospel. Marcion compiled his own canon in which he included about ten letters of Paul and a heavily modified version of the third gospel. All these books were cleansed by him from so-called Jewish stains. In 144 CE he held a dispute with the presbyters of Rome. Among other things he based his considerations on Luke 5,31-38.[6] But the next verse:

"No man also having drunk old [wine] straightway desires new: for he says, The old is better" (Luke 5,39 KJV),

didn't appear in Marcion's version of the third gospel.[7] Small wonder, because within the context of the rest of Jesus' speech it's rather difficult to explain this verse in any other way than as a message of support to the Jewish tradition.[8] On account of this religious dispute Marcion was excommunicated by the congregation of Rome. After that, he rather successfully began to found congregations of his own everywhere, congregations that formed a threat to the orthodox church till the fifth century.[9]

One can imagine that in the fight against Marcion and his followers – and maybe against other heretical currents as well – it became extremely important for the orthodox church to be able to ascribe her gospels to men of authority. For Irenaeus and also for Tertullian (160 – 225 CE) the reliability of a gospel was closely connected with the apostolic authority of him who had written it. A gospel must have been written by an apostle or by a direct disciple of an apostle.[10] Seen against this background it isn't surprising that one looked for the author of the third gospel and the Acts in the circle around Paul, because it is Paul who plays a prominent part in the Acts.

The Luke-tradition

It must be said moreover, that in those days ascribing a writing to an authoritative writer was quite a common feature. One wasn't guided by considerations of historical correctness. A clear example is the Letter to the Hebrews, ascribed, again, to Paul. The majority of the modern Bible-scholars considers this tradition to be incorrect.[11] Many other examples could be given of this – in modern eyes – remarkable custom. That's the reason why we have to be very careful to accept the Luke-tradition too easily. The more so as the oldest tradition about the evangelists doesn't mention Luke's name at all. The church-father Eusebius (267 – 340 CE) quotes Papias on this subject, who was bishop of Hierapolis in Frygia in Asia Minor at the beginning of the second century CE.[12] He ascribes the first gospel to Matthew and the second to Mark, but keeps silent about Luke. This means that a period of more than a century lies between the origin of the third gospel and the Acts – at the end of the first century CE – and the first time Luke is mentioned as an author. A century of tempestuous developments for the church.

As mentioned above, the third gospel and the Acts themselves offer no clues for the authorship of Luke, the physician of Paul. One did try to find indirect support for this tradition in both books. Because they were written in good Greek, this should point at an author of Greek origin. The use of medical terms would give away the fact that he was a physician. In the next chapters I will show that a lot can be put forward against it. Today this Luke-tradition is no longer taken for granted by everybody. Some scholars accept the authorship of Luke simply because they have no better alternative.[13] Others openly express their doubts and leave the question of the authorship unanswered.[14] One fact, however, is clear to most commentators: the author was a Christian from among the gentiles, who wrote for a public of gentiles or Christians from among the gentiles. In this book I'll present another way of looking at this problem.

THE LUKE-TRADITION

I'll show the possible consequences of a Jewish approach of the gospel of Luke and the Acts for the exegesis of both books. It will become clear then that there are a lot of arguments in favour of the fact that Luke *was a Jew, who wrote for a Jewish public*. Information will come forward that makes it improbable that this 'Luke' is the same person as 'Luke, the physician of Paul'. Who the writer of these books was and whether his name was Luke, is - as far as I am concerned - not known. Yet I'll call him – for convenience' sake – 'Luke', not 'Luke the Greek', but 'Luke the author', or better: *'Luke the Jew'*.

2. Do you know Greek?
The language of Luke

The Gospel of Luke and the Acts of the Apostles were written in Greek just like the other books of the New Testament. This Greek, however, is not the Greek of the great Greek literators and philosophers from the centuries before the beginning of the Common Era (CE). The authors of the New Testament used the so-called *Koinè*, the Vulgar Greek of those days. Luke, in a way, is an exception. Now and then the Greek he writes, can stand the test of literary criticism. He sometimes appears to have a complete command of the Greek language, this in contrast to the other New Testament authors. In these cases he writes in a style that shows great similarity to the classical, Attic Greek. Many commentators look upon this as an argument for his gentile, Greek origin.[15] But before one should come to this conclusion, one should answer two questions:

- Why shouldn't a Jew from the first century CE be able to write a book in correct Greek?
- Is Luke's Greek in every aspect as good as can be expected or does it show features that perhaps point at a Jewish origin?

In this chapter I'll look at the language of Luke against the background of the Judaism of those days and come to the conclusion that on account of his Greek there is more reason to suppose that Luke was a Jew rather than a Greek.

2.1 Hebrew and Aramaic as languages of Judaism

Who reads the Bible in the original will meet three different languages: Hebrew, Aramaic and Greek. The greater part of Tanakh (the Hebrew Bible) is written in Hebrew, the original language of the people of Israel. Some parts, however, are written in Aramaic (Daniel 2,4 – 7,28; Ezra 4,7

THE LANGUAGE OF LUKE

– 7,26; Jeremiah 10,11). This language became the language of every day among the Jews during and after the Babylonian Exile (589 – 538 BCE). But already before this exile the Aramaic language played an important part in Israel. In 2 Kings 18, 26 we read that during the siege of Jerusalem by the Assyrians, the Israelite negotiator asks the Assyrian commander-in-chief:

> "Speak, I pray thee, to thy servants in the Syrian language [i.e. in Aramaic]; for we understand [it]: and talk not with us in the Jews' language [i.e. in Hebrew] in the ears of the people that [are] on the wall" (NKJV[a]).

It's clear that Aramaic as the language of a great foreign power was understood and spoken by the higher circles in Jerusalem. In antiquity knowledge of foreign languages was also a common phenomenon in the capital of a country and especially at the royal court.

Had Aramaic been a foreign language in Israel before the Exile, this changed when Judea and Jerusalem were conquered by the Babylonians. The élite of the population was deported to Babel – here Aramaic was the international vernacular – and Judea also came under the Aramaic speaking reign. For the Jews in Babel as well as in the land of Israel, the Aramaic language grew so important that it gradually pushed aside Hebrew as the common language. Even the old Hebrew letters were replaced by the Aramaic square-script which is even today used in written and printed Hebrew. In that situation Hebrew was only used for religious ends. Not only the holy books, the prayers and hymns of praise, but also the most important traditions were worded in Hebrew. It had become the language of the scribes. The people only knew something about their ancient language as far as they came into the study-houses to study the sacred texts. Aramaic was spoken at

---

a   New King James Version 1982

home, in the countryside, in the streets and squares, and so this situation remained in Israel and in later Babylon till the arrival of the Islam in the seventh century CE.

In the land of Israel Aramaic played an important part as well during the divine services in the synagogue. The lectures from Tanakh were held in Hebrew, but there was a so-called *meturgeman* next to the lecturer, who translated the text from Tanakh word for word into Aramaic, and who, if necessary, provided some extra explanation.[16] Gradually one began to write down these translations and commentaries and this developed into the so-called *Targumim*, collections of books from Tanakh translated into Aramaic and provided with paraphrases on its texts. Also the rabbinical tuition was chiefly done in Aramaic. The Talmud, that great compilation of texts about the Jewish life from the first centuries before and after the beginning of the Common Era, is partly written in Aramaic as well, just like a lot of other rabbinical literature. Together Hebrew and Aramaic formed a linguistic complex in the Judaism of those remote days. Like Dutch and German they were sister-languages. Above all things Hebrew was the holy language, Aramaic the colloquial language. But Aramaic was also the language used for the explanation and interpretation of Hebrew texts.[17] Even today it is not possible to become a rabbi without a thorough knowledge of Aramaic, the second language of Judaism.

Both Jesus and his disciples spoke Aramaic as well. And because of the fact that the New Testament was written in Greek we should bear in mind that what we read, are always translations into Greek of what he once said in Aramaic. Besides, we should realize that between us and Jesus there is always someone else: the evangelist. In the New Testament we come across a number of Aramaic words and sentences that remained untranslated. Some examples are:

- *talitha koum*, 'little girl, get up' (Mark 5,41),
- *ephphata*, 'be opened' (Mark 7,34),

- *abba*, 'father' (Mark 14,36),
- *Eloi, Eloi, lama sebachthani*, 'my God, my God, why have you forsaken me?' (Mark 15,34; Matthew 27,46).

Evidently even in the Christian communities outside the land of Israel where Greek was spoken, Aramaic still was a language that had some meaning and influence.

2.2 Greek, the language of the Diaspora

In the domain of linguistics another development had been of great importance in Antiquity. From the end of the 4th century BCE a new language conquered the entire Middle East: Greek. Its rise as a world-language began with the conquests of Alexander the Great (336 – 323 BCE). Even when from the second century BCE the Romans, who spoke Latin, conquered the entire Mediterranean, Greek remained, especially in the eastern part of the Roman Empire, the international language. Many Roman writers and scholars wrote in Greek. For the Romans too, Greek was the language they used outside their own country, Italy.[18] The question of the Roman commander to Paul at his arrest is in this context illustrative: 'Do you know Greek?'(Acts 21,37). Only in the 2nd century CE Latin began to supersede Greek as the international language.

Greek so completely dominated the culture of the entire Middle East around the beginning of the Common Era, that it's important to review the position of Judaism in this respect. After the Babylonian Exile the Jews dispersed all over the eastern part of the Mediterranean-basin. Also in this Diaspora (dispersion) they kept forming their own communities. These were not only religious communities in our western, twentieth-century sense. They were living, highly organized communities:

- they lived together;
- they spoke their own language;
- they lived according to their own traditions;
- they had their own organizations and administration;
- and within their communities they exercised their own limited jurisdiction.

Sometimes they lived in separate districts of a town, as in Alexandria in Egypt. Sometimes they lived scattered all over a town or district as in Antioch in Syria.[19] But these Jewish communities were never isolated islands. A continual interaction existed with the gentile surroundings. There were contacts in the domain of trade and management but also in the domain of religion. Many gentiles joined the Jewish communities and their synagogues as 'those who feared God'. Many of those God-fearing people embraced Judaism as proselytes and were included in it. Some scholars estimate the number of Jews that lived in the Roman Empire at the beginning of the Common Era to be more than three million[20], others even estimate them to be eight million, that is ten percent of the total population.[21] This enormous size of the then Jewry can only be explained from proselytism, the conversion from paganism to Judaism.[22]

Not much is known of the Diaspora Jewry, but there are some exceptions. Only about the Jews in Alexandria in Egypt we are well-informed by an abundance of literature that has been preserved.[23] The language of this literature is Greek. But also from other sources the image emerges that the Diaspora-Jews used Greek as their common language. The dominant position of this language made it unavoidable that all Jews outside the land of Israel used this language. Many Jews were taught to speak Greek, others were also taught to write it. At first Greek was for many of them the second language next to Hebrew or Aramaic, but in the next generations Greek became the 'mother tongue' for most Jews. For proselytes Greek was the first language they had learned in their childhood. Numerous inscriptions were found that confirm the dominance of Greek as the language of the Diaspora Jewry. For example in Rome six catacombs were discovered, which were used by Jews as a cemetery from the second half of the first century CE. There almost 500 inscriptions were found, seventy-five percent in Greek.[24]

The position of the Greek language was so dominant that even Hebrew as the language for religious ends was superseded in many respects. Already in the period of 350 to 150 BCE the Septuagint appeared, a translation of the Hebrew Bible into Greek. This Septuagint became very popular and was widely spread. After ample discussions the rabbis approved of the use of this translation.[25] This approval applied only to Greek that was considered to be the only language that made a somewhat adequate translation possible.[26] The fact that this process was very much discussed about becomes understandable when one reads the warning written by Jesus Sirach's grandson a century before the beginning of the Common Era in the Greek translation of the book of wisdom originally written by his grandfather in Hebrew:

> "You are asked then to read with sympathetic attention, and make allowances if, in spite of all the devote work I have put in the translation, some of the expressions appear inadequate. For it is impossible for a translator to find precise equivalents for the original Hebrew in another language. Not only with this book, but with the Law, the Prophets, and the rest of the writings, it makes no small difference to read them in the original."[27]

Here we see how, in ancient times already, one was conscious of the problematic character of translations. These words should not only be seen as a warning to the readers, but also as a sharp criticism to the Septuagint, whose quality of translation left rather a lot to be desired.[28] That's why, in the long run one attempted to make new and better translations. So, next to the Septuagint, some other translations appeared, among others the one by Aquila (a proselyte) and the one by Theodotion (a Jew) at the beginning and the end of the 2nd century CE respectively.[29] These translations, however, never obtained the authority of the Septuagint. That's why they were lost – with the exception of a couple of fragments.

All these translation activities show that many Jews couldn't read Hebrew any longer. But speaking Hebrew and understanding it has also become difficult, if not impossible for many of them. The praises said over bread and wine, that were part of the daily prayers, might be said in Greek.[30] The divine services in the synagogues were held in Greek and this made it necessary to consent to recite the *Shema-Yisrael-prayer*[a] in Greek.[31] Some scholars suppose that the Septuagint came into existence as a kind of Greek Targum.[32] In the synagogues in the Diaspora Tanakh would have been read in Hebrew but for the sake of the audience the text was translated sentence for sentence in Greek. If the audience had understood Hebrew, all this shouldn't have been necessary. So the conclusion is that Greek was the only or main language they spoke and understood.

The part Greek played in the then Jewry wasn't restricted to the Diaspora. In the land of Israel itself Greek was spoken widely by the Jews, particularly in the higher circles. A lot of information points into this direction. Many Jews in Judea, especially those from the highest strata of society, had Greek names. The first Jew with a Greek name we know of, was Antigonos of Socho, an authoritative scribe from the first half of the second century BCE.[33] Also one of the men sent by Judas Maccabee in 161 BCE to the Romans to enter into a treaty of friendship with them, had the Greek name Eupolemos (1 Maccabee 8,17). The princes from the noble family of the Maccabees had Greek names ever since John Hyrkanos (135-104 BCE). Greek names were quite common in those days among the Jewish inhabitants of the land of Israel.

---

a   The Jewish Confession of Faith built around Deuteronomy 6,4.

Greek played a part in other areas as well. Since the reign of King Alexander Jannaios (103-76 BCE) Jewish coins had been struck with inscriptions in Greek. This kind of coins existed up to the last Jewish king Agrippa II (27-100 CE)[34]. A considerable part of the population of Jerusalem must have spoken Greek. Many Diaspora-Jews must have stayed in this 'capital of Jewry' for some time. They often had their own synagogues (Acts 6,9). Very soon already a decision must be made within the young Jewish-Christian community of this city to create a special organisation for the Greek speaking followers. According to Luke seven men were appointed to this end, six Jews and a proselyte. They had all Greek names (Acts 6,1-5). Greek epitaphs from those days found in Jerusalem are probably epitaphs from these Greek-speaking Jews.[35] But for many Jews who did not come from the Diaspora, Greek had also been their common language. This certainly goes for the Herodians, the followers of the Herodian dynasty, who adjusted themselves to a high degree to the Greco-Roman culture.[36] It's highly remarkable that one comes across documents written in Greek in places where one doesn't expect them. For example a letter in Greek was found in Massada addressed to a certain Judas, one of the last survivors of the Jewish War of 66 – 70 CE. The letter is about something quite ordinary: the provision of vegetables.[37] It's conspicuous in this respect that nowhere in the gospels and in the Acts interpreters are mentioned when conversations take place with Romans who, presumably, didn't speak Aramaic or Hebrew. The conclusion can be that many Jews in the land of Israel were more or less familiar with the Greek language, just like today when many Europeans are more or less familiar with the English language.

What's more, Jerusalem was the centre of Judaism, not only of the temple-service, but also of the study of Torah (the five books of Moses), the fundamental law of Judaism. In this spiritual centre the study of Greek must have taken up an important place for several reasons.[38] The contacts with the Jews in the Diaspora were mainly in Greek, as were the contacts with the Roman government. It's even plausible that Greek was taught and studied to be able to make good translations of Hebrew texts for the benefit of the Diaspora-Jews. The Greek translations of several apocryphal books indicate as much.[a] Several rabbinical pronouncements stress the importance of the knowledge of Greek. But there had been some opposition.

During the Jewish War (66 – 70 CE) the Jewish government in Jerusalem issued a prohibition to teach Jewish children Greek.[39] That such a prohibition was considered necessary shows that teaching Greek to the young people in Jerusalem was a widespread phenomenon. Also the strict pharisaic School of Shammai prohibited the use of Greek as part of a series of measures to lessen the contact between Jews and gentiles. Probably this prohibition was carried through during the Jewish War when the religious-inspired and violent liberation movement of the Zealots, that showed a high degree of affinity with the strict Pharisees, was at the zenith of its power.[40]

These and other measures against the use of Greek were never generally accepted. Particularly the more enlightened pharisaic School of Hillel always understood the importance of the knowledge of the Greek language.[41] At the beginning of the 2nd century CE there were at least four scholars in the study-house of this school in Javne who were fluent in Greek. Two of them monitored Aquila's translation.[42] Rabbi Gamliel II at the beginning of the 2nd century CE had many students who spoke Greek and who were taught by him in this language as well.[43] As a colloquial language Greek lasted a long time in Israel next to Aramaic. It's significant that Bar Kochba, the leader of the Jewish revolt in 135 – 137 CE had a letter written in Greek because there was nobody at hand who was able to write a letter in Hebrew.[44] Greek remained recognizable in the language of the rabbis as well. A typically Jewish institute as the Sanhedrin was and is still defined by this Greek

---

a   Cf. the above-mentioned quotation from the prologue of Ben-Sirah.

name. In the Hebrew and Aramaic of the rabbis more than 3000 Greco-Roman words are found.[45]

From the above it appears that there are few reasons to suppose that a book written in good Greek, could not have been written by a Jew. Very many Jews spoke Greek as their 'mother tongue'. A smaller number of them were also able to write it. Why should a Greek-speaking Jew, especially after having received a good education, not be able to write correct Greek? The good Greek of the gospel of Luke and the Acts isn't an argument at all in favour of a Greek instead of a Jewish origin of Luke. In the next paragraph I'll go further into the matter of Jews writing in Greek in the centuries around the beginning of the Common Era. I'll compare that Greek with Luke's language in order to obtain some arguments to define his identity.

2.3 The Semitic character of the Greek of the Jews

The Greek of many books written by Jews in the centuries just before and after the beginning of the Common Era had a clear Semitic character. I.e. it showed a number of features and expressions that originated more from Hebrew and Aramaic than from Greek. Such features or expressions are called *Semitisms*, or – after their original languages – *Hebraisms* or *Aramaisms*.

A nice example of a Semitism in the translation of Genesis 2,23 can be found in older Dutch Bible translations like the so-called *Statenvertaling* (1637), which can be compared with the famous King James Bible (1611). This Bible translation reads: 'She shall be called Wo-man, because she was taken out of Man'. The English words 'woman' and 'man' are related like the original Hebrew words *ishshah* (woman) and *ish* (man). The Dutch language however knows no linguistic relationship between these words. Woman is 'vrouw' in Dutch whereas man is 'man'. The Dutch translators resorted to the analogy of the names given to female animals in Dutch and translated *ishshah* with "mannin", like "aap" (monkey) and "apin" (she-monkey), "leeuw" (lion) and "leeuwin" (lioness). The Semitism "mannin" however never became part of the Dutch vocabulary. If the English language wouldn't have known the word "woman", maybe the English translators had translated the word *ishshah* with "she-man" to render the word-play in Hebrew.

Another example of a Hebraism in English as well as in Greek, we find in Luke 5,12 and 17. Both verses begin in the Greek text with the words *kai egeneto*. To begin a sentence in Greek with this expression is very clumsy indeed from a Greek linguistic point of view. But in the Septuagint this is the usual translation for the Hebrew word *wajêhie* that can often be found at the beginning of a new story and that indicates that a new episode begins (e.g. Genesis 22,1; Jonah 1,1). In English this expression is often translated – at least in the King James Bible – with: 'And it came to pass ... '. In our language this is not the usual way to begin a story and can therefore be seen as a Hebraism. In some new English Bibles this kind of Hebraisms is 'lost in translation'. As a literal translation of *wajêhie* is *kai egeneto* also in Greek a Hebraism that occurs frequently both in the Septuagint as in the gospels.

Not only words and expressions can occur as Semitisms, but also the place of words in a sentence, the use of certain verbs, whether to use certain tenses or not, the sentence structure, head- and subclauses etc.[46] Nowadays these Semitisms are only found in the older Bible translations such as the King James Bible, but they won't be found in the modern translations because the translators like to write as good English as possible. This was quite another matter for the Greek-speaking Jews in the centuries around the beginning of the Christian Era. Their matrix, even the reason for their existence lay for the Greek-speaking Jews essentially in the Hebrew books of the Bible. The centre of Judaism lay in the Aramaic-speaking land of Israel. Greek became the language of the Diaspora-Jews not because they felt themselves to

The Language of Luke

be Greeks but because of the necessary adaptation to their surroundings. Living in their own Jewish communities, they developed an own kind of Greek that was very much characterized by Semitic elements. The Septuagint was written in that kind of Greek with a lot of Semitisms. But not only translations were written in such Semitic Greek, but original writings as well.[47]

To what extent the Greek of the Diaspora-Jews had a Semitic character is difficult to define. There must have been great differences between places, communities or even between people. The most important factor that determined whether a Jewish author wrote a more or less correct classical Greek, appeared to be his social position, and therefore the degree of his general education.[48] For example the Jewish philosopher Philo of Alexandria, a contemporary of Jesus, wrote excellent Greek in the classical Attic style.[49] Flavius Josephus, the great Jewish historian and contemporary of Luke wrote excellent Greek as well,[50] be it with the help of friends to polish his language.[51] Books written by Jews in Greek can be divided into two groups:[52]

- Books with only a few Semitisms.
- Books with a strong Semitic character.

The work of Philo and Josephus belong to the first group and the Gospels of Mark and Matthew, the fourth gospel[a, 53] and the Book of Revelation belong to the second group.[54] In the next paragraph I'll show why the Gospel of Luke and the Acts of the Apostles must be placed in the second group as well and therefore belong to those books that contain a lot of Semitisms.

---

a I don't call this gospel "the Gospel of John" any longer, because in my opinion it isn't written by the apostle John, but by a disciple of Jesus' friend Lazarus (see endnote).

2.4 The language of Luke

As said before, the Greek of Luke is praised by many scholars as good, classical Greek. In ancient times already it was noticed that he wrote better Greek than many other New Testament-authors. The church-father Jerome (347 – 420 CE) even asserts that Luke didn't know any Hebrew or Aramaic.[55] This opinion is also found with modern scholars.[56] For a long time it was held that the language of Luke contained but few Semitisms. For example it's notable that Luke doesn't copy a number of Aramaic and Hebrew words from the other gospels, and replaces them by Greek words. Some examples:

- *satanas* (Mark 1,13), that he replaces by *diabolos* (Luke 4,2);
- *rabbi* (Mark 9,5) that he translates with *epistata* (Luke 9,33);
- *kananaios* (Matthew 10,4) that he renders with *zelotes* (Luke 6,15).

For some people it's clear: Luke wrote his gospel for Greeks and not for Jews.[57] However, this is disputable, because of the mere fact that there are some examples that contradict this conclusion. Luke also uses a number of Aramaic and Hebrew words he doesn't translate at all:

- the word *mammon* (Luke 16,9, 11, 13) that means 'possession' and that even as an Aramaic loanword turned up in English;
- the word *satanas* ('satan'), which he doesn't always replace by *diabolos* (e.g. Luke 22,3).

But these are not the only examples that point into a Semitic direction. Closer investigation proved that Luke's language is more complicated than is often taken for granted. In the first place Luke appears to know the Septuagint very well. He does not only quote regularly from it, he also often chooses his wording under the influence of this Greek translation of the Hebrew Bible.[58] There are a lot of Hebraisms in the Septuagint and it is hardly surprising that some of them have found their way into the Gospel of Luke and the Acts. For example, the verb 'to say' plays a distinctive part in expressions like 'and he answered and said' (Luke 1,60), 'he praised God and said' (Luke 2,28). This is a Hebraism that is often found in both books of Luke's.[59] If we compare the Greek of Luke with the literary, Attic Greek and with the Koinè (the vernacular) of his days, many Semitic characteristics strike the eye. Luke uses more main verbs and less auxiliaries. His sentences are less complicated than those in classic Greek. The position of a verb in a sentence is usually before the subject and the object. With regard to the classical and post-classical Greek he very often unnecessarily uses personal pronouns. This and a lot more points at the Semitic character of his language.[60] Also one finds in both Luke's books Semitisms that are less frequent elsewhere in the New Testament.[61]

It's striking though that not all parts of his books are equally Semitic in colour. There is a large concentration of Semitisms in the first two chapters of his gospel.[62] There is no other part of the same length in the New Testament that has so many Semitisms.[63] Furthermore we come across an accumulation of Semitisms in some parts of Luke's own material, i.e. in the stories that are not found in the other gospels.[64] The first half of the Acts shows many Semitisms as well, but the second half, particularly in the 'European' parts, a lot less. And finally it's a remarkable fact that Luke's Greek improves towards the end of his books.

How should we interpret these facts? Scholars hold rather different views about this. Some hold the view that Luke imitated the Semitic Greek of the Septuagint.[65] No doubt this idea stems from the supposition that Luke was of Greek origin and that originally he wasn't familiar with the Semitic Greek of the Diaspora-Jews. Others point out that in the Gospel of Luke Semitisms occur that can't be explained with the help of the Septuagint.[66] They suppose that Luke used Hebrew or Aramaic sources for some parts of his gospel and the Acts. In respect to these sources he should have translated many expressions literary into Greek.

Both 'explanations' for the Semitisms of Luke are – as far as I am concerned – questionable. The only known document of which can be said with great certainty that Luke used it as a 'source', is the Gospel of Mark.[a, 67] But it is strange at least that Luke doesn't show any respect at all for this source with regard to linguistic wording. When he copies Mark's stories he corrects his language drastically. He not only deals rather freely with the wording but also with the content of the material of Mark. Let us compare Mark 10,46:

"Now they came to Jericho. As he went out of Jericho with his disciples and a great multitude, blind Bartimaeus, the son of Timaeus, sat by the road begging" (NKJV),

with Luke 18,35:

"Then it happened, as he was coming near Jericho, that a certain blind man sat by the road begging" (NKJV).

Luke made no fewer than three changes in Mark's story:

- He changed the departure from Jericho into the arrival at Jericho.
- He omits the disciples and the great multitude.
- He removes the name of the beggar Bartimeus, the son of Timaeus, from the story.

---

a   In my book "Lukas versus Matteüs" (Luke versus Matthew), published in Dutch, I showed that the supposed existence of the source Q leads to several contradictions after comparing some stories in Matthew with parallel stories in Luke. Therefore the hypothetical source Q should be rejected as a model of explanation of the similarities and differences between both gospels (see endnote).

The Language of Luke

That's not exactly what we would call respect for one's sources! In chapter 6 and 7 I'll compare the geography of Luke with the one of Mark in detail. There it'll appear how Luke rewrote Mark's material after his own ideas time and again. So it's quite clear that respect for the sources couldn't be an explanation for the wording and contents of both books of Luke's. It's more likely that Luke had a concept of his own in mind.[68] Why shouldn't he adapt his language to that concept? All the difficulties the scholars here are up against, originate from the fundamental supposition that Luke was a Greek, who wrote for a Greek public.[69] But then the next problem is: why didn't he, for the benefit of his Greek readers, write his stories in his best Greek? The simplest explanation for this all is that Luke was a well-educated Diaspora-Jew, who was not only familiar with the Semitic Greek of his Jewish environment, but also with the more literary Greek of his gentile environment. This supposition isn't artificial at all. Let us take for example an American rabbi. Of course he'll be able to speak good English, but perhaps also an English interpersed with Semitisms. And this does not only apply to rabbis. A lot of American Jews will be able to do that as well. So, as far as Luke is concerned we can state without any reserve that he, as a man well-educated in religion, must have had a more than average knowledge of Hebrew. From this background almost all characteristics of Luke's language can be explained. Only one problem is left to be solved. Why didn't Luke write an equally-balanced Semitic Greek in all parts of his two books? Why do so many Semitisms appear in Luke 1 and 2, less in the rest of his gospel but still a lot, also many in the beginning of the Acts, but a lot less at the end of it?

Conspicuously the lessening of Semitisms in the course of both books of Luke's runs more or less parallel with the lessening of quotations from Tanakh (the Hebrew Bible).[70] The reason for this is without any doubt that Luke considers his gospel to be a direct continuation of Tanakh, while the Acts continue Tanakh by way of his gospel. Now the explanation for the changes in his language is a simple one indeed: the more substance and form he wants to give his stories against the background of Tanakh, the more Semitic becomes his wording.[71] This is not a matter of imitation or respect for his sources, but a matter of inspiration exclusively. Luke uses the language of the literature that inspires him: the Septuagint against the background of the Hebrew text of Tanakh. When this literature does not directly define the content and the form of his stories, he falls back upon the language of his environment, an environment that contained both Jewish and non-Jewish elements. In that environment he also found the literary motives he could make subservient to his writings. This explains for example the excellent Greek of the preface to his gospel (Luke 1,1-4), that is written entirely in the style of the Greek historiography of those days. However, such prefaces can also be found with other Jewish writers, like Flavius Josephus.[72] Someone who is fluent in the languages of his environment and of his background literature will use these languages either consciously or unconsciously according to the possibilities of the story.[73] Some vivid examples of this phenomenon can be found in his gospel and in the Acts.[74] It appears that Luke is inclined to adapt his language to the person who's speaking in the story:

- In the first half of the Acts the apostles usually speak with a lot of Semitisms. James, the brother of Jesus talks about 'Simeon' instead of 'Simon' or 'Peter' (Acts 15,14). *Simeon* is the Hebrew and *Simon* the Greek form.
- The heavenly voice that calls Saul to order, addresses him with his Hebrew name 'Saul' (*Sja'oel*) in stead of 'Saulos' or 'Paul' (Acts 9,4). *Saul* is the Hebrew form, *Saulos* is the Greek form, whereas *Paul(us)* is his Latin name that has, by the way, a completely different meaning.
- The speech of Tertullus (Acts 24,3-8) is not in Luke's own style, but in the style of the orators of those days.[75] Therefore Tertullus is called an 'orator' (Acts 24.1).[76]

- When Paul during his process addresses both Agrippa, the Jew, and Festus, de Roman, he uses a lot of Semitisms towards Agrippa, but good Greek towards Festus (Acts 25 and 26).[77]

These examples show that Luke was perfectly able to adapt his language to his subject, which befits a good writer.
Our reflections on the language of Luke now lead us to a clear conclusion. Luke's language with all peculiarities that can be found in it, could be best explained if we take it for granted that he was a well-educated Diaspora-Jew. He was able to write Greek in a Semitic style as well as in a classic Attic style. What's more, as a good literator he knew how to adapt his style to the subject of his story. One last question should be asked at the end of this chapter: what public did he have in mind when he wrote his books?

2.5 The public he wrote for

The Semitic character of large parts of his gospel and the Acts raises the question whether Luke wrote for Jews instead of gentiles, as was taken for granted by almost all scholars until recently. The language of both books is too often a kind of Greek that non-Jewish Greeks wouldn't have appreciated and certainly wouldn't have used[78] and that therefore was unsuitable to persuade a public of Greeks. So it was quite understandable that Flavius Josephus had his Greek polished by friends,[79] because he wrote for a Greco-Roman public. Why didn't Luke, who was perfectly able to write good Greek, do the same with so many of his stories? Only Jews must have been able to appreciate the Semitic Greek of these stories. They used to read the Septuagint and they knew about the Hebrew-Aramaic origin of their religion. Therefore, the conclusion that Luke wrote for a Jewish public is more plausible than the supposition that he wrote for a non-Jewish public.

2.6 Conclusions

It is clear that the linguistic facts in the Gospel of Luke and the Acts of the Apostles point rather into the direction of a Jewish author and a Jewish reading public than into the direction of a non-Jewish author and a non-Jewish reading public. However, linguistic data only are not sufficient to 'prove' the conclusion that Luke was a Jew. Because these data allow too many different interpretations. Therefore I am going to look for other facts in the next chapters, facts that may lead to similar or supporting conclusions. But first I'll show in chapter 3 that Luke indeed had been a man with a good general education, who was certainly well-informed on the Greco-Roman world in which he lived and about which he wrote.

3. And they worked together
The use of technical terms by Luke

Many scholars have considered the use of medical terms in the Gospel of Luke and the Acts of the Apostles. They did so in view of the supposition that the writer of both books would have been Luke, the physician of Paul. In this chapter I'll scrutinize Luke's use of medical terms and discuss the eventual conclusions. Next attention will be payed to the use of terms in other fields like shipping and navigation, Roman jurisdiction and politics.

3.1 Medical terms

Medical terms are found in a number of places in the Gospel of Luke and in the Acts:

- In Luke 6,6 a man with 'a withered hand' comes up;
- In Luke 8,43 a woman is described 'having a flow of blood for twelve years';
- In Luke 3,2 we meet 'a certain man lame from his mother's womb'.

Many other examples of the use of medical terms in both books could be mentioned.

Now a lot of extensive considerations have been devoted to the use of medical terms in Luke's books.[80] The main question here is how and in what measure the use of these medical terms supports the authorship of Luke, the physician of Paul. The question, however, remains whether any attention at all would have been paid to this aspect of the Gospel of Luke and the Acts without this Luke-tradition.[a] Comparison of both

---

a See chapter 1.

books with those of other contemporary authors shows that Luke's language bears no testimony whatsoever of a higher medical education and interest than the language of those authors who were no physicians.[81] The medical terms Luke uses, also occur with his contemporaries, like the Jewish philosopher Philo of Alexandria, the Jewish historian Flavius Josephus, and with gentile authors like Seneca, Mark Anthony and others.[82] So Luke's use of medical terms doesn't support the Luke-tradition at all.

Besides, in many discussions about this subject the typically Jewish interest in medical and psychological symptoms[83] is overlooked. Also the relation between sin and illness which turns up rather regularly in Tanakh is drawn too little into the assessment in this respect. For instance an illness can be a metaphor for sin, an indication that one doesn't 'stand in the right relation to God'. A clear example is found in the census taken by David (2 Samuel 24,1-17). More obvious even is this motive in the story of a paralytic (Luke 5,17-26). First the sin is forgiven then the healing follows. It's this emblematic relation between sin and illness the evangelists are interested in and not in illness as a purely medical phenomenon. For example, it's clear that Paul suffered from an ailment which he himself described as a 'thorn in my flesh' (2 Corinthians 12,7). But Luke even doesn't mention it. Probably because he didn't consider this illness to be a metaphor of sin. If so, there was no reason to tell a story about it. What follows, however, is important enough to have a look at as well. Not all his letters were written by Paul himself. In Romans 16,22 there are even some words by his secretary: 'I, Tertius, who wrote *this* epistle, greet you in the Lord'. At the end of the Letter to the Galatians we read: 'See with what large letters I have written to you with my own hand!' Besides-the fact that untrained writers in Antiquity wrote in large letters, it's very well possible that Paul suffered from some (sort of) eye-trouble that made reading and writing difficult for him. This letter to the Galatians offers another clue as well. There Paul writes to the brothers in Galatia because of his 'physical infirmity' that, if that would have been possible, they 'would have plucked out their own eyes and given them to him' (Galatians 4,13-14)! A lot of speculation has been going on about the question what Paul suffered from and whether it was eye-trouble. But in the Acts Luke doesn't mention it, perhaps with one exception. In his story about the conversion of Paul in Damascus he tells us that Paul is temporarily blinded (Acts 9,1-19).[a] Now if Luke derived this blindness of Paul's at his conversion from this supposed eye-trouble[b], then it's conspicuous that Paul appears to be completely cured from it in the Acts exactly *because of* his conversion. And that is not surprising, because who is converted sees matters in the right way, eye-trouble or not! Luke doesn't deal with the 'medical fact' of Paul's blindness as a physician, but as a scribe.

My conclusion now is that the use of medical terms in the Gospel of Luke and the Acts yields no arguments in favour of a physician as an author and certainly not in favour of Luke, the physician of Paul. The medical language of 'Luke the author' is fully explicable from a good general education and from the Jewish-Biblical interest in the metaphorical relation between illness and sin. This interest points sooner into the direction of a Jewish than of a Greek author.

3.2 Nautical terms

In the Acts we come across three so-called 'we-stories':

- Acts 16,10-17;
- Acts 20,5 – 21,18;

---

a   It's remarkable that Paul himself reports on his stay in Damascus (2 Corinthians 11,32-33) just before the passage about the 'thorn in the flesh' (2 Corinthians 12,7).

b   Paul's own letter to the Galatians, in which he writes about his conversion (Galatians 1,15-17) reports no clues for his blindness at that event.

The use of technical terms by Luke

- Acts 27,1 – 28,16.

In the beginning of these stories the storyteller suddenly changes from the third person singular (the he- or she-form) into the first person plural (the we-form). In section 5.2 I'll go further into these we-stories. Now it's important to mention the fact that these three stories occur near the sea or at sea. However, not all stories about sea-voyages in the Acts belong to the we-stories. Paul's first travel begins and ends with a voyage across the sea (Acts 13 and 14). The stories about these voyages aren't we-stories. It's remarkable that there aren't any nautical terms in these stories, with the exception of some simple expressions like 'sail to' (Acts 13,4) and 'set sail' (Acts 13,13). This suddenly changes in the story about Paul's second voyage (Acts 15,36-18,22). Here the we-form is used for the first time in the middle of that story (Acts 16,9). The we-form is especially associated with the sea-voyages, and in these stories a lot of nautical terms turn up as well[84], most of them in the story of the shipwreck (Acts 27,14-44). We read about:

- 'we ran a straight course to Samothrace' (Acts 16,11);
- 'When we had sighted Cyprus' (Acts 21,3);
- 'and could not head into the wind' (Acts 27,15);
- 'they used cables to undergird the ship' (Acts 27,17);
- 'meanwhile loosing the rudder ropes' (Acts 27,40), etc.

Now this nautical language of Luke's could perhaps be explained by assuming that he had been a sailor. And in combination with the Luke-tradition one indeed comes across the opinion that the author of the Acts could have been a ship's surgeon![85] But just as well as there are other explanations possible for an assumed surgeon's profession for Luke's use of medical terms, so it's also perfectly possible to give another explanation for his nautical terms. In the first place he could have been a well-educated and much-travelled man. Besides nowhere in the we-stories the author appears to have done a sailor's job on board during the voyage. He was evidently a passenger, just like Paul and the other fellow-travellers. Still there could have been other reasons why Luke wrote the we-stories in the form of sea-voyage stories. Particularly the special part the sea plays in both books of Luke's will undoubtedly have something to do with it[a]. In the next chapters I'll return to Luke's sea-stories regularly.

3.3 Legal terms

The ample general education of Luke also appears from his knowledge of Roman Law. This is particularly conspicuous in his stories about the trials versus Jesus[86] and Paul[87]. More than the other evangelists he highlights the legal questions in the trial versus Jesus.[88] The trial versus Paul even takes up a quarter of the Acts.[b] So a few random examples.

The letter of the commander Claudius Lysias to the governor Felix (Acts 23,25-30) is written in the same terms as the then official documents dealing with similar cases.[89] Who studies the use of legal terms by Luke is struck again and again by the fact that he never makes a mistake in that respect.[90] Comparison with recovered papyri from those days, which contain official reports, makes this clear. When Luke uses the formula "You have appealed to Caesar? To Caesar you shall go!" (Acts 25,12), it's clear that he was entirely familiar with the language of these official reports.[91] One even managed to repair a damaged papyrus-text by means of the text from the Acts.[92] Without any scientific objection it's possible to borrow data from the Acts about Roman Law that are not found in other sources.[93] Luke is very well informed about the ins and outs of Paul's rights as a Roman citizen (Acts 16,37; 22,25-29). Paul's appeal to the emperor is even the best-documented case of such an event from the first century CE and it concurs with the data

---

a   See section 6.4.
b   Acts 21,27 – 26,32; 28,16-21 and 30.

known from other sources.[94] And what is more, Luke appears to know the routine in Roman prisons thoroughly as well (Acts 12,1 f.; 16,23 ff.).

Luke's interest in and knowledge of legal matters already drew a lot of attention in former times. The Codex Muratori writes: [he's] 'someone who is interested in legal matters'.[95] Some even maintain that Luke meant the Acts to be an apology for Paul in connection with his trial in Rome.[96] Or to persuade the Roman government of the fact that Christians were no danger to the state.[97] In my opinion, however, Luke's interest for and knowledge of Roman Law can only be explained from his attitude towards the Roman Empire. I'll add more information about this in the following chapters[a]. But the interest in matters concerning the Roman Empire need not necessarily point out a non-Jewish background of Luke's. The Roman Empire had been of great importance for the Jews as well, whether they lived in the Diaspora or not. One could even be a Jew and at the same time a Roman citizen, as Luke states about Paul. What's more, for every educated man in those days it was quite possible to have the same legal information at his disposal as Luke appeared to have.[98] On account of the above we could very well explain Luke's knowledge of Roman Law from a wide general education.

3.4 Political terms

Luke was also very well informed about the functions and titles of political figures in the Roman Empire. He mentions the emperors Augustus, Tiberius and Claudius, the last without the title 'emperor' in the correct context (Luke 2,1; 3,1; Acts 18,2). An emperor is also called *Sebastos*[b] (Acts 25,21 and 25). *Sebastos* is the Greek translation of the Latin title *Augustus*, which indicates the elevated, divine status of the

---

a Especially in section 10.3.
b The New English Bible has: 'His Majesty'.

emperor. Originally this title was a name of honour for emperor Octavian, but afterwards it became more or less his proper name. The title *Augustus* then passed to Octavian's successors. Ever since emperor Caligula (37-41 CE) the emperors were addressed as *kurios*[99] in general, Greek for 'Lord'. Luke must have known this title for the emperors as well (Acts 25,26).

Many Roman officials are mentioned in the Gospel of Luke and the Acts in the right manner. As far as the government of the Roman provinces are concerned, Luke recognized the difference between the function of a *proconsul*[a] and a *procurator*[b]. Sergius Paul of Cyprus, Gallio of Achaia and the magistrates of the province of Asia are rightly called *proconsuls* (Acts 13,7 f.; 18,12; 19,38). Besides, Luke knew that Pontius Pilate, Felix and Festus were *procurators* (Luke 20,20; 21,12; Acts 23,24 f.; 26,30 f.).[100] But in the Roman colony of Philippi we're dealing with *praetors*[c] as the highest officials (Acts 16,20 f.). The ranks in the Roman army are mentioned in the right way by Luke as well.[101]

The princes of the Herodian dynasty are also mentioned by their correct title. Herod the Great is 'king of Judea' (Luke 1,5), and in this case Judea must be understood as the entire Jewish country. Herod Antipas, however, is called 'tetrarch', as is his brother Philip (Luke 3,1 and 19; 9,7). But Herod Agrippa I was a king (Acts 12,1), as was his son Herod Agrippa II (Acts 25,13).

The political aspect however, especially in the Acts, isn't restricted to the correct use of titles. A further analysis of the stories of Paul's voyages shows, that they are very political stories indeed. No less than nine times Paul comes into conflict with the population of the cities where he stays. These nine conflicts can be divided into two groups: a group of three and a group of six conflicts. The first group consists of:

---

a Greek *anthupatos*.
b Greek *hegemoon*.
c Greek *strategos*.

- Antioch in Pisidia (Acts 13,14, 44-51);
- Iconium (Acts 13,51; 14,2-6);
- Lystra (Acts 14,8 and 19-20).

These three conflicts remained limited to disturbances by the population only. Within the composition of the Acts these stories are more or less an introduction to the Jerusalem Council (Acts 15). This becomes clearer if one keeps following the text after the Jerusalem Council till Acts 16,4-5.

The second group of conflicts, during Paul's second and third voyage, consists of:

- Philippi (Acts 16,19 f.);
- Thessalonica (Acts 17,1 f.);
- Berea (Acts 17,13-14);
- Athens (Acts 17,15 f.);
- Corinth (Acts 18,1 f.);
- Ephesus (Acts 19,1 f.).

Now these conflicts, with the exception of the conflict in Berea, have clear political dimensions. The often detailed representation and the adapted, political language is rather conspicuous. Luke appears to have a lot of knowledge of local affairs:

- He tells us that Philippi is a *colonia*, a colony, a place where the Romans had Roman citizens and ex-soldiers establish themselves so there was no need to garrison that place (Acts 16,12 and 21). The govenors of this city are called *praetores* (plural of *praetor*) their servants *lictores* (plural of *lictor*) (Acts 16,20 and 35).
- Thessalonica on the other hand is a Greek *polis*. It knew a public meeting (Acts 17,5). The city-governors here are called *politharches* (Acts 17,6), a name also found in the inscriptions of those days.[102]
- As said before, only Berea lacks the political background.

- In Athens the conflict passed off quietly. It has, entirely in the tradition of this city, a philosophical character (Acts 17,18). Paul delivers a speech in front of the *Areopagus* (Acts 17,22). This was both the name of a hill in Athens and the name of the High Council of the city, that used to meet at this hill. Dionysius the Areopagite (Acts 17,34) will have been a member of this council.
- In Corinth, the residence of the proconsul of Achaje, a confrontation takes place between Paul and a number of Corinthian Jews in front of the judgement-seat of Gallio. Entirely in agreement with Roman Law this Gallio refuses to deal with the case, because there are no Roman interests at stake (Acts 18,15).
- Luke describes the conflict in Ephesus in detail as well. Ephesus is the capital of the province of Asia. The governors of this province are called *asiarch* (Acts 19,31), a title that is also found in other contemporary sources.[103] Ephesus was a Greek *polis* as well. This riot, that develops into an illegal public meeting (Acts 19,39), is addressed by the city's *secretary*[a] (Acts 19,35). Excavations proved that the title *secretary* was indeed the title for the head of the official government of this city.[104] In his speech this official points at the existence of a proconsul, who administers justice at set times (Acts 19,38). The description of this public meeting and of the one in Thessalonica agrees entirely with the way in which these city-parliaments in the first century CE functioned.[105]

So Luke appears to have a great knowledge of political affairs when he tells stories that play in the area around the Aegean Sea. This supports the supposition that he was very well educated. But this may also throw some light on the matter of Luke's descent. Therefore the next observation.

---

a Greek: *grammateus*. NKJV has: "city clerk".

The six conflicts in the area around the Aegean Sea are, within the construction of the Acts, the preparation for the seventh and great conflict in Jerusalem (Acts 21,27 f.). Also in this last conflict the political aspect of Paul's action is stressed[106] (Acts 24,5). So the climax of the Acts is very clearly built up from Macedonia, Greece and Asia Minor. There seems to lie Luke's political preoccupation.

Now the over-representation of Macedonia in the group of six is remarkable. This area is represented by no fewer than three cities: Philippi, Thessalonica and Berea. And next to it the regions Attica with Athens, Achaje with Corinth and Asia with Ephesus. And Macedonia bears the brunt: the first three out of six conflicts happen there. Strangely enough, this does not follow directly from the geographical position of the area. After the last conflict in Ephesus Paul passes Macedonia another two times without any mention of conflicts (Acts 20,1-3). The first conflict in Philippi, the first city of Macedonia (Acts 16,12), shows another striking detail. The not unimportant theme *of Paul's Roman citizenship* is introduced here. This theme is going to play a decisive part in the conflict in Jerusalem. And finally there is the fact that the series of six conflicts is introduced by the vision of the Macedonian man (Acts 16,9). This vision is the turning-point in the Acts of the Apostles, and here also starts the first 'we-story', because here Luke suddenly switches from the third person singular into the first person plural.[a] So it's clear now that Luke makes Macedonia the starting-point of the journey-activities of Paul's that result in his last visit to Jerusalem.[107] What possible conclusions could be drawn now? One possibility is that Luke came from Macedonia. Another one is that in the second half of the Acts a certain signification should be attached to Macedonia. But what signification? At the end of this section I'd like to observe, that

---

a   For a more elaborated discussion see section 5.2.

Luke's political interest as emerges from the Acts, asks for a further discussion. Therefore I'll regularly return to this problem in the next chapters.

3.5 Conclusions

At the end of this chapter on Luke's use of technical terms there are three obvious conclusions.

- Luke was in the first place a man with a big general knowledge, who was very well-informed about the Greco-Roman world in which he lived and about which he wrote. This supports my supposition at the end of last chapter, that as a good literator he was able to use the languages of his background literature and of his surroundings in his stories and that he knew how to adapt his own language to the subject of his story.
- Secondly, Luke's interest in medical matters can be easily explained from the background of his general knowledge and from Judaism and Tanakh.
- And finally we can state by virtue of the political preoccupation of the Acts that as far as Luke's geographical origin is concerned we should think of the area around the Aegaen Sea, in particular Macedonia.

After these two chapters on Luke's language and his use of technical terms we'll study his literary method in the next chapter and prove his Jewish identity beyond any doubt.

4. And it began with Moses and with all the prophets
The midrash-character of the gospels

There is this generally propagated belief: Luke had wanted to write a historical work with his Gospel and the Acts.[108] First and foremost he had meant his two books to be a report of historical events. In this way his readers could learn about Jesus' doctrine and life, his death and his resurrection and how the young Christianity spread across the world. In this chapter, however, I intend to show an entirely different approach to the gospels and the Acts. It's my conviction that these early Christian writings belong to a Jewish form of literature that could best be described with the Hebrew term *midrash*. The meaning of this word will become clear if we are prepared to place these books within the then Judaism.

4.1 The origin of the gospels

Jesus was a Jew, lived as a Jew, and taught his disciples as a rabbi.[109] His death at the cross, a form of execution the Romans enforced to subversive people, had made an overwhelming impression upon his disciples. Yet they experienced that their master's life hadn't come to its end with his death at the cross. His words were passed on, stories about him were spread from mouth to mouth and his way of life continued to inspire. Also after his death the circle of his followers grew, perhaps I should say, because of his death. His followers spread, first across the land of Israel but later also among the God-fearing gentiles. The number of stories told about Jesus grew and the stories about his first disciples were added to it.

THE MIDRASH-CHARACTER OF THE GOSPELS

At first this was an oral tradition only. This passing on of stories, sayings and traditions was a common phenomenon in the then Judaism. In general this oral tradition knew a high degree of accuracy, but this could not prevent the fact that all kinds of different versions of the same traditions came into existence. In certain communities and schools only the material that was considered to be important was passed on. One even didn't hesitate, if this was deemed fit, to adapt the traditions to changed circumstances and notions. For the tradition had to stay alive and keep its function in the existence of the community. That's the reason why one regularly meets the same stories in the rabbinical traditions, but in the New Testament as well, either in an altered form or with a slightly changed content. The stories about Jesus and his disciples underwent a certain process of development as well, when they were told, re-told and passed on.

As time went by, one decided in some communities and schools to put in writing the traditions that until then had been handed-down orally. How this process began within the communities of Jesus' followers can't be rediscovered. The question whether the first writings had been collections of words of Jesus or complete gospels, is something one can only speculate about. Anyway it's certain that the literary genre of the gospels prevailed and became widespread. There must have been dozens of them in the 2nd century CE. Only four of them survived the later ecclesiastical censorship. These are the first four books of the New Testament. Many other gospels are only known fragmentarily from the work of the church-fathers who often quoted from them only to dispute them. Since 1946 we have a fifth gospel at our disposal as well: the Gospel of Thomas, found in a Coptic cemetery in Egypt. It's a collection of 114 sayings ascribed to Jesus. After that many other (fragments of) gospels were found back, but none of them is as old as the four gospels in the New Testament. By and large they are gnostic gospels from the 2nd century CE or later which have hardly anything to do with the original Jewish environment of Jesus, his disciples and the four gospel-writers. It's intriguing now that it is Luke's gospel that gives us some insight into the way the gospels came into being. The first sentence of his gospel reads:

> "Inasmuch as many have taken in hand to set in order a narrative of those things which have been fulfilled among us, just as those who from the beginning were eyewitnesses and ministers of the word delivered them to us, it seemed good to me also, having had perfect understanding of all things from the very first, to write to you an orderly account, most excellent Theophilus, that you may know the certainty of those things in which you were instructed" (Luke 1,1-4).

Evidently the writer knew about the existence of other gospels. Luke didn't write his gospel from lack of material about Jesus, but he wanted to tell something not told by others before him.

Most scholars agree that Luke knew and used the Gospel of Mark. A smaller but growing group of scholars holds the view that Luke knew and used the gospel of Matthew as well.[110] Anyway, in writing his own gospel, Luke used the Gospel of Mark as a source. In a lot of research into the text of Luke's gospel, done since the 19th century, it was assumed that Luke not only used Mark's gospel and perhaps Matthew's gospel, but other sources as well. We've already paid some attention to this problem in chapter 2. Thinking about the sources has been dominant for a long time in the research of the gospels. Over the years the number of theories about this problem have become so large and the conclusions from linguistic research are often so conflicting that we can only come to the conclusion that this source-theoretical approach yielded hardly any results at all for the exegesis. What is more, from all the sources supposed to be behind the gospels, only the Gospel of Mark is known as a real source up till now. In chapter 6 and

THE MIDRASH-CHARACTER OF THE GOSPELS

7 we'll see how Luke revised his 'source' Mark and how he adapted it entirely to his own plan.

In the course of the 20th century other approaches of bible-research came up next to the study of the original sources. More attention is paid to the circumstances in which the gospels came about. The various forms of traditions about Jesus became the object of research. And one began to pay more attention to the editorial activities of the gospel-writers themselves.[111] But the big flaw of all these approaches is that one doesn't look at, or hardly looks at the gospels and the Acts from the perspective of the Jewish way of life and the Jewish way of thinking in the last centuries before and the first centuries after the beginning of the Common Era. However, if one is going to do so, there is but one basic assumption for the research and exegesis: the gospels and the Act are a special form of *midrash*.

Midrash means that we're not dealing here with an account of historic events, but with stories that want to teach the audience how to look at life and how to live it in one's own days. The word *midrash* comes from the Hebrew verb *'darash'* which means 'search, research'. In the days of the evangelists it meant 'teaching' as well.[112] In a midrash-story the exact course of events is not important. Even the chief moments in the story needn't always be taken for the historical reality. The aim the storyteller has in mind is teaching the listener or the reader about a specific religious or vital question. It's not about the related events themselves, but about the way one looks at them and about the way of life that can be derived from them. This idea that the gospels should be understood as midrash experiences growing support nowadays.[113] In the next four sections I'll show the midrash-character of the gospels of Matthew and Luke with the help of the stories about John the Baptist. In the last section of this chapter I'll discuss the four main-characteristics of these midrash-stories. And in the next chapters I'll use this midrash-approach in my further research into the Gospel of Luke and the Acts of the Apostles.[114]

4.2 John the Baptist

There is hardly any historical information about John the Baptist. The number of writings that informs us about him is very small and the information is not always historically reliable. That doesn't alter the fact that a rough picture of John the Baptist could be drawn that is important as a historical background of the way in which the evangelists wrote about him. The Jewish historian Flavius Josephus (born in 37 CE) tells us that John was a pious man, who called on the Jews to be baptized by him. Because everyone turned to him, Herod Antipas, always on his guard, feared that John's enormous influence on the people could lead to rebellion. So he had John captured and executed in the citadel of Machaerus.[115] This piece of information deviates on many points from the stories in the gospels on this affair (Mark 6,14-29; Matthew 14,1-12). There is no doubt that Josephus' story is more reliable and in the next sections we'll see why.

Josephus' report on the death of John by Herod makes it also clear that John the Baptist had so many followers that his actions posed a political threat. From the gospels can also be derived that John had disciples, but it's not clear how many (Matthew 11,2; Luke 7,18-19; Mark 11,30-32). There seemed to have been a certain rivalry between John's disciples and those of Jesus' (Mark 2,18). Both religious leaders made their appearance simultaneously each with his own followers (John 3,22-25; 4,1-3). Also after John's death his followers continued as an independent, religious movement. This movement did not only show differences with the movement around Jesus but also affinities (Acts 18,24-25; 19,1-12). One can imagine that in the course of time these differences grew bigger rather than smaller. Up till now there exists in Iraq the religious group of the Mandaeans, who ascribe a special importance to John the Baptist. One can also find a condemnation of Jesus in their writings.[116]

Some information of Christian authors from the 3rd to the 5th century is more important in this respect. This information shows that John's followers looked upon him as the messiah.[117] This idea about John the Baptist goes undoubtedly back to the days of the evangelists Luke and John, because of the fact that in their gospels they emphatically pay attention to this question (Luke 3,15; John 1,20; 3,28). But other ideas and stories about John the Baptist were told as well. So it's quite possible that his resurrection from the dead was preached. This left some traces in the gospels too (Mark 6,14; Matthew 14, 1-2; Luke 9,7). In these circumstances it must have been very important for the evangelists to be very explicit in their ideas about John the Baptist and his relation with Jesus. The connection with the Torah and the Prophets must have been far more important to them than the historical course of events, and I'll explain this in the next sections.

4.3 John the Baptist according to Matthew

In Matthew 11,14 we read that Jesus observes in a sermon about John the Baptist:

"And if you are willing to receive it, he is Elijah who is to come."

This is not a stray observation within the framework of one story only, no, this is what could be called the summary of how Matthew portrayed John the Baptist in his gospel. The number of parallels between John the Baptists and the prophet Elijah in Matthew's gospel is rather large indeed.

- In Matthew 3,4 John's clothes are described as "Now John himself was clothed in camel's hair, with a leather belt around his waist". This is a quotation from 2 Kings 1,8 where Elijah is described as "a hairy man wearing a leather belt around his waist."[118] Elijah is even recognized by these clothes.

- Contrary to many other prophets and certainly to the great prophets like Moses, Samuel, Elisha, Isaiah and Jeremiah, no birth-story neither a story about his vocation is told about Elijah. Without any introduction at all he suddenly appears in 1 Kings 17,1. The same happens to John the Baptist in Matthew 3,1.
- Elijah's action was especially directed against king Ahab and his wife Jezebel, a Phoenician princess. It's exactly because of this, Herod's marriage with Herodias, that John turned against this Herodian prince according to Matthew (Matthew 14,1-4).
- In 1 Kings Jezebel tries to kill Elijah (1 Kings 19,2), and in the gospel of Matthew it's Herodias who causes John's death (Matthew 14,8).

As mentioned in the previous section, Matthew's version of John's death wasn't probably the historical course of events, but he describes the cause of John's death as a midrash all within the scope of his identification of John with Elijah. This identification of figures from their own stories with figures from Tanakh is characteristic for the midrash of the evangelists. They look at their own days 'with Tanakh in mind' (figure 4.1) and in this way they arrive at the explanation of what they see. The reason for Matthew's consistent comparison of John the Baptist with Elijah is the then notion that Elijah would come first to prepare the messianic days.[119] This expectation went back to Malachi 4,5-6. It is clearly worded in Matthew 17,10-13. If Matthew wanted to be able to testify that Jesus was the messiah, he had to show first that Elijah had already done his preparatory work: this was the part played by John the Baptist in Matthew's gospel. It stands to reason that this 'teaching-aim' in Matthew's stories about John was far more important than the exact historical course of events. This becomes even clearer when we put Luke's stories about John the Baptist next to those of Matthew.

4.4 The other vision of Luke

When we compare Luke's stories about John the Baptist with those of Matthew, the first thing that strikes us is that Luke doesn't have all those facts, which in Matthew's gospel point at the identification of John with Elijah.

- In Jesus' speech about John, the words: 'he is Elijah' (Matthew 11,14) can't be found (Luke 7,29-30).
- Also the clothes that point at Elijah are not mentioned at all in Luke's presentation of John as a prophet (Luke 3,7).
- By analogy with the Elijah-stories in 1 Kings Matthew doesn't tell a birth-story nor a story about his vocation, but Luke does! In Luke 1 the annunciation and the birth of John is told at great length, and in Luke 3,2 we read that 'the word of God came to John'. This is a concise reproduction of his calling. These words are absent in Matthew 3,1.

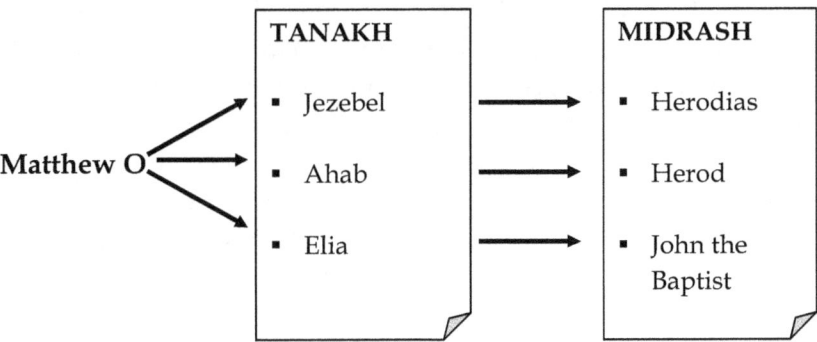

Figure 4.1 *Matthew looks at John the Baptist as an Elijah-figure against the background of Tanakh.*

- In Luke's gospel John's actions against Herod Antipas are not only connected with Herodias but particularly with Herod's atrocities (Luke 3,19-20).
- Herodias, by analogy with Jezebel, is the originator of John's death in the gospel of Mark. No trace of this can be found in Luke. He only uses one verse to inform us of John's death (Luke 9,9).
- In the gospel of Luke one will also look in vain for the conversation about the return of Elijah (Luke 9,36-37) mentioned by Matthew after the transfiguration on the mountain. A conversation that, for the second time in Matthew, results in an obvious identification of John with Elijah (Matthew 17, 10-13).

So Luke omits everything from of the gospel of Matthew that could possibly point at the parallel of John and Elijah. Apparently John the Baptist is no Elijah for Luke. He's at best someone who acts in 'his spirit and power'(Luke 1,17).

There is another striking difference between Luke on the one hand and Matthew on the other: how they represent the relation between John the Baptist and Jesus. In Luke 3,20 Luke ends John's actions with his captivity. Immediately afterwards he tells about Jesus' baptism, however, without referring to John (Luke 3,21-22). He must have inserted this non-chronological order in his story deliberately, because his 'source' Mark mentions Jesus' baptism first and John's arrest next (Mark 1,9-14). Also in comparison with Matthew there is a big difference in the staging. Matthew mentions a discussion between John and Jesus about the question whether Jesus should be baptized or not (Matthew 3,13-15). Luke doesn't mention this conversation and its theme. Presumably Luke tries to limit the contacts between Jesus and John to the utmost. This tendency is pursued in another story as well.

In the story about the fasting of the disciples of John, as told by Matthew, the disciples of John themselves accost Jesus about the fast (Matthew 9,14-15). In the gospel of Luke the Pharisees and the scribes enter into a discussion about this with Jesus (Luke 5,30,33-35). Here it also appears that Luke makes the relation between Jesus and John less direct. Now what is behind Luke's entirely different approach of John the Baptist? That question can only be answered against the background of Tanakh.

4.5 John the Baptist according to Luke

Who reads the beginning of the story about the annunciation of John the Baptist in Luke1,5-25, is powerfully reminded of Samuel's birth-story in 1 Samuel 1. On closer investigation the number of similarities between the birth-stories of Samuel and of John the Baptist appears to be very large in the gospel of Luke:

- Both stories begin with the words 'And it came to pass'.[a] This is an indication that Luke must have had the Hebrew text in mind, because the Septuagint[b] didn't translate these words from 1 Samuel 1 literally. The result is that Luke starts this story about John the Baptist with an ugly Greek sentence. For the sake of the resemblance to Tanakh he apparently puts up with it.
- The expression 'a certain priest'[c] (Luke 1,5) is a quotation of 'a certain man'[d] (1 Samuel 1,1). Here Luke used the Hebrew text again and not the Septuagint.
- In both stories the men are first introduced and then the women: first Elkanah and Zacharias and then Hannah, Peninnah and Elizabeth (1 Samuel 1,2; Luke 1,5).

---

a   Hebrew: *wajehie*, Greek: *egeneto*.
b   The Greek translation of Tanakh from the 3rd and 2nd century BCE.
c   Greek: *hiereus tis*.
d   Hebrew: *iesh èchad*. The Greek word *tis* could be looked upon as a translation of the Hebrew word *èchad*.

- Both stories bear dates: the priesthood of Hophni and Phinehas and the kingship of Herod (1 Samuel 1,3; Luke 1,5).
- The scene of action is in both stories the sanctuary: the tabernacle in Shiloh and the temple in Jerusalem (1 Samuel 1,3; Luke 1,9).
- In both stories the father is going to bring a sacrifice (1 Samuel 1,3; Luke 1,9).
- At first both mothers are barren (1 Samuel 1,11-12; Luke 1,13).
- Both children were prayed for (1 Samuel 1,11-12; Luke 1,13).
- In both cases someone intervenes who promises that their prayers will be answered: Eli and Gabriel (1 Samuel 1,17); Luke 1,13).
- Both children will be devoted to the service of the LORD (1 Samuel 1,11 and 24-28; Luke 1,15-17).
- In both stories the motive of the loss of voice plays a part (1 Samuel 1,13, Luke 1,20 and 22).
- After some days both women conceive (1 Samuel 1,20; Luke 1,24).
- Both children are named by their mothers (1 Samuel 1,20; Luke 1,60).
- From both children something is said about their youth and about their task with regard of the whole of Israel (1 Samuel 3,19-21; Luke 1,80).

Now it's perfectly clear how Luke sees John the Baptist: as a *Samuel-figure*. This identification influences his entire gospel. The so-called admonitions to the people Luke adds to the story of John's actions and that can't be found in the gospel of Matthew, are about the same three themes that appear in Samuel's speech to the people (1 Samuel 8,11-18):

- The daily needs (Luke 3,11; 1 Samuel 8,13).
- The levying of taxes (Luke 3,12-13; 1 Samuel 8,14-17).
- The military (Luke 3,14; 1 Samuel 8,11-12).

THE MIDRASH-CHARACTER OF THE GOSPELS

Here we find also an explanation of Luke's version of the "facts" in which he first finishes the story of John's actions and only then begins with his story of Jesus' actions. The same sudden change of a principal character is seen in 1 Samuel 16,13 between Samuel and David. There too, the spirit of the LORD came upon David, like it came upon Jesus at the beginning of his appearance in public according to Luke. After this change of principal characters we only meet Samuel only once and in a minor function (1 Samuel 19,18-20). The same applies to John the Baptist in Luke (Luke 7,18-19). And finally we discover that the deaths of Samuel and John the Baptist are only mentioned casually (1 Samuel 25,1; Luke 9,9). Luke always looks at John the Baptist with Tanakh in mind, and what he sees is a Samuel-figure (figure 4.2).

4.6 The Song of Mary ..., or of Elizabeth?

Luke's identification of John with Samuel and the parallel between Zacharias and Elkanah on the one hand and between Elizabeth and Hannah on the other make it possible to look at the so-called *Song of Mary* (Luke 1,46-55) in another way. A comparison of this song of

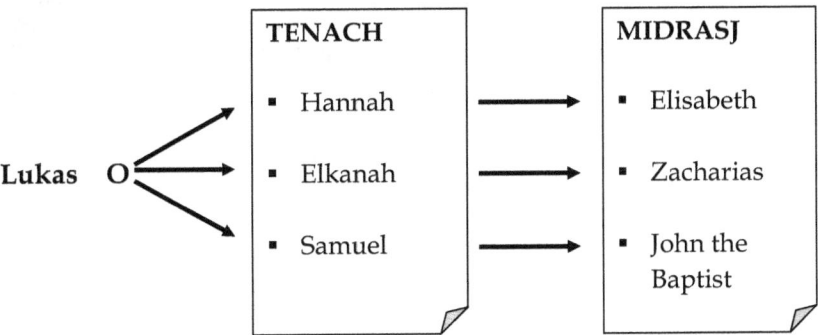

Figure 4.2   *Luke looks at John the Baptist as a Samuel-figure against the background of Tanakh.*

praise with the *Song of Hannah* shows many similarities (see table 4.1). It's clear that the *Song of Hannah* was the very Tanakh-background for Luke. This insight now causes the following problem: because of the fact that Luke identifies Hannah with Elizabeth it's rather peculiar that the song of praise in Luke 1,46-55 is pronounced by Mary and not by Elizabeth. Did Luke consciously deviate from his scheme 'Hannah is Elizabeth'? Or is something else going on?

In this respect it's remarkable that the manuscripts of the gospel of Luke with regard to Luke 1,46 aren't identical. In some manuscripts from the 4th and 5th century we read that not Mary, but Elizabeth pronounced the song of praise! Also the church-fathers Irenaeus (130-202 BC) and Origen (185-254 BC) knew this song of praise as the *Song of Elizabeth*. If we take the possibility for granted that this was indeed

Table 4.1

Comparison of the Song of Elizabeth (Luke 1,46-55) with the Song of Hannah (1 Samuel 2,1-10).

Luke 1,46-55	1 Samuel 2,1-10
My soul magnifies the LORD, and my spirit has rejoiced in God my Savior.	My heart rejoices in the LORD, my horn is exalted in the LORD. I smile at my enemies, because I rejoice in Your salvation.
For He has regarded the lowly state of His maidservant; for behold, henceforth all generations will call me blessed. For He who is mighty has done great things for me, and holy is His name. And His mercy is on those who fear Him from generation to generation.	No one is holy like the LORD, for there is none besides You, nor is there any rock like our God.

The Midrash-Character of the Gospels

Luke 1,46-55	1 Samuel 2,1-10
He has shown strength with His arm, He has scattered the <u>proud</u> in the imagination of their hearts.	Talk no more so very <u>proudly</u>, let no arrogance come from your mouth, for the Lord is the God of knowledge and by Him actions are weighed.
He has put down the <u>mighty</u> from their thrones, and <u>exalted the lowly</u>.	The bows of the <u>mighty</u> men are broken, and those <u>who stumbled are girded with strength</u>.
He has filled the <u>hungry</u> with <u>good things</u>, and <u>the rich</u> He has sent away <u>empty</u>.	Those <u>who were full</u> have hired themselves out for <u>bread</u>, and the <u>hungry</u> have <u>ceased to hunger</u>. Even the barren has borne seven, and she who has many children has become feeble. The Lord kills and makes alive, He brings down to the grave and brings up. The Lord makes <u>poor</u> and makes <u>rich</u>, He brings low and lifts up. He raises the poor from the dust and lifts the beggar from the ash heap to set them among princes and make them inherit the throne of glory. For the pillars of the earth are the Lord's, and He has set the world upon them.
He has helped <u>His servant Israel</u>, in remembrance of His mercy, as He spoke to our fathers, to <u>Abraham</u> and to <u>his seed</u> forever.	He will guard the feet of <u>His saints</u>, but the wicked shall be silent in darkness, for by strength no man shall prevail. The adversaries of the Lord shall be broken in pieces, from heaven He will thunder against them. The Lord will judge the ends of the earth. He will give strength to <u>His king</u> and exalt the horn of <u>His anointed</u>.

the original version then it's conspicuous that the pericope Luke 1,39-56 shows a much larger unity. In that case this song of praise is the logical sequel of the words of Elizabeth in Luke 1,42-45. Also the word 'her', which refers to Elizabeth, in the last sentence of this pericope, is easier to understand because in that case she, Elizabeth, only stopped speaking in the preceding verse (verse 55) and not ten verses earlier (verse 45). Now the most plausible explanation for all this is that Luke 1,46 originally read: 'And Elizabeth said', or: 'And she said'. Later copyists changed this – under the growing religious importance of Mary – in: 'And Mary said'. However, reading this text against the background of Tanakh, there is more reason to speak about the Song of Elizabeth than about the Song of Mary. Here we see that reading the gospels against the background of Tanakh yields strong arguments to settle certain manuscript-problems. This way of reading the gospels could be, in many cases, an important instrument to reach a reconstruction of the original gospel-text. In the next section I'll discuss a number of characteristics of gospel-stories written in this way.

4.7 The gospels as midrash

The way in which the evangelists wrote their gospels can best be described with the term *midrash*. This narrative method shows a lot of resemblance with the way in which some parts of Tanakh were written, and also with the way in which rabbis from the first centuries taught their students with the help of stories. Therefore the many rabbinical *midrashim* (plural of *midrash*) constitute a background of inestimable value for the exegesis of the gospels. This not only applies to their literary form, but also to their religious contents. In this section I'll examine the form and the function of the midrash-stories. To that end I'll deal with four of the most important characteristics of the narrative-

The Midrash-Character of the Gospels

midrash.[a] In the following chapters I'll sometimes return to these four characteristics explicitly, sometimes implicitly. They are of the utmost importance for an exegesis of the Gospel of Luke and the Act of the Apostles based on the Jewish tradition.

a. Tanakh as a starting-point

Matthew's and Luke's midrash-stories are, just like many rabbinical midrashim, somehow connected with Tanakh. The argument that is delivered, the language and the images that are used, the themes that are discussed about and the argumentation that is enunciated, they have especially been borrowed either from Tanakh or from other midrashim which in their turn build on Tanakh themselves. Therefore a midrash-story can always be seen as an explanatory commentary on Tanakh, or – if you want to – as an application of Tanakh to contemporary people and situations. This also holds good when stories are told about personalities from Tanakh. That's why the rabbis for their midrashim about proselitism go back to Abraham, 'the father of all proselytes', although proselytism only appeared long after Abraham.[120]

The connection between the gospel-story and Tanakh is made with the help of a number of literary means. We'll briefly talk about five of them. In the first four we'll refer to the stories of John the Baptist, we already talked about before. The fifth we'll meet a number of times in later chapters.

- In the first place there are the quotations of the text of Tanakh in the Greek translation. More often than not the text of the Septuagint is used but sometimes the evangelist corrects this text

---

a   Next to the narrative midrash (*aggadic midrash*) there is also a Jewish-legal midrash, the so-called *halachic-midrash*. In this study on Luke/Acts I'll deal with the narrative midrash only.

THE MIDRASH-CHARACTER OF THE GOSPELS

towards Hebrew. We already saw an example of this phenomenon in Luke 1,5.[a] This quoting can appear in different forms that vary from a complete text to the use of certain more or less loose words.

- In the second place a gospel story can be built on a story from Tanakh thematically. The parallels we found between Luke's story about Zacharias in the temple and the Samuel-stories about Elkanah and Hannah in the tabernacle[b] show this thematic relation clearly. Another example is the comparison of John's teaching with Samuel's speech to the people.[c]
- The third method the evangelist used is the identification of personalities. Sometimes this identification is mentioned explicitly, as in the case of John the Baptist and Elijah in the gospel of Matthew.
- In the fourth place a corresponding literary form of a series of stories can be mentioned here. Luke's cycle of stories about John the Baptist shows a same literary form as the one about Samuel: the announcement of his birth, the birth itself, the naming, his youth, his actions, the teaching of the people, the sudden move to the background, a short action once again and the brief mention of his death. Such a corresponding form of a series of stories can be connected to the identification of individual persons.
- These four literary 'tools' of the evangelists are certainly not the only ones that connect their stories with Tanakh. Also the function of the names and their meanings within a story will sometimes have to play a part in the exegesis. In the first place the meaning of a name in a story can be of some importance, as is often the case

---

a   See section 4.5 the first two items.
b   See section 4.5
c   See section 4.5, 2nd paragraph.

in Tanakh. A second possibility in the gospels is that a name can refer to the same name in Tanakh. This is for example the case with Zacharias (Luke 1,5). This name reminds us of the prophet Zechariah, son of Berechiah (Zecheriah 1,1), and the high priest Zechariah, son of Jehoiada (2 Chronicles 24,20-22), who lived three hundred years earlier. Who reads Matthew 23,25 closely, sees that both Zecheriahs in Tanakh are even identified with eachother there.[121] In this context it's notable that the officiating high priest isn't mentioned in Luke 1,5. Does Zacharias perhaps play the part of a substitute of the high priest here?[a]

Perhaps it would be possible to mention more literary means the evangelists use to connect their stories with Tanakh. The five mentioned above, however, offer us sufficient support to examine the links of the gospels with Tanakh. Tanakh was the very starting-point for the evangelists when they wrote their stories. This starting-point influences the essence of the gospel of Luke as well as the Acts of the Apostles. In the next chapters I'll show some additional examples of this phenomenon. Next to 'Tanakh as a starting-point' there are three other characteristics of midrash-stories that matter. They are all dealing with the function of the midrash in the days when these stories were told for the first time.

b. The transformation of history
The narrator of a midrash doesn't bother about a historical account of the actual events. It's true that the midrash often incorporates historical facts and situations, but the main line as well as the details of midrash-stories are mainly defined by the purpose the narrator or the writer of a story has in mind. If it suits his purpose to tell something that historically seen never happened or has happened quite differently, then neither the narrator nor the listener will have any problems with the story.

---

a   There are more indications for this in Luke 1,5-25. A further analysis, however, would carry too far here.

The Midrash-Character of the Gospels

The purpose of the midrash surpasses real history. Thus history is transformed so to speak into 'biblical history'. Not what really happened, but what should have happened to give us a better insight in our faith, is what the midrash tells us.

This transformation of history can be seen most clearly when different narrators use the same historical facts in their stories. In Tanakh one can study this characteristic of midrash by comparing the books of Samuel and Kings on the one hand and the books of Chronicles on the other. Also the comparison of the gospels of Matthew and Luke on the basis of the stories about John the Baptist[a] causes a deeper understanding of this transformation of history. How this transformation is carried out, is determined by the stories in Tanakh that serve as a starting-point when they are told. Matthew transforms the history of John the Baptist by means of the stories about Elijah, as does Luke with those about Samuel. In doing so they add stories or leave them out as their Tanakh starting-point may require.

Also in the rabbinical midrashim a similar transformation of history is a matter of course.[122] For example it's told of the great rabbis Hillel, Jochanan ben Zakkai and Akiva, who lived between 50 BCE and 135 CE, that they reached the age of 120 years, just like Moses. Just like Moses' life their lives were divided into three periods of 40 years: they practised a craft for 40 years, they studied Torah for 40 years and they taught Torah for 40 years.[123] Of course, this is a tradition and not exact history, but it teaches us to look at these three rabbis as Torah-scholars of the same level as Moses. Therefore one transfers, so to speak, the facts from Tanakh about the age and life of Moses (see for instance Deuteronomy 34,7) to these rabbis. This raises the question of the purpose of the midrashim.

---

a   See previous sections.

c. The didactic-polemic character of midrash

The third characteristic of midrash, that is closely connected with both previous ones, is the fact that a midrash has *always* a didactic aim. It's told or written to teach, or better still to enable the listener or reader to 'teach' themselves, to 'learn'. The story is told to invite the listeners to reach a certain insight in his or her own life-situation. This also holds good when these stories are about situations or personalities from the past. When the rabbis speak about the past their eyes are directed towards the present.[124] For the gospels this means that the stories about John the Baptist and about Jesus are never stories about them or about the time and circumstances they lived in only. Also the time and the circumstances of the evangelists and of their public are of decisive importance for the form and the contents of the gospel-stories. The evangelists who lived about half a century after Jesus, each made their own transformation of the history of Jesus. They did so with a view to their own circumstances and their own public. And of course, each of them must have had his own didactic-target in mind.

A midrash can not only have a didactic but also a polemic character. Very often the border between didactics and polemics can't be indicated clearly and depends on the public the narrator had in mind with his story. The element of polemics is as old as Tanakh itself. In the very first story of the Creation (Genesis 1,1 - 2,3) a clear polemic against the sun- and moon-worship from the days of the Babylonian Exile can be recognized in the way the creation of the sun and the moon is described.[125] Both in the gospels and in the midrashim of the rabbis these polemics are clearly recognizable.[126] Discussions with Pharisees, Sadducees and Samaritans are openly described. But all the same the stories that don't describe explicit discussions, can be polemic of character as well.[127] Indeed Matthew's and Luke's stories about John the Baptist could be meant as a polemic against the messianic pretentions of John's followers. John's resurrection and his messianism are rejected by the evangelists with these stories. John is introduced as a messianic prophet instead of a messiah. This means that in the eyes of the evangelists he was a preparer and not an executor of the messianic time. Also in the old rabbinical literature one comes across a similar, implicit polemic.[128] It is of great importance for the research and the exegesis of the gospels to keep this didactic-polemic character in mind.

d. Difference of opinion
Congenial narrators of midrashim are able to deal with the same subject in their stories in entirely different ways. On the one hand this can be caused by the difference of the circumstances in which they tell their midrashim, on the other hand a difference of insight in all kinds of questions can be the reason for it. The existence of various visions of the same case is quite customary in the rabbinical Judaism of the first centuries CE. It sometimes involves fierce discussions and it is certainly not always needed to reach a uniform point of view.[129] In many cases the Talmud records the conflicting views of the School of Shammai and the School of Hillel without coming to a decision. The preference of the Talmud-editors for the point of view of the School of Hillel is only subtly expressed by always giving this school the final word.

These differences of opinion and the resulting discussions between congenial rabbis are essential to the Jewish way of thought. Contemplating, discussing and testing one's own and another man's opinion again and again prevent rigidity and decay. Entirely in agreement with this line of thought one can consider the various notions of Matthew and Luke about John the Baptist. For Matthew John is a second Elijah. In the then Judaism Elijah was seen as the herald of the messianic era. His appearance heralds the last stage of the redemption.[130] In this respect Luke's expectations run less high. For him John is a second Samuel, a prophet with a more modest task. In Luke's eyes Jesus' appearance isn't the last stage of the redemption. After his gospel he writes the Acts. Jesus' life is not the end of a prophetic chain for him, but a link

THE MIDRASH-CHARACTER OF THE GOSPELS

in the history of the redemption which still continues.[131] This perspective is the reason why Luke couldn't use the identification of John the Baptist with Elijah. That's why he took another story as starting-point in Tanakh than Matthew did. Such differences in opinion between both evangelists don't confine themselves to the figure of John the Baptist. Their visions on Jesus and his actions differ thoroughly from each other.[132] The same applies to their outlook upon the Pharisees.[a]

Now in this context the so-called sources-theory can be put in another light as well. Differences of opinion can lead a Jewish narrator to tell the stories of his predecessors anew, but adapted to his own vision. This happens frequently in the rabbinic midrashim. Numerous stories happen in different versions with sometimes essentially changed contents. In fact this process can already be discovered in Tanakh, for example in the way the books of Samuel and the Kings are retold in 1 and 2 Chronicles. This process of retelling in an adapted form and with an adapted content explains furthermore both the similarities and the differences between the gospels of Mark and Luke. Especially the differences should be considered to be very important, because they can give us insight into the evangelists' conception of their own gospels. In the chapters 6 and 7 I'll show how Luke took his own line in his adaptation of the Gospel of Mark. But first, in the light of the idea that the gospels are midrash, we'll examine what the Gospel of Luke and the Acts of the Apostles can tell us about their author and why they were written and who they were meant for.

---

a   See section 9.1

5. Among ourselves
Author, adressee and purpose

In some parts of the Gospel of Luke and the Acts of the Apostles Luke speaks about himself. These passages can be divided into two groups:

- The two prefaces in which Luke writes about himself in the I-form (Luke 1,1-4; Acts 1,1-3).
- The three so-called we-stories, in which he writes about himself and the others in the we-form, and which happen, all three of them, in the second half of the Acts (Acts 16,10-18; 20,4 – 21,6; 27.1 – 28,16).

The person to whom Luke dedicated his work is mentioned at the beginning of both books as well: a certain Theophilus (Luke 1,3; Acts 1,1). In this chapter I'll discuss the prefaces and the we-stories. After that I'll check what may be concluded about Luke, if we consider these passages to be midrash. Next I'll devote a short discussion to the public that Luke must have had in mind and to which this Theophilus belonged. At last I'll round off with a section about the purpose Luke had in mind with his twofold work.

5.1 The prefaces

In the preface to his gospel Luke gives in one long, rather artificial sentence a number of interesting data:

> "¹ Inasmuch as many have taken in hand to set in order a narrative of those things which have been fulfilled among us, ² just as those who from the beginning were eyewitnesses and ministers of the word delivered them to us, ³ it seemed good to me also, having had perfect understanding of all things from the

very first, to write to you an orderly account, most excellent Theophilus, 4 that you may know the certainty of those things in which you were instructed" (Luke 1,1-4).

Not only the address, the why, the what and the how are briefly mentioned here, but also the group he considered himself to belong to and in which, apparently, the reported events had happened, is mentioned - be it vaguely. In the first verse we read that Luke wants to make it clear that his book is about 'a narrative of those things which have been fulfilled *among us*'. We now have to consider two questions: what 'things' are meant here and who are meant here with the words 'among us'? Moreover, it's important to pay some attention to the word 'fulfilled', because this theme-word is used again at the end of the Gospel of Luke. There we read:

> "Then he said to them, 'These are the words which I spoke to you while I was still with you, that all things must be fulfilled which were written in the Law of Moses and the Prophets and the Psalms concerning me.'"

From this verse and from Luke 24,26-27 one could gather that with the suffering and the resurrection of Jesus the fulfillment Luke was aiming at in his preface has been achieved. This is supported by another word of Jesus:

> "For the things concerning me have an end" (Luke 22,37).

This means that with the phrase 'with those things which have been fulfilled among us' is meant what is described in the Gospel of Luke. There is no reason to relate the preface of the Gospel to the Acts of the

Apostles as well. The Acts have a preface of their own, and in this preface is referred to the Gospel of Luke and a summary of the gospel is given:

> "¹ The former account I made, O Theophilus, of all that Jesus began both to do and teach, ² until the day in which he was taken up, after he through the holy spirit had given commandments to the apostles whom he had chosen, ³ to whom he also presented himself alive after his suffering by many infallible proofs, being seen by them during forty days and speaking of the things pertaining to the kingdom of God" (Acts 1,1-3).

The meaning of the words *'those things which have been fulfilled among us'* (Luke 1,1) can be looked for in *'all that Jesus began both to do and teach, until the day in which he was taken up'* (Acts 1,1-2).[a] This has consequences for the words *'among us'* in Luke 1,3. What group does Luke indicate with these words? Within what community has Jesus' life played as the fulfillment of the scriptures? What group did Luke consider himself to belong to? In the next sections I'll review five possible meanings of the words *'among us'*. His gospel and the Acts will have to give us the information to reach the most probable interpretation.

a. Among us: Christians?
In the Acts Luke caused the 'birth' of the Christian community to take place during Pentecost, ten days after Jesus' Ascension (Acts 1 and 2). That ascension, or the separation between Jesus and his disciples,[b] is also the end of the Gospel. So Pentecost doesn't belong *to 'the narrative of those things which have been fulfilled among us'* (Luke 1,1). Besides, the word "Christians" is only mentioned for the first time in the Acts when the story about the community of Jesus' followers has already

---

[a] See in this respect Luke 24,51.
[b] There is no real ascension to be found in the Gospel of Luke, only in the Acts.

advanced considerably (Acts 11,26)[a]. Consequently, the *'among us'* in Luke 1,1 can't have the meaning 'among us, Christians'. Therefore, we'll have to look for a group in the Gospel of Luke in which Jesus' appearance took place. Four possibilities remain.

b. Among us, the Apostles?
Luke's is the only gospel that distinguishes clearly and repeatedly the apostles from the other disciples of Jesus. The word 'apostle' means 'messenger, envoy'. It's a translation of the Hebrew word *sheliach*. In the then Jewish law the rule held good: 'the *sheliach* of a man is (as) the man himself'.[133] In Luke 6,13 Luke states that the title 'apostle' for the twelve disciples was given to them by Jesus himself. In this way Luke lays the foundation for their later position in the community of Jerusalem. Also after Judas' death the dozen should be restored. Matthias is chosen in his place (Acts 1,26).

Remarkably no one else is mentioned by the word 'apostle' than the twelve in the Gospel of Luke and the Acts. Even Paul isn't called 'apostle' in the Acts, except in Acts 14,14. Some manuscripts however, don't mention the word 'apostle' in this verse, and the question could be asked whether the word had been there originally.[134] That Luke didn't consider Paul an apostle of Jesus', appears from his definition of the term 'apostle' in Acts 1,21-22. There we read that an apostle must have witnessed all Jesus' public actions. And Paul clearly doesn't come up to this condition. This restriction of the apostleship to the twelve also means that Luke can't have considered himself to belong to them. That's why we can't restrict the words 'among us' (Luke 1,1) to the circle of the apostles. We'll have to search in a wider circle of people in Luke's gospel for the meaning of these words.

---

[a] See section 8.2 as well.

c. Among us, disciples?
Jesus' disciples form a wider circle than the apostles.[a] At first sight it seems to be possible to restrict the meaning of the words *'among us'* (Luke 1,1) to this group of disciples. There are, however, some features of Luke's gospel that resist this notion. First of all, the disciples play a less important part in Luke's gospel than in Matthew's. Counting the verses in both gospels will soon prove the point. If we restrict ourselves to the stories between Jesus' baptism and his death (Matthew 3,13 – 27,50 and Luke 3,21 – 23,46), we'll discover that almost 50% of the verses in Matthew's gospel describes something that only plays within the circle of the disciples, or in which the disciples occupy a special place. In Luke's gospel this is not yet 30%.[135]

Besides, in the Gospel of Luke we find a number of stories and texts that stress the publicity of Jesus' actions. The parallel of the Sermon on the Mount (Matthew 5,6 and 7) - a better name should be here the Sermon in the Field (Luke 6,20-49) - is explicitly situated in a 'great multitude of people' (Luke 6,17). Elsewhere Jesus is described as a man *'who was a prophet mighty in deed and word before God and all the people'* (Luke 24,19). When he tries to keep his actions hidden, he fails to do so (Luke 5,14-15). Luke sees it as Paul describes in his apologia for Agrippa: *'since this thing was not done in a corner'* (Acts 26,26). That's why it's not possible to restrict the meaning of the words 'among us' to the circle of the disciples. For *'those things which have been fulfilled among us'* we'll have to go in search of an even larger group of people.

d. Among us, eye-witnesses and servants of the word?
Luke himself, in his preface, supplies us the possibility of the meaning of the words 'among us' (Luke 1,2). Many textbooks and commentaries identify this group of eye-witnesses and servants with the circle of disciples and apostles. The words 'from the beginning' should refer to the beginning of Jesus' public actions. The 'word' should be understood as

---

[a] See Luke 6,13 and the Acts 1,21-22.

the word of Jesus or the word of God as it appears to the world in the words of Jesus and in his actions.[136] However, with an appeal to the midrash-character of the gospels, as discussed in the preceding chapter, a very different explanation could be given.

In Judaism, 'the word' is the word of the LORD, in the form of Tanakh (Torah, Prophets and Writings) that comes to Israel and through Israel to the nations. Greek uses the word *logos* for 'word'. This is the translation of the Hebrew word *davar*. But *davar* does not only mean 'word', but also and at the same time 'cause, case, matter, thing etc.'. The word of the God of Israel is a word that 'makes things happen'. It can be observed, seen in the things it does. That's why this word has 'eye-witnesses': those who observe the fulfillment of the 'word', and it has 'servants': those who 'do' or fulfill it. In this context the expression 'from the beginning' ought to refer to the first words of the word of God: 'In the beginning'(Genesis 1,1), the more so because here in these verses we're dealing with the beginning of the Gospel of Luke. It's about eye-witnesses and servants from the beginning of Tanakh: Adam, Noah, Isaac, Jacob, Moses, the prophets, the writers of Tanakh, the scribes since Ezra and Nehemiah, the teachers in Israel up to John the Baptist, Jesus, his apostles and disciples. In Luke 1,1-2 not only the life and teaching of Jesus is meant. Luke points here at the course of God's word through world and history.

In the previous chapter we saw how Luke grafted the description of John the Baptist upon Tanakh. This will turn out to be the same with his description of Jesus. The life of Jesus is not even the crux of the whole question. It's the continuity of God's actions that is characteristic for Luke's gospel and the Acts. More than the other evangelists Luke presents Jesus as a link in the chain of the redemption: Tanakh, John the Baptist, Jesus, the twelve apostles, Paul ....[137] His gospel begins with the story of Zacharias in the tempel (Luke 1,5 ff.). It's a part full of words, quotations and themes from Tanakh. Luke describes Jesus' life as *a* fulfillment of Tanakh, not the only or the final fulfillment. In the Acts he shows how Tanakh continues to be fulfilled, also *after* Jesus. Then, however, no longer *without* Jesus, as one can't serve the God of Israel since Moses without Moses. This means that the group of 'eye-witnesses and servants of the word' is larger than the group of the apostles and disciples. It even includes people who we, with respect to Luke, would consider to belong to the past. But from the biblical point of view this is no problem at all. Events from the past are sometimes represented as happening in the present. People from the past are considered to be alive (Luke 20,38) or appear in later generations (Matthew 11,14; 14,1-2; Luke 9,7-9). The blending of present and past is in the consciousness of the Jewish-biblical man a lot bigger and more self-evident than in our 20th-century, western approach of history. Modern historical thought is especially defined by actual, time-tied events that take place in a straight line of time. In the Jewish-biblical imaginative world past and present are not clearly defined. The biblical notion of time is more spatial than linear. At the celebration of the Seder, the Jewish Passover-meal, the leader of this meal, confronts those present with the words:

> "It was we who were slaves of Pharao in Egypt and God, Our God lead us from there with a mighty hand and an outstretched arm."

So the present-day generation had been there as well when Israel left Egypt! This flowing together now of past and present makes it possible to interpret the words 'among us' (Luke 1,1) as the 'eye-witnesses and servants' from the past. And finally the question may be asked whether Luke considers himself to belong to the eye-witnesses and servants as well. In that case we can restrict the words 'among us' to this group. The words 'delivered them to us' (Luke 1,2) however, point at a distinction between 'us' and 'the eye-witnesses and servants'. Therefore it's obvious that we'll have to look for the meaning of the words 'among us' at a group that not only contains the apostles and the disciples, the eye-witnesses and the servants from the past, but that is still greater. In that case there is only one possibility left.

e. Among us, Jews
In the Gospel of Luke a number of clear indications can be found that support this meaning of the words 'among us'. Twelve times the name of Israel occurs in this gospel, as often as the number of the tribes of Israel, and as often as in the Gospel of Matthew and twice as many as in Mark's and John's gospel together. If we consider the relevant texts and contexts we will be able to distinguish four groups of texts.

- The task of John the Baptist is restricted to Israel, which in those days meant to the Jews (Luke 1,16 and 54a,68 and 80).
- The task and significance of Jesus is also restricted to Israel, with one exception. This is the case in the Annunciation, but here, however, we don't find the name of Israel (Luke 1,31-33). Also in the story of the men of Emmaus we read that Jesus' task was directed towards Israel (Luke 24,21). We find three texts in the story about Simeon in the Temple. He expects 'the consolation of Israel' (Luke 2,25). When he sees the child Jesus he associates it with 'a light to [bring] revelation to the gentiles', but immediately continues with the words 'and [to] the glory of Your people Israel' (Luke 2,32). In Luke's gospel this is the first time that is spoken about the consequences Jesus' life will have outside the boundaries of Israel. And it is the last time as well, for we won't find words like that anywhere else in the Gospel of Luke! Now the mission to be a light to the gentiles is a task the prophets regularly impress upon Israel, (for example in Isaiah 42,6; 49,6).138 The addition in Simeon's words 'and [to] the glory of Your people Israel' shows that it's

---

a   In section 4.5 we substantiated that Mary's Magnificat is in fact Elizabeth's Magnificat. So this text refers to John the Baptist and not to Jesus.

about a task of Israel as a whole, essentially. But Simeon restricts his next words entirely to Israel: 'Behold, this [child] is destined for the fall and rising of many in Israel ....' (Luke 2,34). So the task and significance of Jesus is mainly directed towards Israel. In as much the gentiles are involved, it's about the task of Israel worded in Tanakh to be a light to the nations.

- This restriction to Israel can also be found in a text about the task of the twelve apostles in the kingdom of God (Luke 22,30). And in this respect it is remarkable as well that they, the apostles, never leave the land of Israel in the Acts.
- And finally there are a number of three sayings of Jesus in which the name Israel is mentioned. Twice in the speech Jesus delivers in the synagogue in Nazareth (Luke 4,25 and 27). This speech is a call to the Jews to accept their mission to the world. The reference in this speech to gentile regions and the gentiles, serves within Israel the aim of conversion to and answering the task formulated in Tanakh.[a] The same applies to the mention of Israel in the words of Jesus. He says about the centurion of Capernaum, that he hadn't found such great faith, even in Israel (Luke 7,9). It's true, Israel's belief is compared here with the belief of a non-Jew, but the purpose of these words is to show the Jewish crowd something they can take an example from.[b]

A provisional conclusion can be drawn now from all this. In Luke's eyes Jesus' task and actions were especially aimed at Israel. By confronting Israel with its mission in the world, a mission worded by the prophets in Tanakh, Jesus became indirectly significant to the gentiles as well. However, his work has never been aimed at the gentiles directly. This is clearly demonstrated in the story about the centurion of Capernaum

---

[a] I'll return to this story more explicitly in section 6.8.a.
[b] In section 6.8.b I'll discuss this story in more detail.

(Luke 7,1-11). If we compare Luke's version of this story with Matthew's version (Matthew 8,5-13) there are two points that ask for our attention.

- First of all there is no question in Luke of direct contact between Jesus and the centurion, as indeed there is in Matthew (Matthew 8,5 and 13). First some elders of the Jews mediate between Jesus and the centurion, and next some friends of the centurion (Luke 7,3 and 6). One gathers that Luke wrote the face-to-face meeting between Jesus and the non-Jewish centurion out of the story.
- And there is a second difference with Matthew. Luke describes the centurion as someone who 'loves our nation, and has built us a synagogue' (Luke 7,5). Apparently Luke felt the need to underline the centurion's positive attitude towards Israel.

By doing so he provided this story with two important features, that also characterize the Acts of the Apostles:

- the relation of Jesus towards the gentiles only consists through the agency of others and
- the gentiles are only entitled to expect something of Jesus if they should convert to Israel's heritage.

There are three other stories about meetings of Jesus' that should be discussed in this context. At the beginning of the Sermon in the Field, a great multitude of people is mentioned, not only from the entire Jewish country and Jerusalem, but also from the gentile parts of the country Tyre and Sidon (Luke 6,17). This story is a midrash on Joshua 8,30-35. There it is Joshua (in Greek: Jesus!) who delivers a speech to Israel. There also were 'the strangers who were living among them' (verse 33 and 35). Moses had ordered Joshua to deliver this speech (compare Joshua 8,30-33 with Deuteronomy 27,11-14). The blessing and the curse in the words of Joshua (Joshua 8,34; Deuteronomy 27,15 - 28,68), constitute the clearest similarity with Jesus' words in the Sermon in the Field. This sermon begins with four blessings and four curses (Luke 6,20-26). It is essential that the strangers in Joshua went and committed themselves to Israel, just like the inhabitants of Tyre and Sidon did to Jesus. Doing so they shared in the words of Jesus and Joshua. Jesus' actions towards the gentiles in this story didn't continue and didn't go beyond the example given in Tanakh towards the strangers in the midst of Israel.

Also in the story of Jesus' visit to the region of the Gerasenes a meeting took place between Jesus and someone who, perhaps, was a stranger (Luke 8,26-39). In section 6.7 I'll discuss this story in detail. The Tanakh-background of this story will show that its purpose is directed towards Israel.

Then there is this meeting of Jesus and Pilate during the trial (Luke 23,1-7, 13-25). It's also conspicuous here that Luke provides the story with more Jewish elements than the other evangelists. He is the only one who gives the Jewish tetrarch Herod Antipas a part in this trial (Luke 23,8-12). The contrast between Jesus and Herod Antipas focuses this story on the internally Jewish political situation in those days. Here the setting of the events shows a clearer involvement with Israel as well.

And finally there is another important story in the gospels of Mark and Matthew not found in Luke: Jesus left his way and went to the Syro-Phoenician country, a country of gentiles (Mark 7,24-30; Matthew 15, 21-28). This removal too fits in with the image Luke paints of Jesus' actions. With the exception of the region of the Gerasenes Jesus' action takes place entirely in the Jewish land west of the river Jordan. It's only in the Acts that not Jesus himself but the testimony of his actions and teachings crosses the borders of the land of Israel.

The most obvious conclusion that can be made on account of all this, is that Luke in the 'narrative of those things which have been fulfilled among us' describes those events that happened 'among us, Jews'. This means that the idea, cherished for centuries, that Luke was a Christian from the gentiles who wrote for a gentile public, needs to be revised.

5.2 The we-stories

The second cluster of information Luke gives about 'himself', is formed by the so-called we-stories. These are found in the second half of the book of the Acts. The we-form in these stories points to Luke's travelling party. From this we can gather that Luke kept Paul company:
- from Troas to Philippi (Acts 16,10-17);
- from Philippi to Jerusalem (Acts 20,5 – 21,18);
- from Caesarea to Rome (Acts 27,1 – 28,16).

Notably in all three we-stories a sea-voyage is described. Each time Paul puts to sea the we-figure turns up in his company. When Paul once interrupts his voyage by travelling by land, the we-figure continues his journey by boat (Acts 20,13-14). The coastal regions seem to fix the borders of the we-stories.[139] As soon as the voyage has ended, the we-figure disappeares from Paul's company as sudden as he had turned up. It's also notable that in the last verse of each we-story Paul is differentiated from the we-company:[140]

- Paul and us (Acts 16,17),
- Paul with us (Acts 21,18),
- Paul by himself (Acts 28,16).

This means that the we-figure accompanies Paul to Philippi, to Jerusalem and to Rome, but seems to leave him almost immediately after arrival. It is remarkable how easily some commentators conclude from the last we-story that Luke stayed with Paul in Rome for two years.[141] Acts 28,16-31 mentions Paul's two years of imprisonment in Rome. This imprisonment was presumably the same as the one mentioned in 2 Timothy 4,6-18. Luke, the physician, would have kept Paul company during his imprisonment (2 Timothy 4,11). But in the Acts the mention of the story of this imprisonment is also the end of the last we-story.[142] Nowhere in the Acts evidence can be found of the fact that the we-figure had been in the company of Paul in Rome. For example, the leaders of the Jewish community of Rome came to visit Paul in *his* lodging and not in *our* lodging (Acts 28,23). This could lead to the rather odd conclusion that Luke, the physician, did keep Paul company in Rome, but that 'Luke', the author of the Gospel and the Acts, did not!

This kind of considerations is, in fact, based too much on a historical way of reading the Acts and takes too little into account the midrash-character, that characterizes the Acts of the Apostles in many respects as well. If we look carefully at the beginning of the first we-story we discover that this story is a turning-point in Paul's activities. Twice the holy spirit prevented Paul to preach the word in Asia-Minor (Acts 16,6-7). Then, in the night, he perceives a Macedonian man. The said man summons him to go into quite another direction (Acts 16,9). In this summons the we-form is introduced, so to speak: 'Come over .... and help *us*'. Immediately after that the first we-story begins (Acts 16,10). Why did Luke begin this story in this peculiar way? The first thought that crosses one's mind is that in this Macedonian man he shows us a self-portrait.[143] If that is the case, he was a native of Macedonia. This however, is no indication for a Jewish or Greek identity. Jews from the diaspora were also described after their country of origin. See for instance the Alexandrians and the Cyrenians in Acts 6,9 (as well as in Acts 2,9-11). A vivid example of this is also found in John 7,35 and 12,30. Here Jews from the diaspora are called 'Greeks'. In chapter 8 however, I will show that the part Macedonia plays in the second half of the Acts, reaches much further than can be explained from an author's pseudonym. That's why we'll have to look elsewhere for the meaning of this story of the Macedonian man and the following we-stories. It is the character of the relation between Paul and Luke that could be the essence of these stories.

AUTHOR, ADRESSEE AND PURPOSE

Who compares the contents of the Acts with the letters of Paul will soon be able to enumerate a great number of differences. These differences do not only touch the reproduction of historical events (as far as we, with regard to Luke's texts, could use the word 'historical' here), but also the contents of the ideas propagated by both. A few examples will suffice. Paul himself states that he only returned to Jerusalem three years after his conversion (Galatians 1,17-18). Luke on the other hand relates that Paul left for Jerusalem immediately after his conversion (Acts 9,19b-26). Though Paul himself explicitly demands the apostolate for himself (1 Corinthians 9,1-2), Luke doesn't call him an apostle anywhere in the Acts and Paul doesn't come within Luke's definition of the apostolate either (Acts 1,21-22). Paul's ideas about the Torah are very controversial for the Jews indeed, but in the Acts Luke presents him as a Jew faithful to Torah (Acts 21,23-26). Does Paul himself write about a conflict with Peter (Galatians 2,11-14), nothing of this can be found in the Acts. This list could be extended with many more examples. Now the most important observation one could make in the Acts in this respect is, that Luke doesn't mention one letter of Paul anywhere and doesn't show that Paul wrote any letters anyhow! There is only one decisive explanation for all this: Luke wrote the Acts among other things as a 'critical correction' on the historical Paul and his ideas. In Luke's description Paul is more Jewish than he was indeed. The Paul of the Acts is a *midrash-transformation* of the historical Paul.[a]

The meaning of the we-form in the second half of the Acts becomes clear against the above-mentioned background. Luke was not concerned about the fact that he should have been in Paul's company and therefore should have been able to give a correct account as far as the facts are concerned.[b, 144] Luke's presence at the events is a presence seen from the perspective of Tanakh. By means of the we-stories he makes it

---

[a] In section 4.6.b I discussed this characteristic of midrash.
[b] As is the case in contemporary literature when an author switches to the first person.

clear that in the Acts we are dealing with 'his' Paul, whose Jewishness can't be questioned (Acts 22,3). This, however, doesn't explain everything of the we-stories. Why are they limited to the coastal regions? Why are they about sea-voyages in particular? Why do they make such a clear link between Philippi, Jerusalem and Rome? A number of these and related question will be dealt with in the chapters 8 and 10.

Concerning Luke's identity, these we-stories don't yield any direct information. But one could find in them an argument in favour of Luke's Macedonian origin. The fact that, in the Acts, Paul is more Jewish than the 'historical' Paul had ever been, as we know him from his own letters, is however a very strong indication in favour of a Jewish identity of Luke's. What possible reasons could he have had for his emphasizing this Jewish aspect, if he had been a Christian from among the gentiles? That's why the we-stories indirectly support the idea of a Jewish author.

5.3 Most excellent Theophilus

The Gospel of Luke and the Acts are dedicated to someone who's called Theophilus. In the preface of the gospel he's provided with the title 'most excellent' (Luke 1,3). In the preface to the Acts this title isn't mentioned (Acts 1,1). What can we say about someone of the name of 'Theophilus' and who, evidently, held high office?

Theophilus is of course a Greek name. But so is almost every name in the New Testament to begin with the name *Jesus*. Now many of these names are Greek translations or transformations of originally Hebrew or Aramaic names. The original name of Jesus was in Aramaic *Jehoshua*. Yet in the Acts and the letters of Paul we are often dealing with original Greek names, as is the case with the name 'Theophilus'. Now, is that the reason why we have to suppose that he is Greek?

AUTHOR, ADRESSEE AND PURPOSE

The important part Greek played in the first-century Jewry, both in the land of Israel and in the diaspora, has come up before[a], and we already saw that many Jews even in the land of Israel had Greek names. The father of the high priest Matthias, appointed by Herod, was called 'Theophilus', just like a certain Theophilus, son of Hannas, who was the high priest from 37 to 41 CE.[145] Originally many Jews in antiquity had Hebrew names, made up of the syllable *ja* from *jahu*, an abbreviation of the tetragrammaton, the four letter Name of God. When they translated their name into Greek, they preferred to do so with the help of the Greek word *theos*.[146] But that doesn't mean that all names made up with the syllable *theos* were names of Jews. We know of many Greeks, non-Jews, with such names: Theognis, Theopompus, Theokritus etc. However, we can take it for granted that the name *Theophilus* was mainly used by Jews and was the second in popularity among them after the name *Dositheos*.[147] Undoubtedly this has something to do with the meaning of the name: 'beloved of God'. The notion that God loves man is characteristic for the Jewish religion, this as distinct from the gentile religions in which, generally speaking, the relation between the gods and man has nothing to do with love. Therefore we could assume that the name Theophilus sooner belongs to a Jew than to a gentile, converted to Christianity.

From the title 'most excellent' given to Theophilus it can be deduced that he was a very distinguished man. Pontius Pilate was addressed as 'most excellent', and Paul addressed the other governors with the same title (Acts 23,26; 24,3; 26,25). Some deduce from this title that Theophilus was a very distinguished gentile, even a god-fearing man.[148] However, few reasons support that theory. True, the main part of the Jews, especially in the diaspora, belonged to the lower and lower-middle classes, yet a lot of Jews rose to high and influential positions. One can

---

[a] See section 2.2.

easily imagine that they were addressed with the title 'most excellent'. Just a few examples in illustration.[149]

Two generals of Ptoleme VI Philometer of Egypt (224-205 BCE), Onias and Dositheos, were Jews.[150] Joseph bar Tobias was one of the most important tax-collectors (publicans) in the Middle East in those days.[151] Cleopatra III of Egypt too, was served by two Jewish generals: Chelkias and Ananias, sons of the high priest Onias III.[152] From 46 to 48 CE Tiberius Julius Alexander was governor of Judea. His father was head of the Jewish community in Alexandria in Egypt and Tiberius was a nephew of the Jewish philosopher Philo of Alexandria. So he was of unquestionable Jewish origin.[153] These are but some examples of Jews in high positions in non-Jewish governments.

Besides, the possibility can't be ignored that also within Judaism itself there were functions that carried the title 'most excellent'. This could have been the case with the *archon*, the head of a Jewish community in the diaspora. This was, especially in the Jewish communities in the big cities, an important function that in many places had grown into hereditary leadership and was in the hands of well-to-do families.[154] One could easily imagine that Theophilus had been the *archon* of an important Jewish community, for instance in a city like Antioch, Ephesus or Rome. But in that case the question arises about Luke's aim, his purpose with his gospel and the Acts.

5.4 *The purpose of the Gospel of Luke and the Acts*

In the literature concerning the Gospel of Luke and the Acts of the Apostles there is no agreement about the purpose Luke could have in mind with both books. One thing, however, is clear. Purpose and public for which they were written, were closely connected. Most commentators hold the view that Luke wrote for Christians from the gentiles. A certain Theophilus could have belonged to them. In that case Luke's books were possibly meant to give them the certainty they needed to their faith by power of argument.[155] Some even underline the historical facts the Christian faith is supposed to be based on.[156] Another notion wants that Luke wrote for gentile outsiders. He presumably wanted to show that Christianity wasn't as bad as it was known, but on the contrary had good characteristics only.[157] And others suppose that Luke wrote for the Romans and especially for the Roman government: his books were thought to be an apology to propitiate the Roman authorities towards the Christians.[158] However, an insurmountable objection could be put forward against all these opinions. The means Luke used when writing his books were not exactly attuned to all these target groups.

- In the first place he takes it for granted that his readers have an almost unlimited knowledge of Tanakh or Septuagint.
- Secondly he uses all kinds of Jewish ideas and notions like messiah (= christos), redemption, the kingdom of God, son of men etc. very much as a matter of course.
- And finally one should be very well informed about the Jewish culture and history to be able to understand Luke's work.[159]

Therefore it's more obvious to suppose that he has written both his books for a public of religious Jews. In that case the next question is: to what end? I'll try to find an answer to that question in the rest of this book.

6. In the entire Jewish land
Jesus' stay in Galilea-Judea

It's very much possible to draw detailed maps of the various journeys of Paul with the help of the geographical data from the Acts, but it's absolutely impossible to make an accurate map of Jesus' wanderings through the land of Israel with the help of Luke's gospel. Luke appears to situate Jesus in his gospel in an imaginary landscape and not in the real map and landscape of Israel. This now points – according to a number of commentators – to the fact that he didn't know the lie of the land.[160] Yet many of the geographically coloured expressions with regard to the land of Israel in both books are correct. For instance: 'went down' (Luke 4,31; 10,30; Acts 8,5 and 26; 9,3) and 'went up' or 'came up' (Luke 2,4; 19,28; Acts 11,2). In the chapters 6, 7 and 8 we'll further investigate Luke's geography and show that it's especially Jewish, if one approached his geography from the midrash-character of the gospels.

6.1 Geography and composition

Many geographical indications in the Gospel of Luke are rather vague: 'a deserted place' (Luke 4,42), 'the synagogues of Galilee' (Luke 4,44), 'a certain city' (Luke 5,12), 'through the grainfields' (Luke 6,1), 'the Pharisee's house' (Luke 7,36), etc. The other gospels are usually not clearer in this respect, so Luke is no bewildering exception. Yet there are some geographical indications that offer more support for a 'spot on the map' where, according to Luke, Jesus did his work. Several parts of the country and places are mentioned: Galilee (Luke 4,14), Judea (Luke 4,44), Nazareth (Luke 4,16), Capernaum (Luke 4,31), Bethsaida (Luke 9,10), Jericho (Luke 18,35), Jerusalem (Luke 19,11), etc. For a correct assessment of this material it's important to examine in what way

Jesus' stay in Galilea-Judea

geography and composition in the Gospel of Luke are interwoven with each other.[161] Here we'll especially occupy ourselves with the data of the chapters 4 to 21 of the Gospel of Luke.

After a number of introductory stories the real story of Jesus' activities begins in Luke 4,14. Then a clear division into three parts can be noticed:[162]

- Jesus' activities in Galilee-Judea (Luke 4,14 – 9,50);
- The journey to Jerusalem (Luke 9,51 – 19,28);
- Jesus' stay in Jerusalem (Luke 19,29 f.).

Luke made this division consciously, which can be gathered from several data. In the first place journeys are mentioned regularly, more precisely journeys to Jerusalem (Luke 9,51; 10,38; 13,22 and 33; 14,25; 17,11; 19,28), whereas further geographical facts are scarce in this travel-story. Two stories are important for the theological meaning of this travel-motive: Luke 9,57-62 about following Jesus, immediately at the beginning of the journey, and Luke 13,31-35 about the prophetic purpose of the journey, exactly in the middle.

A second indication for a conscious division into three parts is to be found in the repetition of the various themes through the three parts.

Table 6.1

Examples of repetitions of the themes in the three main parts of the Gospel of Luke (Luke 4,14 – 9,50; 9,51 – 19,28; 19,29 f.).

Theme	Part 1	Part 2	Part 3
• rejection at the beginning of each period	4,16-30	9,51-56	19,47-48
• the theme of the sending out	9,1-6	10,1-20	22,35-38
• a Herod-scene	9,7-9	13,31-35	23,8-12
• the women who served Jesus	8,1-3	10,38-42	23,49
• the theme of the first and the last	9,46-48	14,7-11	22,24-27

Table 6.2

Examples of thematic repetition in the first two main parts of the Gospel of Luke (Luke 4,14 – 9,50; 9,51 – 19,28).

Theme	Part 1	Part 2
• the calling of a publican, who's mentioned by his name and a stay in his house.	5,27-32	19,1-11
• a pronouncement about lamp and light	8,16-17	11,33-36
• the theme of tree and fruit	6,43-45	13,6-9
• the healing in a synagogue on a sabbath	6,6-11	13,10-17
• the healing of lepers	5,12-16	17,11-19
• the praying of John's disciples	5,33	11,1
• the motive of the seed	8,4-15	13,18-19
• Jesus' relatives	8,19-21	14,25-35
• the objection of the Pharisees and the Scribes against eating together with publicans and sinners	5,29-32	15,1-2

Without aiming at completeness we collected a number of examples in table 6.1.[163] Also when comparing the story of Jesus' stay in Galilee-Judea with the travel-story, a lot of thematic repetitions are noticeable, as shown in table 6.2. Both tables contain examples of clear similarities of themes. It is possible, for example on exegetical grounds to indicate more parallels between the first and second period or between all three of them. An example is found in both 'Jonah-stories' (Luke 8,22-25 and 11,29-32). Here 'the storm at the lake' betrays the background of Jonah 1. The division into three parts is sufficiently illustrated by these examples and I'll use it when trying to explain the geographical notes that are found in these three parts. In this chapter I'll restrict myself to Jesus' stay in Galilee-Judea (Luke 4,14 – 9,50).

6.2 The comparison with Mark

In the first part of Luke's story on Jesus' activities (Luke 4,14 – 9,50) a lot of geographical indications can be found. It's important for the stu-

Table 6.3
The geographical notations in Luke 4,14 – 5,39 compared with those in Mark 1,14 – 2,22.

Mark	Luke
1,14-15 Galilee (preaching)	4,14-15 Galilee (teaching)
1,16-20 Sea of Galilee (calling of 4 disciples)	
(6,1-6a)	4,16-30 Nazareth (synagogue; rejection)
1,21-34 Capernaum (synagogue, house of Simon)	4,31-41 Capernaum, town in Galilee (synagogue, house of Simon)
1.35-38 lonely place (Simon and others follow him)	4,42-43 lonely place (the crowds are looking for him)
1,39 Galilee (preaching in synagogues)	4,44 Judea (preaching in synagogues)
	5,1-11 Lake of Gennesareth (the fishing of Peter's)
1.40-44 (healing of a leper)	5,12-15 One of the cities (healing of a leper)
1,45 lonely places (banned from the city)	5,16 lonely place (praying)
2,1-12 Capernaum (many people together; healing a paralytic)	5,17-26 (Pharisees and Scribes from Galilee, Judea, Jerusalem; healing of a paralytic)
2,13-14 at the seaside (calling of Levi)	5,27-28 at his tax office (calling of Levi)
2,15-22 in his house (meal with publicians; discussion about fasting)	5,29-39 in his house (meal with publicians; discussion about fasting)

dy of these data to compare the Gospel of Luke with the Gospel of Mark, that served as a 'source' for Luke.[164] This comparison is especially important because Luke, as far as the geography is concerned, adds a

JESUS' STAY IN GALILEA-JUDEA

large number of changes with respect to Mark. In the tables 6.3 to 6.7 the geographical indications of Luke are printed next to those of Mark's. On account of a number of important differences between both gospels we'll try to decode Luke's geography.

Table 6.4
The geographical notations in Luke 6,1 – 7,50 compared with those in Mark 2,33 – 3,30.

Mark	Luke
2,23-28 grainfields (plucking the heads of grain on a Sabbath)	6,1-5 grainfields (plucking the heads of grain on a sabbath)
3,1-6 synagogue (healing on sabbath)	6,6-11 synagogue (healing on sabbath)
3,7-12 to the sea (crowds from Galilee, Judea, Jerusalem, Idumea, beyond the Jordan, Tyre, Sidon; healings)	6,12-16 the mountain (choosing the twelve apostles)
3,13-19 the mountain (appointment of the twelve disciples)	6,17-49 a level place (crowds from the entire Jewish land, Jerusalem, Tyre, Sidon; healings, Sermon in the Field)
3,20-30 in a house (Beelzebub, Jesus' relatives)	(11,14-23; 8,19-21)
	7,1-10 Capernaum (a centurion's slave) 7,11-16 Nain (the raising of an only son) 7,17 the entire Jewish country (rumour) 7,18-35 (Jesus about John)
(14,3-9)	7,36-50 house of a Pharisee (Jesus anointed by a woman who was a sinner)

6.3 Extra information about geographical sites

Luke adds extra information about the location to some geographical names. To Capernaum (Mark 1,21) is added 'a city of Galilee' (Luke 4,31), to the country of the Gadarenes (Mark 5,1) 'which is opposite Galilee' (Luke 8,26). Such extra information can also be found elsewhere in the Gospel of Luke and in the Acts, for example at Nazareth, Bethlehem, Emmaus and the Mount of Olives (Luke 1,26,39; 2,4; 24,13; Acts 1,12). These indications are all correct but one. Only the indication at Emmaus is disputable.[165] It's certainly not a matter of course to conclude from this material that Luke hadn't known the land of Israel. It's more likely to explain this information by assuming that Luke wrote for a public that didn't know much about the lie of the land. It's certainly not necessary either to consider this public as non-Jewish on this ground. We have already seen that the greater part of the Jews lived outside the land of Israel.[a] Many of them never visited the land and so they won't have been very well-informed about the geographical situation. Extra information about the location of places and regions would have been welcome and necessary with the Jews in the Diaspora. Yet the question is whether that is all there is to it. In the Gospel of Luke and in the Acts we find many places without such extra information: Nain, Bethsaida, Jericho, Gaza, Azotus (Asdod), Lydda, Saron, Joppe, etc. (Luke 7,11; 9,10; 18,35; Acts 8,26, 40; 9,32,35, 36.). It can't be understood why Luke should hold the
view that his public should know indeed the location of these places on the map, and should *not* know the location of the places mentioned before. One should consider the possibility that the indication of places and regions is influenced by other factors than the supposed geographical knowledge of the public Luke wrote for.

---

[a] Section 2.2

JESUS' STAY IN GALILEA-JUDEA

Table 6.5

The geographical notations in Luke 8,1 – 9,10a compared with those in Mark 4,1 – 6,31.

Mark	Luke
	8,1-3 from town to town, from village to village (the women who serve Jesus)
4,1-25 by the sea, in a ship (the sower, the lamp, the basket)	8,4-18 (the sower, the lamp)
4,26-34 (the mustard seed)	(13,18-21)
(3,31-35)	8,19-21 (Jesus' relatives)
4,35-41 to the other side (storm at sea)	8,22-25 to the other side of the lake (storm at the lake)
5,1-19 to the other side of the sea in the country of the Gadarenes (healing a man with an unclean spirit)	8,26-39a the country of the Gadarenes opposite Galilee (healing a man with an unclean spirit)
5,20 Decapolis (preaching)	8,39b the whole city (proclaiming)
5,21-37 the other side, by the sea (daughter of Jairus, a woman who'd had a flow of blood)	8,40-50 (returning, daughter of Jairus, woman who'd had a flow of blood)
5,38-43 the house (resuscitation)	8,51-56 the house (resuscitation)
6,1-6a his home town (rejection)	(4,16-30)
6,6b the surrounding villages (Jesus teaches)	9,1-5 (the sending out of the twelve)
6,7-13 (the sending out of the twelve)	9,6 throughout the villages (the twelve are preaching)
6,14-29 (death of John)	9,7-9 (Herod and Jesus)
6,30-31 (return of the apostles)	9,10a (return of the apostles)

Jesus' stay in Galilea-Judea

Now I'd like to point out that for the Diaspora-Jews the most important sources of geographical knowledge of the land of Israel were undoubtedly Tanakh and Septuagint. Besides, it's equally clear that Nazareth, Capernaum, the land of the Gerasenes and Emmaus, - and Luke provided each of them with an extra indication -, don't occur in Tanakh. This also holds for Nain and Bethsaida, which didn't get any extra indication. However, in section 6.8 I'll show that the mention of these two places should be explained exegetically, not geographically. As for Bethlehem, the extra information 'the city of David'(Luke 2,4) evokes rich memories from Tanakh, for instance from the first and the last verse of the book of Ruth. For that matter, there was a Bethlehem in Galilee[166], so that even from a geographical point of view this extra information wasn't superfluous. And finally as for the Mount of Olives, 'which is near Jerusalem, a Sabbath day's journey'[a] (Acts 1,12), this extra information has undoubtedly something to do with Jesus' instruction to the apostles not to leave Jerusalem (Acts 1,4). They complied to Jesus' instruction within the prevailing practice of the law of the then Pharisaic Judaism.

Here we discover that geography and exegesis can go hand in hand, as in the previous section where geography and composition went hand in hand in Luke. This relation between geography and midrash-exegesis will become even clearer in the next sections.

---

[a] A Sabbath day's journey is a distance of about 800 meters. According to Pharisee law one was allowed to walk this distance from one's home. The Sadducees didn't recognize this rule, because it's not found in the Torah, but derived from it exegetically.

6.4 The lake and the sea

A striking phenomenon is that Luke omitted the sea (*thalassa* in Greek) completely from the story.[a] In Mark 6,32-34 the sea plays a prominent part in the story. However, in Luke 9,10b-11 the sea has disappeared completely and consequently the order of arrival of the 'crowd first – Jesus second' (in Mark) should be changed into 'Jesus first – crowd second' (in Luke). Even in the stories in which the Lake of Galilee *should* play a part, as in the stories about the big catch, the storm and the madman of Gerasa, Luke doesn't use the word 'sea', but only the word 'lake' (in Greek: *limne*). And he twice replaces the word 'sea' (Mark 4,39 and 41) by 'water' (Luke 8,24-25). In this way Luke appears to reserve the sea for the Acts. But in that book he's very thrifty with the word 'sea' as well. The word is only found once during Paul's first three yourneys in Acts 17,14 after his departure from Berea. In the other travel-indications the noun 'sea' is absent.[b] Then, quite suddenly, during Paul's fourth voyage, in the tempest, the sea (Greek; *thalassa*) is mentioned thrice (Acts 27,38, 40, 41).

All this can't be explained from Luke's eventual unfamiliarity with the geography of the land of Israel. No doubt a midrash-motif forms the basis of the way in which he deals with the sea and thus corrects Mark. The Sea of Galilee (Mark 1,16) seems an almost daily reality for Mark. For Luke the sea is a 'theological' idea, as is also the case in Tanakh and with the rabbis: the sea as the 'face of the deep'.[c] In this context the sea is the remainder of the primeval flood, from which God called forth the dry land on the third day of the creation. He set bounds to it (Genesis 9,14-15; Job 38,8-11). However, by doing so the primeval

---

[a] Compare in table 6.3 to 6.6 the texts of Luke 5,27; 6,17; 8,4, 26 and 40; 9,10b-11 with those of Mark's.
[b] See: Acts 13,4 and 13; 14,26; 16,11; 18,18 and 21; 20,1, 3, 5, 6, 13-16 and 38; 21,1-3, 6 and 7.
[c] Literary translation of Genesis 1,2 (NKJV).

flood has not yet overcome. The victory over the primeval flood awaits the end of times when the sea will be no more (Revelation 21,1). Until then death and destruction shall reign beyond the bounds set by God. This is the primeval flood that engulfed Pharaoh's chariots and his army (Exodus 15,4-5). And the same fate shall befall Tyre when she rejoices at the downfall of Jerusalem (Ezekiel 26,2-3 and 19). Thus, in many stories and texts the sea and the primeval flood are connected with the enmity against God and Israel, with the enmity of the people that live outside God's revelation and with the realm of the dead (Isaiah 17,12-13; 51,9-10; Jonah 2,2; Revelation 17,15; 20,13). In this context both the sea and the realm of the dead symbolize all those places and situations where God isn't praised and neither knowledge nor wisdom is found (Psalm 6,6; Job 28,14; Ecclesiastes 9,10). Therefore it's across the sea Jonah flies 'from the presence of the Lord' (Jonah 1,3). Rabbi Eliezer, a contemporary of Luke's, says about this:[167]

> "[Jonah said to himself:] Behold, I want to escape from His Presence to a place where His Glory isn't proclaimed. Do I ascend to the heavens, it is written: His glory [is] above the heavens (Psalm 113,4). Do I ascend above the earth [it is written]: the whole earth [is] full of His glory (Isaiah 6,8). Behold, I shall flee to *the sea*, to a *place where His glory isn't proclaimed*".

It's against this background that we have to consider Luke's approach of the sea. I have reached the following conclusions accordingly.

Evidently Luke doesn't consider the Lake of Gennesareth as the sea in the above-meant sense. He's of the opinion that it *does* belong to the place where the glory of God has already been proclaimed. In the story of Jesus in the storm we could recognize an attempt of the underworld to regain the 'lake' (Greek: *limne*) in order to make it a 'sea' (*thalassa*) again. Jesus repels this attack for the glory of God needn't be proclaimed there indeed. But the sea between Jerusalem and Rome is something else. In the Acts 27,35 the glory of God is proclaimed in the midst of the tempest with the blessing over the bread. Thus the frontiers of God's revelation are extended towards the ends of the earth in Luke's eyes (see also Acts 1,8). In Luke's mind this had been Paul's job, not Jesus'.

In this context another mention of the sea in the Acts is of interest. In Acts 10,6 and 32 Peter is at the seaside in Joppe. Joppe is the seaport of Israel, the same town as Jafo in Jonah 1,3. But for Peter his field of activity is confined by the sea. In the Acts he never leaves the land of Israel. His mission lies in Israel, not in the Diaspora. His work and that of his fellow-apostles is directed towards Israel and doesn't extend beyond the foreigners who live in the country (Acts 10). Only at the end of the Acts the wide gap between Jerusalem and Rome, formed by the sea, is bridged by Paul. In the following sections I'll show why especially Rome, in Luke's eyes, was situated across the sea at the far side of the realm of the dead. For now it's obvious, however, that Luke's dealing with the sea is explicable only when we take the meaning for granted the sea has in Tanakh and in the rabbinic tradition.

6.5 Extension from Galilee to Galilee-Judea

A third striking element in Luke's first part of Jesus' activities is, that he widens their area, from Galilee to Galilee-Judea (compare Luke 4,44 with Mark 1,39). In his own material on the resurrection of a widow's only son in Nain Luke states, that the 'report about Jesus went throughout all Judea' (Luke 7,17). Another translation is possible here as well: 'throughout the entire Jewish country', a possibility I'll return to later. And it's also remarkable that the mention of a journey of Jesus throughout Galilee isn't taken up by Luke (Luke 9,43b).

One could conclude from the above-mentioned data that Judea has become more important than Galilee. This however is doubtful. In contrast with Mark and Matthew, Luke ascribes Galilee a bigger part in the

Jesus' Stay in Galilea-Judea

trial against Jesus by inserting a confrontation with Herod Antipas, who ruled Galilee and therefore had jurisdiction over Jesus (Luke 23,6-7). Also the apostles' origin from Galilee is mentioned explicitly in the Acts (1,11; 2,7). Strictly speaking Luke adds Judea to Galilee as the area of Jesus' activities. Even in the first chapters of his gospel the place of action changes from one to another region all the time (Luke 1:9, 23, 26, 39, 56, 65; 2:4, 22, 39, 41, 51). Now there are in the Gospel of Luke and in the Acts a number of places from which may be concluded that there is more at stake here than a simple extension of a working area. True, there are texts in which Galilee and Judea seem to be two different regions (Luke 5,17; 23,5; Acts 9,31), but in a greater number of cases only Judea is mentioned, when Galilee is meant as well. For example, Herod the Great is called King of Judea, but the entire Jewish country came under his power (Luke 1,5). We also perceive that Luke removes Mark's distinction between Galilee and Judea (Mark 3,7) and unites both regions under the name of Judea (Luke 6,17). Remarkably, in the Acts Galilee is absent from many geographical indications (Acts 1,8; 8,1; 10,39; 11,1 and 29). When Galilee is mentioned, it is situated between Judea and Samaria (Acts 9,31), entirely contrary to the geographical reality. In this context two descriptions of the area of Jesus' activities are important:

- 'both in the land of the Jews and in Jerusalem' (Acts 10,39),
- 'from Galilee to Jerusalem' (Acts 13,31).

Luke sees Galilee-Judea-Jerusalem very much as a unit. So he ascribes two meanings to the word 'Judea': on the one hand the region of the province of Judea, on the other the (entire) Jewish country, Galilee inclusive. A twofold meaning like that is, in fact, nothing special for geographical names and it happens very often elsewhere, especially as far as capitals and the main provinces or countries are concerned.

Jesus' stay in Galilea-Judea

Table 6.7

The geographical notations in Luke 9,51 – 19,29 compared with those in Mark 10,1 – 11,1.

Mark	Luke
10,1-12 To the other side of the Jordan (divorce)	
	9,51 travelling to Jerusalem
	9,52-55 village of Samaritans
	9,56 another village
	9,57 – 10,37 under way
	10,38-42 under way, a certain village
	11,1-37 somewhere
	11,38-52 inside
	11,53 – 13,9 left that place
	13,10-21 one of the synagogues
	13,22-30 through cities and villages, travelling to Jerusalem
	13,31-35 depart from here
	14,1-24 in the house of one of the rulers of the Pharisees
	14,25 – 17,10 travelled with him
	17,11 journey to Jerusalem through the midst of Samaria and Galilee
	17,12 – 18,14 a certain village
10,13 – 34 (children, the rich young man, following Jesus, the third prediction of his suffering)	18,15-34 (children, the rich young man, following Jesus, the third prediction of his suffering)
10,35-45 (James and John)	(22,24-27)
10,46-52 Jericho, arrival and departure (healing of Bartimaeus)	18,35-43 near Jericho (healing of a blind)
	19,1-10 in Jericho and through (Zacchaeus)
	19,11-27 near Jerusalem (parable of the ten minas)
	19,28 to Jerusalem (going up)
11,1 near Jerusalem, Bethphage and Bethany at the mountain of Olives	19,29 near Bethphage and Bethany, at the mountain of Olives

"Washington" for example often means: the United States. Continental Europeans often say "England" meaning the whole of Great-Britain. In the first century CE the Romans used the word 'Judea' in this double meaning.[168] And the word 'Judea'[a] had been used earlier for the Hasmonean kingdoms and the kingdom of Herod the Great, although they covered a much larger area than Judea only.[169] It now begins to look as if Luke in his gospel as well as in the Acts presents the idea that the provinces of Galilee and Judea adjoined each other and so constituted one region.[170]

So what is the meaning of the extension of Galilee (in Mark) to Galilee-Judea (in Luke) for the first part of Jesus' activities? Although the stories of this part of the Gospel of Luke don't seem to play anywhere special in the province of Judea and all places mentioned are outside this province, Luke, in this way, makes it clear to his readers that also the first part of Jesus' mission had been directed towards all Jews and not towards his disciples or towards the Jews of Galilee exclusively. The entire land of Israel had been the area of Jesus' activities from the beginning. Here again we find support for the meaning 'among us, Jews', we already mentioned with regard to Luke 1,1.[b] More important so, seeing that Luke doesn't include many stories of Mark's that play abroad.

6.6 *Removal of gentile regions*

Mark mentions certain regions that aren't part of the Jewish land and it is quite remarkable to see how Luke deals with this.[c] In Luke 6,17 Idumea (Edom) and the Transjordanian region are left out of the story.

---

[a] In Aramaic: *Jehud*.
[b] See section 5.1.e.
[c] See tables 6.3 to 6.7.

Jesus' stay in Galilea-Judea

Only Tyre and Sidon are mentioned.[a] In Luke 8,39b the mention of Decapolis is removed. And a journey of Jesus to Caesarea Philippi north of Galilee isn't taken over in the Gospel of Luke as well (compare Luke 9,18 with Mark 8,27).

Equally important is the absence of a series of stories that play abroad and which we do find in the Gospel of Mark (Mark 7,24 – 8,10):

- the meeting with a Syro-Phoenician woman in Tire,
- a journey through Sidon,
- the healing of a deaf-mute,
- the second feeding in Decapolis.

These stories belong to the so-called 'grosse Lücke' (Mark 6,45 – 8,10), a joined series of Mark-stories that are not in the Gospel of Luke. Some scholars explain this phenomenon from the supposition that Luke only had an incomplete text of the Gospel of Mark at his disposal.[171] Further consideration of these stories however, makes us suppose something else. The *first* story of this 'grosse Lücke' is a sea-story: Jesus walking on the sea (Mark 6,45-52). We already noted that Luke exercised restraint with regard to the sea, both in his gospel as in the Acts.[b] The third story from the 'grosse Lücke' is a passionate speech of Jesus' against the Pharisees (Mark 7,1-23). Later on we'll see that Luke's attitude towards the Pharisees is a lot more positive than the one of Mark and Matthew.[c] Probably he hadn't been able to use both Mark-stories. Owing to the three omissions of the stories that played abroad we began this section with, it can be taken for granted that Luke consciously didn't take over these stories from the 'grosse Lücke' as well. They presumably didn't fit in the concept of his gospel Luke had in

---

[a] See section 5.1.e. as well.
[b] See section 6.4.
[c] See section 9.1.

mind.[172] In his concept Jesus' mission had especially been pointed at the Jewish land and not at the regions abroad.

Quite another light is being shed now upon the supposition that Luke wouldn't have known the land of Israel. How should he *not* have known the country if he *did* know how to distinguish the neighbouring regions so that next he could remove them almost everywhere? An urgent question can be raised here: how is it possible that an evangelist like Luke, who in the Acts attaches so much importance to the preaching of the gospel among the gentiles, removes exactly these gentile regions from his gospel? To answer this question the only exception to this concept will be of great importance. We'll discuss this exception in the next section.

6.7 The land of the Gerasenes

Only one example of Jesus visiting a gentile region can be found in the Gospel of Luke: the land of the Gerasenes (Luke 8,26-39). The following can be said about this story of the healing of a demoniac. First of all, this story follows immediately on the story of the 'squall' at the lake. I have already mentioned the fact that this story was written with Jonah 1 in mind (compare Luke 8,23-24 with Jonah 1,4-6).[a] In the book of Jonah the journey to the gentile city of Nineveh (Jonah 3) follows immediately after the storm at sea and in Luke's gospel Jesus visits the gentile region of the Gerasenes immediately after the storm at the lake as well. A clear example of how Luke uses the Tanakh-background in his own stories! Besides, this story of Luke's is in its turn the background of the parallel-story in Acts 27 about Paul in the storm at sea, as already stated in section 6.4. Paul's stay in Rome, the Nineveh of its days, follows immediately after Acts 27! So there are three parallel stories here:

---

[a] See section 6.1.

JESUS' STAY IN GALILEA-JUDEA

a. Jonah in the storm → Nineveh
b. Jesus in the storm → the land of the Gerasenes
c. Paul in the storm → Rome

These facts now make it possible to compare the story in the Gospel of Luke about the demoniac of Gerasa with the story in the Acts of Paul's stay in Rome. And there are some striking similarities too, so that we can't escape the conclusion that here we are dealing with a conscious composition of Luke's.

- What is obvious immediately is the Latin name of the demoniac: Legion (Luke 8,30). Which of Luke's contemporaries wouldn't have associated this name with the Roman legions?
- The demonic spirits are driven into a herd of swine (Luke 8,32). The Jews in Luke's days regularly compared the Romans with pigs.173 Very probably this comparison originated from the fact that the Roman legion that occupied the land of Israel carried a pig as a symbol in its standard.
- Next we see the herd of swine perish into the abyss (Luke 8,31-33). This of course, reminds us of what I wrote before about the link between the sea, the abyss and the realm of the dead on the one hand and the people that are hostile to Israel on the other.a Obviously the theme of this story is the eventual fall of the military power and rule of Rome.b
- From this perspective of the eventual fall of the Roman Empire another detail in the story about the healing of the demoniac

---

[a] See section 6.4.
[b] Also in the Revelation the fall of Rome (the 'harlot of Babylon' in Revelation 17,4-5) is described as an act of being thrown into the sea (Revelation 18,21). The images used there correspond with the perishing of the army of Pharao in the Red Sea (Exodus 15,4-5) and the perishing of the Babylonian Empire into the Eufrates (Jeremiah 51,63-64).

comes forward. Contrary to Mark's version of this story the demoniac comes from the town (compare Luke 8,27 with Mark 5,2). Also at the end of the story the action of the healed man is only directed towards the town and not towards the whole region (compare Luke 8,39 with Mark 5,20). This fits completely into the comparison with Nineveh (Jonah 3) and with Rome (Acts 28).

Next we should ask what this Gerasa-story, in addition to the reference to Rome, has to do with Paul's stay in Rome in Acts 28. When we compare both stories we discover six points of agreement, entirely in the same order throughout both stories:

- The meeting (Luke 8,27a; Acts 28,15);
- The living-quarters (Luke 8,27b; Acts 28,16);
- The wearing of chains (Luke 8,29; Acts 28,20);
- The rejection (Luke 8,37; Acts 28,26-27);
- The living-quarters again (Luke 8,39a; Acts 28,30);
- The proclaiming (Luke 8,39b; Acts 28,31).

As a seventh point of agreement can be put forward that at the end of both stories nothing is told about a supposed conversion of the town. And here we find the difference with Jonah 3. True enough, the conversion of Nineveh is a model for the conversion of the gentiles, but the Rome of Paul's days (and that of Luke's days as well) must still be converted! In Acts 28 Luke, in the person of Paul, incites the Jews of Rome to fulfil Jonah's mission. But the connection with the story about the healing of the demoniac of Gerasa urges us to go one step farther.

In the above we saw that Luke on the one hand restricts Jesus' mission to the Jewish land but on the other hand extends it to the *entire* Jewish Land. As said before the Sermon in the Field in Luke 6,17-26 should be read against the background of the entry into the land of

JESUS' STAY IN GALILEA-JUDEA

Israel under Joshua.[a] There Luke depicts Jesus as a Joshua-figure who pursues the liberation and the cleansing of the land of Israel in order to make it reach its true destiny. Other Jewish groups during and after Jesus' days knew this aspiration too. But the big problem was always how to liberate the land of Israel from the Roman legions. The group of the Zealots wanted to reach this end with a violent uprising. It's quite possible now to reconstruct Luke's opinion in this matter from a combination of the Gerasa-story and the story of Paul's stay in Rome: the battle for the liberation and cleansing of the land of Israel shouldn't be fought in the land itself but abroad. And the weapon used shouldn't be violence, but the teachings in Torah and the Prophets. By moving this spiritual battle to Rome the Roman military oppression will eventually perish in the abyss of history. That was what Luke hoped for.

It's clearer now why Luke wrote the sea out of his gospel and kept it for Acts 27. Not the lake of Gennesareth, but the sea between Jerusalem and Rome is the great barrier that must be taken within the framework of this liberation-strategy. This hasn't been Jesus' work but Paul's. In Luke 8,26-39 Jesus points at the road, that Paul in Acts 27 and 28 has to go.

The conclusion is that the only story in the Gospel of Luke that plays outside Israel isn't an essential exception to Luke's concept that Jesus' actions were primarily directed towards the Jewish Land. It's more likely that the story points at the conversion of the gentiles, and especially the conversion of Rome into a god-fearing city, and thus will be the means to the liberation and cleansing of the land of Israel. The aim of Jesus' mission will especially be pursued in Rome by the Jews in the Diaspora. Nothing else remains to be concluded than the fact that Luke had clear Jewish intentions with his gospel and with the Acts, and that he wrote for a Jewish public.

---

[a] See section 5.1.e.

JESUS' STAY IN GALILEA-JUDEA

6.8 Mentioning Galilean places

In the first part of Jesus' activities during his stay in Galilee-Judea four places are called by their names. They are all in Galilee: Nazareth, Capernaum, Nain and Bethsaida.[a] With the exception of Nain these places are also mentioned in the Gospel of Mark. Luke however, follows his own path in mentioning these places, a path that can only be understood from midrash-motives and not from purely geographical or historical considerations. I'll discuss all four places.

a. Nazareth
The first place we arrive at during Jesus' stay in Galilee-Judea is Nazareth (Luke 4,16-30). In comparison with the parallel-story in Mark 6,1-6 two things come forward. First Luke presents us with an entirely own version of this story in which he refers to the Tanakh three times:

- Isaiah's prophesy of the messianic times (Luke 4,18-19; Isaiah 61,1-2);
- a quotation of Elijah's stay with the widow of Zarephath (Luke 4,25-26; 1 Kings 17,1-16);
- a quotation of the healing of Naaman the Syrian by Elisha (Luke 4,27; 2 Kings 5,1-14).

Secondly Luke put this story at the beginning of the public actions of Jesus. By doing so the story gets the character of a programme that shows Jesus' goal and teaching. In Luke's eyes the relation between Israel and the nations was an important element in this programme. This does not only appear from the reference to Naaman the Syrian. Who reads the whole of Isaiah 61 will see that this chapter deals with – among other things – Israel's function towards the nations (Isaiah 61,9 and 11). In many commentaries the widow of Zarephath is looked upon

---

[a] For the geographical position of Bethsaida: see the discussion in section 6.8.d.

as a gentile woman.[174] However, is that a correct interpretation? The text in Luke 4,25-26 isn't clear about this. Indeed, Elijah isn't sent to the widows of 'the entire land', but to the widow of Zarephath, who lived outside the land of Israel, but could have really been an Israelitic woman. In some Jewish traditions from Luke's days she is seen as an Israelitic woman from the tribe of Asher. Supposedly her by Elijah resuscitated son was the prophet Jonah.[175] When discussing Capernaum and Nain I'll show that Luke too, saw her as a Jewess. And this allows for the following interpretation of the Nazareth-story.

With the quotation from Isaiah 61 Luke indicates that Jesus' actions were aimed at persuading the Jews in the land of Israel and especially those of Jerusalem (Zion in Isaiah 61,3) to live as a messianic people after Isaiah's model in order to be the salvation of the other nations. If they fail, Jesus prophecies, this mission will go to the Jews of the Diaspora (the widow of Zarephath), in order to bring the gentiles (Naaman the Syrian, see 2 Kings 5,2-3 in particular) to Israel to teach them the wisdom of the LORD. And this is exactly the programme that Luke develops in his gospel and in the Acts. In these books Jesus is above all things the messianic man whose task it is to make Israel a messianic people (Luke 4,18). Consequently he clashes with certain groups in the Jewish society of his days. In this way the rejection in Nazareth (Luke 4,28-29) points forward to Jesus' execution in Jerusalem. Strangely enough the brow of the hill and the cliff they wanted to throw him from (Luke 4,29) can't be found in the surroundings of Nazareth. But this is not a geographical error of Luke's, but an indication that it's about an execution. In those days a stoning usually began by throwing the convict from a heigh steep rock.[176]

The reference to what will happen in Jerusalem later on is also found somewhere else in the story. In Luke 4,23 and 24 Jesus' hometown is mentioned. The question is whether only Nazareth is meant. Is Nazareth Jesus' hometown, because he had been brought up there? In Luke 2,49 Jesus, a boy of twelve, is in the temple in Jerusalem studying with the teachers, and there he calls God his father. So is Jerusalem, the city of God[a], perhaps his hometown? The theme 'no prophet is accepted in his own country' results in Jesus' complaint 'O Jerusalem, Jerusalem, the one who kills the prophets and stones those who are sent to her ...' (Luke 13,34). And there is a striking similarity as well between Jesus' actions in Nazareth and the one in Jerusalem: he doesn't heal or perform other miracles there, but teaches only. The reason why Luke sets this story about the 'programme' of Jesus' actions in Nazareth lies in this two-fold meaning of the word 'hometown' (Nazareth as well as Jerusalem)[b].

So the rejection in Nazareth in the Gospel of Luke symbolizes those groups in the then Jewry which reject the purpose of Jesus' actions and in doing so don't shrink from violence to silence him. In chapter 7 and 9 we'll examine which groups could be meant here. Anyway, it's clear from the story following the Nazareth-story and that plays in Capernaum that Luke didn't have the entire Jewish people in view here. Many commentators suppose or suggest this mistakenly.[177] In this Nazareth-story there is no support for the explanation that this is a story about an initial rejection of Jesus' by his family and relatives.[178, c] For Luke Nazareth is the starting-point of Jesus' actions. It points at its final consequence in Jerusalem: his willingness to suffer and to die for the cause of the LORD. So Nazareth is not so much a geographical indication, as a 'theological' or 'midrashic' one. This now makes the question

---

[a] Zion; see Psalm 46,2 and 9; 87,3

[b] As we'll see in section7.2, there is no place on earth that plays a bigger part in the Gospel of Luke and the Acts than Jerusalem.

[c] James, Jesus' brother, will later be the leader of the Jerusalem community (Acts 12,17; 15,13; 21,18). That's why it's out of proportion to present the initial rejection by his family as an attempt to kill him. We observe that none of Jesus' relatives plays a part in Luke's Nazareth-story. The observation about his father Joseph (Luke 4,22) sooner indicates that those who are speaking there are not his immediate relatives.

arise whether something like that is also the case with the other three mentions of Galilean cities.

b. Capernaum

The second place mentioned during Jesus' Galilean-Judean stay is Capernaum. Also with this entry Luke has a purpose of his own. Compared with Mark, Luke removed Capernaum twice, viz. at the healing of a paralytic (Luke 5,17) and at the fight to be the greatest (Luke 9,46). In both cases it's about a remark of Mark's from which appeared that Jesus once lived in Capernaum. Obviously Luke wanted to avoid that this could be gathered from his gospel. Has Capernaum perhaps another meaning for him?

Luke takes over one Capernaum-story only from Mark, about healing and exorcizing. And, what's more, in his own text he tells a second Capernaum-story about the healing of a slave of a centurion (Luke 7,1-10). The first of these two stories follows immediately after the Nazareth-story. We'll discover that these stories are closely connected. Because the first time Capernaum is mentioned is in the Nazareth-story itself (Luke 4,23). Some commentators have problems with that verse[179], because it refers to an action of Jesus' about which Luke hasn't told us anything yet. In my view, however, it's about an indication that the Nazareth-story has something to do with the following Capernaum-story. In this connection it's noteworthy that in the Capernaum-story the name of Nazareth is found as well (Luke 4,34). Considering the structure of both stories we see a striking resemblance and contrast as well. Apart from some opening and closing sentences both stories show a clear division into three parts with related or contrasting themes (see table 6.8). In the Nazareth-story it's about a programme of Jesus' mission. The most important objective is to turn Israel into a messianic people. On account of the parallelism between both stories we are now able to conclude that for Luke Capernaum was presumably the first place where this objective should be pursued. Apart from that, we find a first

Table 6.8
The Nazareth-story (Luke 4,16-30) compared with the Capernaum-story (Luke 4, 31-44).

Division	Nazareth-story (Luke 4,16-30)	Capernaum-story (Luke 4,31-44)
opening	v. 16 - place and situation	v. 31-32 - place and situation
1st part	vv. 17-22 - spirit of the LORD - agreement	vv. 33-37 - exorcizing an unclean spirit, - ashtonishment
2nd part	vv. 23-26 - physician, heal yourself, - the widow of Zarephath	vv. 38-39 - healing, - Simon's mother-in-law
3rd part	vv. 27-29 - cleansing of Naaman, - rejection of Jesus	vv. 40-43 - healings and exorcisms, - keeping Jesus
closing	v. 30 - departure	v. 44 - actions elsewhere

argument for the supposition here that Luke saw the widow of Zarephath as an Israelitic woman: he puts her on a level with Simon Peter's mother-in-law, who was a Jewess.

In the parallelism of both stories however, one element of the Nazareth-story is missing in the Capernaum-story: the pagan Naaman and his cleansing. What could have moved Luke to make the theme of healing and exorcism come back more specifically in the third part of the Capernaum-story, instead of incorporating an event related to the healing of Naaman? This own approach of Luke's urges us to look for another explanation than the conclusion that he kept on following Mark's story. We find the answer in the second Capernaum-story about the healing of the slave of a centurion (Luke 7,1-11).

After comparison of this second Capernaum-story with Matthew's version (Matthew 8,5-13), we'll discover again Luke's own approach. He writes this very story against the background of Naaman the Syrian

(2 Kings 5,1-14). Comparison of Luke 7,1-11 with 2 Kings 5,1-14 yields at least five thematic similarities:

- Naaman and the centurion are not only gentiles, but they are also soldiers (2 Kings 5,1; Luke 7,2);
- in both stories the sick person is a subordinate, who's found favour with his master (2 Kings 5,1; Luke 7,2);
- in the first story an Israelitic girl is the go-between (2 Kings 5,2-3) and in the second one some elders of the Jews (Luke 7,3) – in both cases the mediators are representatives of Israel;
- a second mediation takes place by the king of Aram (2 Kings 5,5) and by some friends of the centurion's (Luke 7,6) – in both stories representatives of the gentiles;
- no meeting takes place before the healing, neither with Elisha (2 Kings 5,9-10), nor with Jesus (Luke 7,9-10).

Of course there are contrasts as well, but they all indicate that the centurion of Capernaum has made more progress on the way of all nations towards Israel than has Naaman the Syrian. Does Naaman refuse to bathe in the Jordan from disbelief (2 Kings 5.11-12), the centurion refuses to receive Jesus from modesty and belief. However, Israel has also made some progress in its relation towards the gentiles. Whereas the king of Israel sees the arrival of Naaman as a threat of war (2 Kings 5,7), some elders of the Jews intercede actively for the centurion (Luke7,4). Luke cuts his story short at the moment of the healing. A meeting of the centurion with Jesus is not mentioned. Apparently such a meeting isn't needed for what Luke has to tell us with this story!

It's now clear why Luke doesn't insert a parallel with Naaman the Syrian in his first Capernaum-story: he saves it for the second Capernaum-story. In this way Capernaum is the first place where Jesus' programme, derived from Tanakh and explained in the Nazareth-story, is completely realized, be it in two stages, in the situation of Jesus' days:

when the Jews decide to live as a messianic people, there is not only a place for god-fearing gentiles in Israel, but there is also the possibility that they are an example for Israel (Luke 7,9). Of course there was no need for Luke to persuade the god-fearing gentiles of this. But many Jews in the first century would have had a lot of trouble with this idea of Luke's. That's why, in the light of the midrash-exegesis of the Capernaum-stories, everything can be said for the supposition that Luke wrote for a Jewish public.

In his gospel Luke deals with the Galilean places according to his own concept and this finally confronts us with the question why the realisation of Jesus' programme should take place in Capernaum in the first place. In my opinion, also this question could only be answered against the background of Tanakh. For *Kfarna'um* means 'village of Nahum'. The little prophetical book of Nahum is about the fall of Nineveh, the muster-place of all anti-Israelitic forces in the world. As contrasted with the book of *Jonah* the book of *Nahum* considers that foretold fall as a prospect full of comfort for Israel. *Nahum* means 'comforter'. It needs no argument that this little prophetical book was a source of inspiration for the Zealotic liberation movement in Jesus' days. Therefore it's a matter of course that Capernaum, the 'village of Nahum', is the first of all places where Jesus' programme will have to be realized. In Israel, the Zealotic spirit of a violent uprising against the Romans will have to give way to a spirit of healing and cleansing, a spirit that eventually will be extended even to the slaves of the gentiles. After Luke has finished this argumentation with the second Capernaum-story, he will be able to show which 'Nineveh-prophet', Nahum or Jonah, corresponds to the way of Jesus. He shows this in the Nain-story that follows the second Capernaum-story immediately.

c. Nain
Nain is mentioned only once in the Gospel of Luke, that is in Luke's own material. In this place the resuscitation of the only son of a widow

is enacted (Luke 7,11-17). At first sight the mention of the name of Nain has no significance in the whole of the story. But also this story should be read against the background of Tanakh. The dead boy is in the story the only son of a widow. In Tanakh there is only one story with a comparable theme: the story of the widow of Zarephath (1 Kings 17,7-24). This story served apparently as the background of the Nain-story, because there are not only some thematic similarities but also a number of similar wordings:

- the mention of the gate of the city (1 Kings 17,10; Luke 7,12);
- the woman has only got one son (1 Kings 17,12; Luke 7,12);
- the woman is a widow (1 Kings 17,9; Luke 7,12);
- after the resuscitation the son is given back to his mother (1 Kings 17,23; Luke 7,15);
- both stories end with a saying about the prophet (1 Kings 17,24a; Luke 7,16a) and a saying about God (1 Kings 17,24b; Luke 7,16b).

As mentioned before in the discussion on Nazareth, in the Jewish tradition in the first century CE the resuscitated son of the widow of Zarephtah is identified with the prophet Jonah. Undoubtedly, the then Jewish readers of the Gospel of Luke will have experienced this association as well. That's why we'll be able to suppose that Luke inserted this story here, directly after the second Capernaum-story, with a view to this tradition about Jonah. After having rejected the Zealotic appeal to Nahum[a], he shows his readers that Jesus' actions from Nain on are completely in line with the book of Jonah. Central in this book is not the fall but the conversion of Nineveh. Remarkable too is the exclamation 'a great prophet has risen up among us' (Luke 7,16). Now, should we think of Jesus, of Jonah (the resuscitated son) or of both? The argument Luke begins with in this story, ends in the stories of the storm at the

---

[a] See the previous subsection.

lake and the healing of the demoniac of Gerasa (Luke 8,22-39), the Jonah-background of which I already discussed.[a]

The question now is why this resuscitation-story had to play in Nain, of all places. *Nain* means 'the lovely one'[180] and has the same meaning as the name of *Naomi*. Now Naomi is the prototype of a widow whose sons have died (Ruth 1,3-5). Just like de widow of Zarephath she lives abroad. Here we see a second argument why Luke saw the widow of Zarephath as an Israelitic woman: he put her on one level with the widow of Nain who, in his eyes, was undoubtedly a Jewess, and he indirectly identifies her with Naomi as well. So the name of Nain connects the story of the resuscitation by Jesus directly with the book of Ruth. And the road Naomi takes with Ruth towards Israel is a continuation of the road of Jonah towards Nineveh. The purpose of both roads is the same: to bring the gentiles to the point that they will say:

'Your people shall be my people, and your God, my God' (Ruth 1,16).

The order of words in this sentence shows a biblical characteristic: as a gentile one should come to know the people of Israel first and only then one could come to know the God of this people. And this also explains the strong appeal of the Prophets to Israel to fulfil its mission in the world. If Israel doesn't fulfil its mission, things look black for the relation between God and the rest of mankind.

The question for the author of the Gospel of Luke should be answered in the light of these Tanakh-backgrounds. The books of Jonah and of Ruth were not written by a gentile author or for a gentile public, nor is it necessary to consider Luke's argument as destined for non-Jewish readers. As Jonah and Ruth were written to remind the Israelites of their worldwide mission, so it is quite possible that Luke wrote his

---

[a] See section 6.7.

gospel for Jews to make them understand how they could fulfil that mission in their own days as best as they could. The Jewish background with and the midrash-exegesis of the geographical material in the Gospel of Luke lead us again and again to the conclusion, that Luke was a Jew who wrote for a Jewish public.

d. Bethsaida

Bethsaida is the fourth and the last place we come across during Jesus' stay in Galilee-Judea. This place is mentioned twice in the Gospel of Mark (6,45; 8,22), but none of these entries was taken over by Luke. On the contrary, it's remarkable that the 'grosse Lücke', the series of stories Luke doesn't take over from Mark, begins and ends with Bethsaida. Luke follows his own path with Bethsaida, too. Contrary to Mark he puts Bethsaida at the beginning of the story about the feeding of the 5000 (Luke 9,10b). It's of some importance as well that, till the beginning of the travel-story (Luke 9,51), he leaves out all mentions from which could have been concluded that Jesus had gone beyond Bethsaida or its immediate surroundings. Comparison with Mark shows that it's about three mutations in the text: the villages of Caesarea Philippi (Mark 8,27), the journey through Galilee (Mark 9,30) and a stay in Capernaum (Mark 9,33). However, the corresponding stories, albeit with variations, are found in the Gospel of Luke as well. It's obvious that Luke meant to situate all stories of 9,10b-50 in Bethsaida and its surroundings. This evokes the question after the meaning of all this. But before going further into this question we'll make another observation.

Bethsaida is situated at the north-eastern side of the Lake of Galilee, at the eastern side of the river Jordan, and didn't belong to the Roman province of Galilee in the first century CE.[a] In connection with the already discussed limitation of Jesus' actions to the Jewish land, as Luke

---

[a] See map 7.1.

introduces them in his gospel[a], one can now ask the question whether we're dealing here with an exception or with an error of Luke's. We observe that there is no assertion whatsoever in the Gospel of Luke itself that Bethsaida should have been outside Galilee. Careful comparison with Mark shows that Luke has repositioned Bethsaida in Galilee, so to speak. In Mark 6,32-35 there is some talk of a voyage of Jesus'. In the parallel-text of Luke 9,10b-12, however, Luke avoids the impression that Bethsaida was situated at the other side of the lake. Besides, both times Mark mentions Bethsaida it is reached by boat. We already saw that Luke didn't take over these entries. Next Luke situates the feeding of the 5000 (Luke 9,12-17; Mark 6,35-44) near Bethsaida and not the feeding of the 4000 (Mark 8,1-9), a story not found at all in the Gospel of Luke. One of the keys to these stories is the number of baskets of bread that remains after the end of the meal: 12 in the 5000-story and 7 in the 4000. In the Jewish tradition 12 is the number of the tribes of Israel and 7 (interchangeable with 70) the number of the nations of the world.[181] So Luke makes the story of the feeding of Israel take place in or near Bethsaida, but he doesn't take up the feeding of the nations of the world into his gospel! We're now able to derive from this that for Luke Bethsaida functions as a place within the Jewish land, particularly in Galilee. This is confirmed in Luke 24,6 that states that Jesus announced his suffering to the disciples in Galilee. Two out of the three announcements of his suffering however, are situated in Bethsaida (Luke 9,22 and 44). Here too, Luke's concept is that Bethsaida was in Galilee, but why Bethsaida?

The literal meaning of the word *Beth-saida* is 'house of fish', but because of the fact that fish was one of the most important staples of food around the Lake of Galilee[182], the word *Bethsaida* can also be translated with 'place of provisions'[183]. This points at the fact that Luke considers Jesus' stay at *Bethsaida* as a period of provisioning: he provides

---

[a] See section 6.6.

his followers of the necessary 'provision' preceding the journey to Jerusalem. In fact, this journey begins immediately after the stay in Bethsaida. It's striking as well that the series of Bethsaida-stories begin with the feeding. At the same time the involvement in the aim of the journey is stated thrice clearly (Luke 9,22 and 31 and 44). All this could be compared with a campaign: the soldiers must be provided with provisions and insight how to reach the planned aim. Associations crop up with a march on Jerusalem of various Zealotic groups, in order to liberate this city from the Roman yoke. I'll return to this comparison when I'll discuss the travel-story. However, it's perfectly clear that the Bethsaida-stories play a presumably important part as a preparation to the travel-story. The mention of Bethsaida has no geographical, but a midrash-function in the story as such.

The general conclusion we can draw at the end of this chapter, is that the geographical notations Luke makes in the first part of Jesus' actions, if read from the midrash-character of his gospel, don't point at Luke's unfamiliarity with the situation in the land of Israel, but, as part of his dissertation, strongly support the supposition that Luke was a Jewish author who wrote for a Jewish public.

7. The things that make for your peace
Jesus' travel to and stay in Jerusalem

7.1 The travel story (Luke 9,51 – 19,28)

The travel story shows at least three important aspects: the geography, the Tanakh-background and the character of Jesus' actions during the journey. I'll devote a section to all three of them.

a. The map of Luke's gospel

Once arrived at Luke 9,51 the parallellism of the gospels of Luke and Mark (from 10,1) begins to abandon us. Their roads part when in both gospels Jesus' journey to Jerusalem begins. When we first look at Mark's travel story we'll soon discover that it's only one chapter in length and has only five travel notes (Mark 10,1, 17, 32, 46, 52). These notes link up perfectly with the geographical situation at that time and the route can be easily drawn on the map (see map 7.1). They travel via the eastern side of the river Jordan, avoiding Samaria, and near Jericho they cross the river again to reach Judea. This was the common route for the Galilean Jews who went on a pilgrimage to Jerusalem. In this way they avoided contact with the Samaritans who, true enough, were related to the Jews, but who lived and thought differently in so many respects, that there was a great measure of enmity between both groups. So in the Gospel of Mark Jesus doesn't meet any Samaritans. His journey to Jerusalem is described as a common pilgrimage to Jerusalem.

In Luke it's a different matter altogether. A journey via the eastern side of the river Jordan isn't even mentioned. On the contrary, it seems that he wants to prevent the impression that Jesus had travelled via the eastern side of the river Jordan in order to avoid Samaria. Because the first place Jesus calls at during his journey is a village of the Samaritans (Luke 9,52). It should be clear from the beginning that here we're not

Jesus' Travel to and Stay in Jerusalem

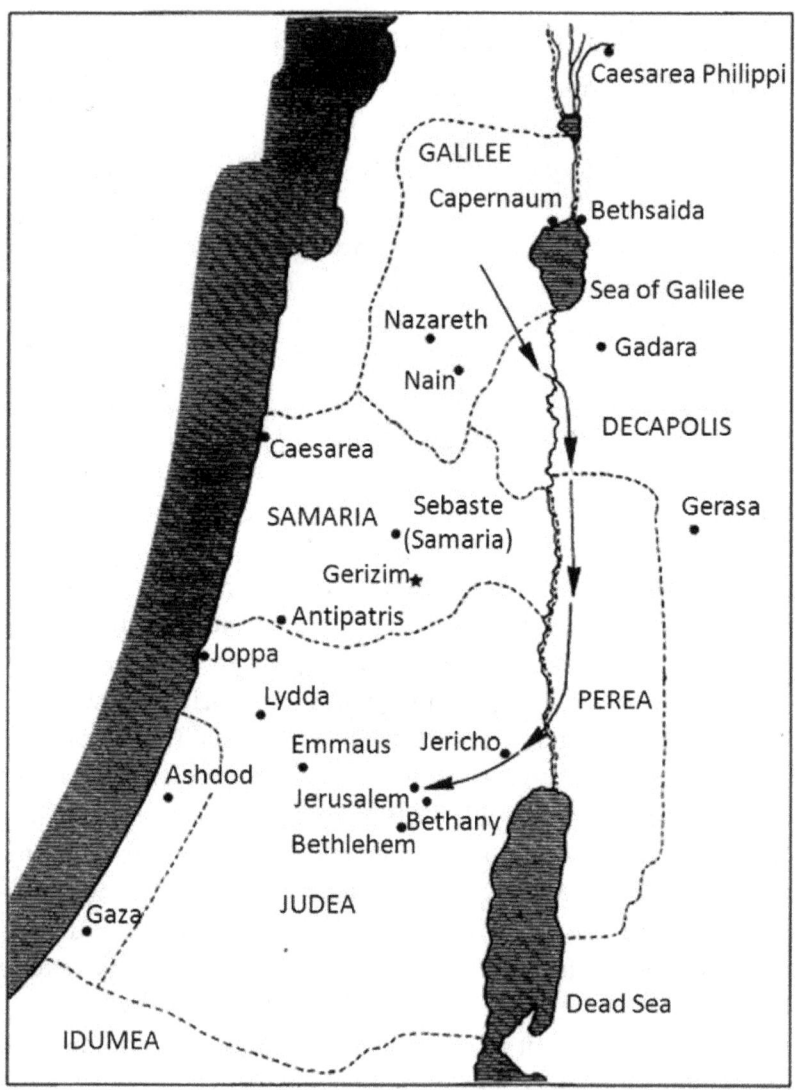

Map 7.1 *The map of the land of Israel according to the Gospel of Mark.*

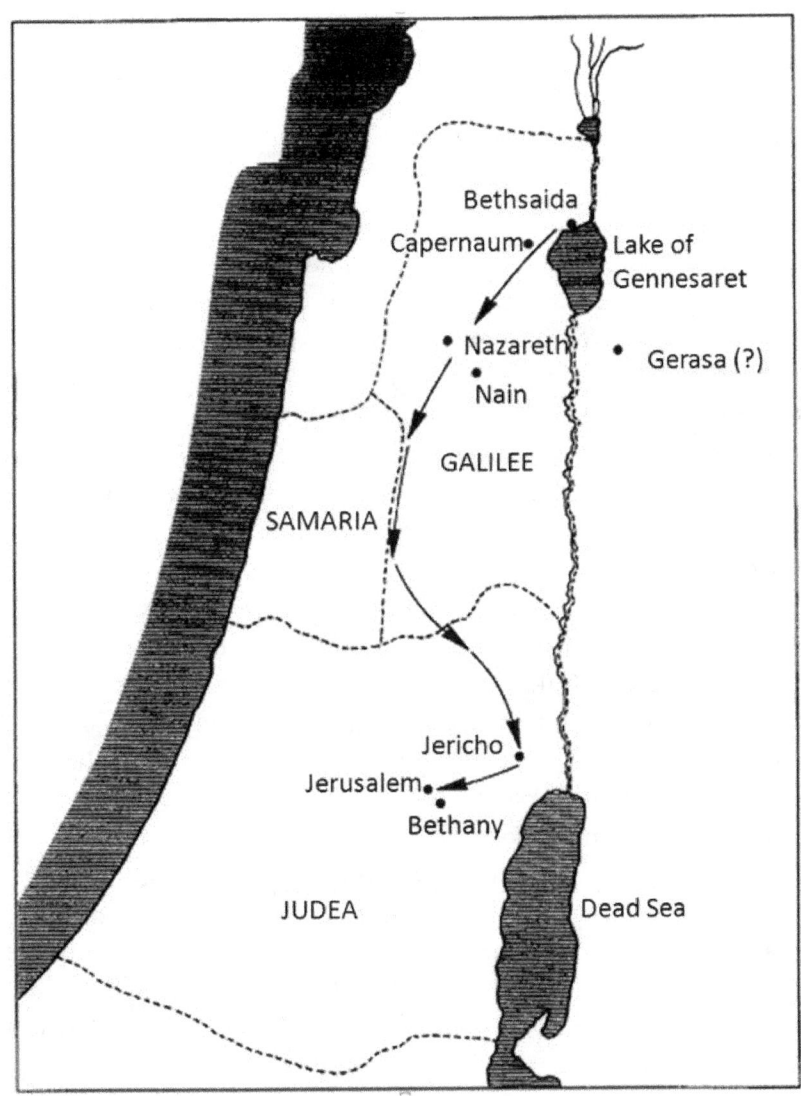

Map 7.2 *The map of the land of Israel according to the Gospel of Luke.*

JESUS' TRAVEL TO AND STAY IN JERUSALEM

dealing with a common pilgrimage. In the Gospel of Luke the going up to Jerusalem probably has quite another meaning. We'll return to this in the following sections.

Who, aided by Luke's geographical notes in the travel story[a], wants to fill in Jesus' journey in the map, will be confronted with a good many problems. It's true, the first stay is in Samaria (Luke 9,51-56), but later on we find Jesus in Galilee. The warning of some Pharisees "Get out and depart from here, for Herod wants to kill you" (Luke 13,31), must have been given in Galilee, as Herod Antipas ruled in Galilee and Perea, but not in Samaria and Judea. Also most other stories during the journey are only conceivable in Jewish, that is to say in Galilean or Judean surroundings. However, a clear crossing between Galilee and Judea is not given, although in Luke 18,35 Jesus suddenly appears to be in Jericho in Judea.

I have already observed that presumably Luke saw Galilee and Judea as adjacent to each other.[b] A geographical note in Luke 17,11 can throw some light on Luke's idea of the land of Israel. This text can be translated into two essentially different ways. The NKJV has: '... that he passed through the midst of Samaria and Galilee', but the second possibility is: '... that he passed *along between* Samaria and Galilee'.[c, 184] The image of the land Luke evidently had in mind was: Samaria and Galilee are adjacent and north of Judea, so that Galilee bordered directly on Judea. The possible route as described by Luke could have been as drawn in map 7.2 approximately. All this made a number of commentators conclude that Luke had little or no knowledge of the land. However, the underlying assumption of this conclusion is that Luke would have written his gospel differently had he known more about the land. And here I begin to doubt, because first the question

---

[a] See table 6.7
[b] See section 6.5
[c] The NETbible.

should be answered whether Luke used, consciously and with good intentions, another map in his gospel than the map of the historical geography.

In the first place I recall the correctness of many geographical notes in the Gospel of Luke and in the Acts.[a] In Acts 15,3 the territories Phoenicia and Samaria are mentioned in the correct order. In Acts 23,31-32 Luke knows exactly where to locate the border between Judea and Samaria. The soldiers accompany Paul as guards to Antipatris. This was a border town between both provinces. As soon as the company left Judea and continues through Samaria to Caesarea extra guards are no longer needed.

In the second place we have seen how Luke regularly adapted the geographical data to the midrash-aims of his stories.[b] He does so with towns and villages, so why shouldn't he do the same with provinces? Besides, there is a third point worth considering in this context.
Someone who studies the rabbinical method of dealing with the geography of the land of Israel in the first centuries CE, will discover that they always adapt the map in such a way that it supports the meaning of their midrash as well as possible. The earth and its seas were seen as concentric circles in an ocean. The centre of these circles was the so-called 'stone of foundation' in the Holy of Holies of the temple which therefore became the centre of the earth. Around this centre concentric areas are assumed in order of importance: the Holy of Holiest, the temple, Jerusalem, the land of Israel and the rest of the world.[185] A literary interpretation of Deuteronomy 17,8 is: 'The land of Israel is higher than all the countries of the world, Jerusalem is higher than the entire land of Israel and the temple is higher than the whole of Jerusalem'.[186] The source of Etam, however, that irrigated the temple, was higher than the

---

[a] See the preface of chapter 6
[b] See chapter 6

temple itself and the rabbis who said so knew this very well of course.[187] Another tradition goes that the land of Israel was washed by seven seas:

- The Great Sea or the Mediterranean,
- The Sea of Gennesareth, the Samachonitic Sea,[a, 188]
- The Sea of Salt or the Sea of Sedom,
- The Sea of Akko (Gulf of Akaba),
- The Sheliath,
- The Apamea.[b, 189]

Another tradition says that Israel had four rivers:

- the Jordan,
- the Jarmuk,
- the Kermion,
- the Pigah.

One has never been able to identify the last two of these four.[190] Moreover, it's clear that the numbers seven and four in these traditions didn't have any geographical but some symbolical meaning.

We are also informed that the excellence of the land of Israel and its position in the centre of the world didn't change after the destruction of the temple in 70 CE. What didn't change as well was the weight of its stones, which was larger than the weight of the stones of the surrounding countries.[191] Of course the rabbis' object was not the geodesical and geophysical reality. The geographical data in such traditions were subordinated to the religious meanings and intentions of the philosophy of life from which they told their stories. Therefore I think and presume that Luke appears to show the same attitude with regard to

---

[a] The Lake Huleh.
[b] The Sheliath and the Apamea probably are disappeared Idumean lakes.

JESUS' TRAVEL TO AND STAY IN JERUSALEM

Table 7.1
The Deuteronomic background of the travel-story (from this: Luke 9 – 11).

Luke	Deutero-nomy	Explanatory notes
9,51-56	4,1-40 5,1-32	Luke 9,54 – fire from heaven to consume them / Deuteronomy 4,24; 5,25 – the LORD, your God, is a consuming fire
10,27	6,5	'You shall love the LORD your God with all your heart, with all your soul, and with all your strength'
10,30-37	7,1-26	Luke – relation Israel-Samaritans/ Deuteronomy – relation Israel-Canaanitic peoples
10,38-42	8,3	Luke 10,42 – choose the good part / Deuteronomy 8,3 – not by bread alone
11,3	8,9	Luke – daily bread / Deuteronomy 8,12 – [is the core of the Jewish thanksgiving after meals][191]
11,5-13	8,11-18	Luke 11,5 – borrowing bread / Deuteronomy 8,12 – eating and being satisfied Luke 11,9 – praying and being forgiven / Deuteronomy 8,18 – for it is he who gives you power to get wealth Luke 11,11-12 – serpents, scorpions / Deuteronomy 8,15 – serpents and scorpions
11,14-20	9,1-11	Luke – casting out demons not by Beelzebub but with the finger of God / Deuteronomy – driving out the Anakim, not because of (Israel's) righteousness but because of the wickedness (of the Anakim) Luke 11,20 and Deuteronomy 9,10 – the finger of God
11,29-32	13,1-5	Luke – asking a sign / Deuteronomy – a prophet who announces a sign
11,33-36	14,1-2	Luke and Deuteronomy – body care
11,37-52	12,1-17 14,3-29	Luke 11,39-42; Deuteronomy 12,15-17; 14,3-29 – cleanliness, followed by tithes Luke 11,51; Deuteronomy 12,13-14 – temple and sacrificial services

123

the geographical material. This does not only argue in favour of a Jewish identity, but it also solves the apparent contrast of an author who on the one hand uses the geographical data correctly but on the other hand not. This raises the following question: what were Luke's exegetical purposes with his deviating geography of the land of Israel? Before being able to answer this question we'll have to make another important observation.

b.   The Deuteronomic background of the travel-story
The first part of the travel-story (Luke 9,51 – 17,10) was entirely written against the background of the book of Deuteronomy. This becomes clear from a thematic comparison of the successive stories. Without laying claim to completeness I brought twenty-seven thematic similarities of the relevant Luke- and Deuteronomy-stories[a] together in the tables 7.1 to 7.3. The purpose and the meaning of the travel-story and the deviating geography should be explained against this Deuteronomy-background. In this respect I recall the fact that Luke wrote the story of the sermon in the field (Luke 6,17 f.) against the background of the entry into the country of Canaan under the leadership of Joshua. In this sermon Luke pictures Jesus as a Joshua-figure.[b] Deuteronomy is for the greater part a speech Moses made to Israel at the other side of the Jordan (Deuteronomy 1,1 and 5; 4,46) just before the entry into the land of Canaan took place (Deuteronomy 1,3). The book contains the code of conduct for Israel's life in the land of Canaan (Deuteronomy 33,11-20). Joshua is the one under whose leadership Israel has to enter the land to

---

[a]   It's quite possible to find more parallels or to support the parallels given in the tables with the help of other means as linguistic similarities, mediating midrashim, social-cultural backgrounds etc. In this way also the parallellism between Luke 15,8-9 and Deuteronomy 21,10-14 could be shown. In the context of this book, however, it would go too far to treat these Deuteronomic backgrounds extensively.

[b]   See section 5.1.e.

Table 7.2
The Deuteronomic background of the travel-story (from this: Luke 12 – 15).

Luke	Deutero-nomy	Explanatory notes
12,2-3	13,6-11	Luke: there is nothing covered that will not be revealed / Deuteronomy: secret temptation will not be covered
12,16-21	12,17-19	Luke & Deuteronomy: the attitude of man towards the yield of the land and towards his cattle
12,22-34	15,7-18	Luke 12,31: God will bless who seeks his Kingdom / Deuteronomy 15,10 and 18: idem who keeps the sabbatical year
12,51-53	13,6-11	Luke: discord between five in one house / Deuteronomy: seduction by brother, son, daughter, woman or friend (five persons)
12,57-59	16,18-20	Luke & Deuteronomy: judge and jurisdiction
13,1-5	16,21; 17,1; 17,2-7	Luke: sacrifices and sinners / Deuteronomy: altar and offence Luke & Deuteronomy: offence and punishment
13,10-17	15,1-8	Luke: healing on sabbath / Deuteronomy: sabbatical year
13,31-35	17,14-20	Luke – Herod / Deuteronomy – set a king over you[a]
14,1-6	15,1-8	See Luke 13,10-17
14,16-20	20,1-9	Luke – three reasons not to join a banquet: a piece of ground, five yoke of oxen, wife / Deuteronomy – three reasons not to join a battle: house, vineyard, wife
14,31-32	20,10-11	Luke & Deuteronomy – peace instead of war
15,11-32	21,18-21	Luke – the lost son / Deuteronomy – the rebellious son; Luke 15,14 – he had spent all / Deuteronomy 21,20 – a glutton

---

[a] Also in the Talmud this part is connected with a Herod (the Great) and there is talk of the killing of rabbis (Bawa Batra 4a).

Table 7.3
The Deuteronomic backgroud of the travel-story (from this: Luke 16 and 17).

Luke	Deuteronomy	Explanatory notes
16,1-8	22,1-4	Luke and Deuteronomy – attitude towards someone else's possessions
16,10-13	22,5-12	Luke and Deuteronomy – faithful in very little Luke 16,13 – serving two masters / Deuteronomy 22,9-12 – different kinds of seed, beasts of draught, garments
16,18	22,13-30 24,1-5	Luke and Deuteronomy – marriage and divorce
16,19-31	24,6-15	Luke and Deuteronomy – attitude towards the neighbour
17,7-10	26,16-19	Luke and Deuteronomy – conclusion with an incitement to complete servitude

begin with this Deuteronomic life in the land'.[a] This means for the travel-story in Luke's gospel that it could be read as an application of Deuteronomy to the life in the land of Israel in Jesus' days. The travel-story shows three striking characteristics, which gain in meaning by the Deuteronomic background.

During Jesus' stay in Galilee-Judea the kingdom of God is spoken about as something more or less taken for granted[b], but in the travel-story this speaking intensifies, and issues like the character and the coming of the kingdom of God come up for discussion more explicitly.[c] So there is a close relation between Luke's idea of the kingdom of God and the way in which he makes Jesus apply. Deuteronomy to his days and circumstances. Particularly through the parallellism of Luke 12,22-

---

[a] Deuteronomy 3,21-22 and 28; 31,7-8 and 23; 34,9; Joshua 1,7-8; 8,30-35.
[b] Luke 4,43; 6,20; 7,28; 8,1 and 10; 9,2; 11,27.
[c] Luke 9,60 and 62; 10,9 and 11;11,2 and 20; 12,31-32; 13,18, 20 and 28-29;14,15; 16,16; 17,20-21; 18,16-17, 24-25 and 29; 19,11.

34 and Deuteronomy 15,7-18 this relation becomes clear: seeking God's kingdom goes hand in hand with keeping the Deuteronomic commandments, the rules of conduct for the life in the promised land. For Luke Deuteronomy is clearly the foundation for the realization of the kingdom of God. The following is in agreement with this.

In the travel-story Jerusalem plays a central part.[a] From Luke 13,33-35 it's quite clear that this is not a mere geographical part. In Deuteronomy there is such a central part for 'the place .... the Lord your God chooses'.[b] For the Jews this place was and is Jerusalem only. But another explanation also occurred in Jesus' days and here we see a third, clear characteristic of the travel-story: there are only three stories about Samaritans in the Gospel of Luke and they're all in the travel-story (Luke 9,51-56; 10,25-37; 17,11-19).

In the parallel construction of the travel-story and Deuteronomy the expulsion of the Canaanitic nations (Deuteronomy 7) and the story of the Good Samaritan (Luke 10,25-37) appear next to each other. It's not only clear that Luke compares the Samaritans with the Canaanitic tribes from Joshua's days, but also that he considers another attitude towards them necessary in his days: the possibility that a Samaritan turns out to be an example for Israel. In the third Samaritan-story (Luke 17,11-19) this idea is propagated as well. Yet Luke's attitude towards the Samaritans isn't just a sympathetic one. In the first Samaritan-story a whole Samaritan village is described as averse to Jesus, because *his face was [set] for the journey to Jerusalem* (Luke 9,53). The five books of Moses were for the Samaritans the Holy Scripture as well, but they interpreted 'the place the Lord your God will choose' as Mount Gerizim where once their temple stood.[c] The Samaritan version of Deuteronomy even has in Deuteronomy 12,14 'the place the Lord *has chosen*' instead

---

[a] Luke 9,51 and 53; 10,30; 13,4, 22 and 33-35; 17,11; 18,31; 19,11 and 28.
[b] Deuteronomy 12,5, 11, 14, 18, 21 and 26; 14,23, 24 and 25; 15,20; 16,2, 6, 7, 11, 15 and 16; 17,8 and 10; 18,6; 26,2.
[c] See e.g. John 4,20.

of *'chooses'*. So Mount Gerizim was the most important point of difference between Jews and Samaritans. A rabbinical tradition from those days tells that the Samaritans belong to Judaism if they should reject from their belief with respect to Mount Gerizim.[192] It's clear that Luke's point of view in this question agrees with that of the Jews and not with that of the Samaritans. Besides, his attitude towards the Samaritans looks very much like the one of the rabbis: in fact the Samaritans belong to Israel, but place themselves outside Israel by their different ideas. They are more or less in between the Jews and the gentiles.

Now Luke's ideas on the geography of the land of Israel become clear by the above-mentioned characteristics of the travel-stories. The kingdom of God with its Deuteronomic foundation should be realized in the first place in the Jewish land west of the Jordan and with Jerusalem as its centre. That's the reason why Jesus' actions are almost entirely restricted to this area. But there is an obstacle for this argumentation: Samaria lies just between the Jewish regions Galilee and Judea. Now Luke transforms the map in such a way that the position of Samaria towards the rest of the Jewish land agrees with the relation of the Samaritans with the Jews: they are between the Jews and the gentiles. Indeed, Samaria is visited by Jesus, but then it's a border town of the Jewish land. Luke places the geography entirely second to his argumentation rooted in Tanakh. If there is one argument that argues strongly in favour of a Jewish identity of Luke's, the author, than it's this one.

c. The character of Jesus' actions

To complete this discussion of the travel-story we still have to pursue the question why Luke models this part of his gospel explicitly as a journey. Surely the matter isn't exactly suited for the purpose, and reading it one gathers that Jesus makes only little progress during his journey to Jerusalem.[193] The answer to this question should be found in the function a journey from Galilee to Jerusalem could possibly have. A function that differs from the function of a pilgrimage.[a] It'll be remembered that Jesus' speaking about the kingdom of God intensifies during the journey. Following Jesus during the journey is also seen within the scope of the kingdom of God (Luke 9,59-62). The aim Jerusalem and the theme of the kingdom of God meet at the end of the journey, when Jesus approaches Jerusalem and the disciples think that the kingdom of God will be revealed then and there (Luke 19,11). In response to this he tells them the parable of the ten minas (Luke 19,12-27), a parable with a pre-eminently political character.[b] The words 'will be revealed' in Luke 19,11 don't indicate the actual *coming* of the kingdom of God, because in Luke 17,21 it is said that the kingdom of God already *exists*. It's beyond doubt that 'it will be revealed' means that the kingdom will reveal its political form and will become visible to everyone. According to the ideas of many Jewish groups in those days it was the task of the messiah, and especially of the messiah from the house of David, to realize the kingdom of God politically as well, by breaking the Roman yoke and by reigning over a renewed kingdom of Israel afterwards.[194] The general belief was that Jerusalem would be the place where the Messiah would manifest himself as such for the first time.[195]

Against this background it goes without saying to compare Jesus' journey to Jerusalem with the setting up of a campaign in order to conquer the city of God, to liberate it from the Roman occupation and to cleanse it from pagan taints. This was the ideal of the Zealots' resistance movement and at several times indeed the Zealots tried to give shape to this ideal by force of arms. And yes, there are many indications that Luke wrote his gospel against the background of the Zealotic movement.[c] For Luke is the only evangelist that left us rather a lot of information on this movement. Now it will become clear from the following

---

[a] See section 7.1.a.
[b] I'll discuss this parable in section 9.3.c.
[c] See e.g. sections 6.8 and 9.3

that Luke didn't present Jesus as a Zealot, but chose the travel-story as a form of polemics directed against Zealotism.

In Jesus' actions during and after the journey hardly anything can be discerned of armed resistance, revolt or other forms of violence against the Roman occupation. His actions are almost entirely peaceful. The only exception, the cleansing of the temple, will be dealt with in the next section. This nonviolent character of Jesus' actions becomes almost immediately clear, as a kind of motto, in the first story of the journey (Luke 9,51-56). When a Samaritan village doesn't want to receive them and the disciples James and John ask his permission to command fire to come down from heaven and consume the Samaritans, Jesus rebukes them and reject this and goes to another village. In this rather peculiar exclamation of both disciples, Luke summarizes the hostile inclination of many Jews towards the Samaritans. This enmity though was mutual and already very old. In the days of Ezra (5th century BCE) already there was some talk of conflicts between Samaritans and Judeans (Ezra 4). Such conflicts did not always finish without violence.[196] In 128 BCE the Samaritan temple on Mount Gerizim was destroyed by the Jewish king John Hyrkanos. In 9 CE the Samaritans desecreted the temple in Jerusalem. In the autumn of 51 CE a Galilean pilgrim is murdered by Samaritans. When the Roman governor Cumanus Venditius refuses to punish the culprits, a multitude of Jews commanded by the Zealotic leader Eleazar ben Dinai carries out a bloody retaliation among the Samaritans. One can easily assume that especially the Zealotic-minded Jews in the first century CE were only too willing to use violence towards the Samaritans. Obviously this disposition was so widespread that Luke could have Jesus' disciples put it into words.

It can be substantiated by another way as well that this opening-story of the journey is about an anti-Zealotic stand. The story of the rejection of Jesus by a Samaritan village was written against the background of Elijah's action in 2 Kings 1. There are several connections:

- Samaria as the place of action (Luke 9,52; 2 Kings 1,2);
- Dispatching messengers (Luke 9,52; 2 Kings 1,2);
- The consuming fire from heaven (Luke 9,54; 2 Kings 1,10, 12 and 14).

In some manuscripts of the Gospel of Luke this Tanakh-background is even expressed by means of the addition 'just as Elijah did'. Now Elijah is described as a 'Zealot' in Tanakh and the Apocrypha (in Greek *zèlootès*), owing to his action against Ahab and Jezebel (1 Kings 19,10 and 14; 1 Maccabees 2,58; Jesus Sirach 48,2). But Elijah is not the only character in Tanakh whose zeal became the very characteristic of his person. Also Phinehas, the grandson of Aaron, is characterized with the words 'zeal' and 'zealous' and in the Apocrypha the descriptions of both figures differ very little only (Numbers 25,11 and 13; 1 Maccabees 2,26 and 54; Jesus Sirach 45,23). That's the reason why in the old Jewish tradition Phinehas and Elijah were identified with one another. This identification was so strong that, in the stories told about both of them, they got each other's characteristics.[197] And it is precisely this Phinehas-Elijah-figure who inspired the Zealots in their violent actions against the Romans and against their fellow-Jews they considered to be traitors.[198]

The rabbinic tradition however, especially the one that became authoritative through the Talmud, is not favourable to Phinehas and Elijah in all respects. In particular Phinehas' high-handed action (Numbers 25) and Elijah's inflexibility (1 Kings 17 and 18) are the targets of their criticism.[199] Also the identification of Phinehas and Elijah was kept out of the Talmud.[200] Although a positive appreciation of both prevails, the anti-Zealotic rabbis deemed it necessary, evidently, to mitigate an appeal to the extreme sides of the actions of both.[201] We now see in Luke 9,51-56, that Luke takes the same view: the appeal to violent means à la Elijah is no longer expedient in Jesus' days. In this context it is conspicuous that not only the consuming fire but also the being-zealous of God form parts of the Deuteronomy background we found earlier in this

Luke-story (Deuteronomy 4,24; 5,9).[a] In Luke's view one should leave the decision to use violence or not to heaven. In spite of this one can be a Zealot: for Torah (Acts 21,20).

The peace-loving, non-violent character of Jesus' action and teaching appears too, from the parallellism of some stories from the Gospel of Luke and Deuteronomy.[b] The parallellism of Luke 10,30-37 and Deuteronomy 7,1-26 shows that Luke is more positive about the relation to the Samaritans than Israel's relation was to the Canaanitic tribes in the days of Joshua.[c] The expulsion of the Anakites (Deuteronomy 9,1-11) is parallelled by the expulsion of evil spirits without violent means (Luke 11,14-20). Herod, having the intention to kill Jesus, is undoubtedly the contrast of the king in Deuteronomy 17,14-20. However, Jesus doesn't react with counterviolence, but with the readiness to suffer violence for the sake of his prophetic task (Luke 13,31-35). And subsequently it's more than significant that Luke pacifies, so to speak, the war-laws (Luke 14,16-20; Deuteronomy 20,1-9). This doesn't mean that he annuls them, on the contrary. Jesus' actions are non-violent, so within the scope of his teachings a military interpretation or adaption of this Deuteronomic law doesn't come up for discussion. This Deuteronomic law remains the basis for action, when Israel's future is at stake (mark especially Deuteronomy 20,1), even without military action.

What does this all boil down to, especially to the public Luke was writing his gospel for? The kingdom of God should be realized, in political and social aspect as well. All Jews agreed on that in the first century CE, but considerable differences of opinion existed about how this should happen and about the means permissible. The Zealotic resistance movement in particular aimed at, if need be only with a few, starting the revolt against the Romans. They firmly counted on heavenly intervention in the thick of the battle.[202] Other Jewish groups such

---

[a] See Table 7.1.
[b] See Table 7.1.
[c] See section 7.1.b.

Table 7.4
Geographical synopsis of Jesus' stay in Jerusalem according to Mark 11 – 13 and Luke 19,29 – 21,38.

Mark	Luke
11,1 Near Jerusalem, to Bethphage and Bethany at the Mount of Olives	19,29 Near to Bethphage and Bethany, at the mountain called Olivet
11,2-6 'The village opposite you' (dispatching 2 disciples for a colt)	19,30-34 'The vilage opposite you' (dispatching 2 disciples for a colt)
11,7-10 (Riding to Jerusalem)	19,35-36 (Riding to the Mount of Olives)
	19,37-40 Drawing near the descent of the Mount of Olives (praises by the disciples, the Pharisees rebuke)
	19,41-44 Drawing nearer and watching the city (prophecy with regard to the destruction of Jerusalem)
11,11a At Jerusalem in the temple (looking around at all things) 11,11b To Bethany (late in the day) 11,12-14 From Bethany (the withered fig tree)	
11,15-18 Jerusalem (the cleansing of the temple)	19,45-48 Entering the temple and the cleansing thereof
11,19 'When evening had come, He went out of the city' 11,20-26 Passing the fig tree (faith and prayer)	
11,27 – 12,27 In Jerusalem again (authority, the wicked tenants, paying taxes to Caesar, Sadducees and the resurrection)	20,1-40 One day in the temple (authority, the wicked tenants, paying taxes to Caesar, Sadducees and the resurrection)
12,28-34 (The first commandment)	

Jesus' travel to and stay in Jerusalem

Mark	Luke
12,35-44 (Son of David, warning against the scribes, the widow's two mites)	20,41 – 21,4 (Son of David, warning against the scribes, the widow's two mites)
13,1-37 Out of the temple, on the Mount of Olives opposite the temple (speech about Jerusalem's future)	21,5-36 (Speech about Jerusalem's future)
	21,37-38 In the daytime in the temple, at night on the Mount of Olives

as the Pharisees who, in the future, would determine the rabbinic Judaism, were very critical towards this Zealotic movement. Within the scope of these internally Jewish opposites, the travel-story may be read as an anti-Zealotic polemic, or, if you want, as an alternative for the military-political messiah-expectation of the Jewish liberation movement of the first century. Anyway, one shouldn't gather from this that in Luke's eyes the kingdom of God shouldn't also be realized 'earthly and nationally'.[203] What could rather be said about Luke's point of view is, that this realization in the political circumstances of the first century shouldn't occur with the help of violence, revolt and armed resistance. There had been no need for him to convince a gentile public of this, not even a public of Christians from the gentiles. This means that the Gospel of Luke was written with the intention to show certain groups of Jews another, non-violent way to fulfil the task God had given the people of Israel. Once again the conclusion must be that not only the Gospel of Luke was written by a Jewish author, but also with a view to a Jewish public.

7.2 Jerusalem

There is no city in the world that is of such paramount importance as Jerusalem in the Gospel of Luke and the Acts of the Apostles. There is no New Testamentary writing that ascribes such a pivotal place to

JESUS' TRAVEL TO AND STAY IN JERUSALEM

Jerusalem as this two-volume work of Luke's.[204] This fact now, should make us very suspicious towards the idea supported by many, that the central theme of both books would be the fact that Jerusalem gives up its place to Rome.[205] Before pursuing this in greater depth I'll list a number of points about Luke's dealing with Jerusalem.

We already noticed the important part Jerusalem plays during the travel-story as 'the place the Lord your God chooses'.[a] Though the city was emphatically mentioned earlier in Luke's gospel. So does this Gospel begin in Jerusalem in the temple too, with the announcement of the birth of John the Baptist (Luke 1,5-23). After the birth of Jesus the story turns back to his 'introduction to the LORD', and once again the temple is the scene of action (Luke 2,22-39). Then, after one verse only we arrive in Jerusalem for the third time at Passover when Jesus is twelve years old and again the temple is at the centre (Luke 2,41-51). All this contrasts strangely with the indirect and rather negative part Jerusalem plays in the birth-story in Matthew. In his gospel Jerusalem is especially the city where the king of the Jews is *not* born but where Herod resides, Jesus' great adversary (Matthew 2,1-9). Before Jesus begins to appear in public in Galilee-Judea, Jerusalem appears for the fourth time in Luke's story when he is tested in the wilderness. And again the action takes place in the temple (Luke 4,9-12). Comparison with the parallel story of Matthew's shows once more, that in the Gospel of Luke Jerusalem is more important: the third test, the climax of the story, takes place in Jerusalem, whereas in Matthew the same scene is the second test only (Matthew 4,5-7).

Also in the last chapters of the Gospel of Luke we find, with regard to Mark and Matthew, a tendency to enlarge Jerusalem's part and to restrict the action to the temple-complex. In table 7.4 a comparison is made with Mark. It's conspicuous that Luke doesn't borrow from Mark

---

[a] See section 7.1.b.

Jesus' travel to and stay in Jerusalem

the travelling to and fro between Jerusalem (in the daytime) and Bethany (at night) (Mark 11,11b-12, 19-20).[a] Luke even removes two stories from this period of Jesus' actions:

- The story about the withered fig tree on the road from Bethany to Jerusalem (Mark 11,12-14, 20-26). Luke moves this story and he revises it into a parable with a completely different end (Luke 13,6-9).
- The story about the anointing in Bethany in Simon the Leper's house (Mark 14,3-9). Luke moves this story to Jesus' stay in Galilee-Judea. And he adapts it and gives it quite another meaning (Luke 7,36-50).

The speech about Jerusalem's future isn't situated on the slope of the Mount of Olives, but in the temple, just like Jesus' preceding teaching.[b] It's remarkable as well that the issue of 'destroying the temple', in the trial against Jesus told by the other evangelists though in different versions, is completely left out by Luke (c.f. Mark 14,58; Matthew 26,61; John 2,19).

When we compare the stories about Jesus' appearances after his resurrection, found in the gospels of Luke and Matthew, the unique position of Jerusalem in the gospel of Luke attracts our attention once and again. In Matthew's gospel the disciples are ordered to go to Galilee and it is there that the last meeting with Jesus takes place (Matthew 28,7, 10 and 16-20). In Luke's gospel on the other hand the disciples are explicitly told not to leave Jerusalem (Luke 24,49; Acts 1,4). The two disciples who nonetheless leave Jerusalem are so to speak intercepted by Jesus himself (Luke 24,13 and 33). And so the last meeting of Jesus and his disciples takes place on the Mount of Olives near Jerusalem (Acts 1,12). From then on Jerusalem remains the place of action in the

---

[a] Cf. Mark 11,27 with Luke 20,1.
[b] There is no indication in Luke 21,5 that Jesus would have left the city.

JESUS' TRAVEL TO AND STAY IN JERUSALEM

Acts for chapters on end (Acts 1-7). Even when Jesus' followers moved away from Jerusalem slowly but surely, it's this city one returns to again and again (Acts 9,26-29; 11,2-19; 12,1-19 and 24-25; 15,2b-29; 21,15 – 23,30).

If we compare Paul's action after his conversion, according to Luke in the Acts, with Paul's own description in the letter to the Galatians, we discover once more how Luke enlarges the part of Jerusalem continuously. Paul himself states explicitly that after his conversion he didn't travel to Jerusalem but returned to Damascus via Arabia (Galatians 1,17). However, in the Acts things are represented quite differently. There Paul travels to Jerusalem almost immediately after his conversion (Acts 9,26). A journey to Arabia and a return to Damascus aren't mentioned at all. But a departure from Jerusalem to Tarsus, Paul's place of birth, is mentioned indeed (Acts 9,30). This representation of Luke's fits in perfectly with his pursuit to make Jerusalem the centre of his gospel and the Acts. How could it be possible to reconcile all these data with the idea that Jerusalem should yield its place to Rome? Jerusalem is for Luke the religious centre not only for Judaism, but also for the communities of Jesus' followers, either Christians or Jews. That the Acts ends in Rome is by no means inconsistent. It stems from Luke's idea that by following Jesus the Jewish people could realize its significance for the nations of the world. Jerusalem, however, will always be the 'base of operations'. Here every new development in the spreading of the message should begin and should be sanctioned.

This central position of Jerusalem in Luke's thinking is all the more remarkable, since he wrote *after* the destruction of city and temple by the Romans. While writing his books Luke must have had this historical disaster in mind. This can be gathered from Jesus' speech on Jerusalem's future:

'But when you see Jerusalem surrounded by armies, then know that its desolation is near' (Luke 21,20).

JESUS' TRAVEL TO AND STAY IN JERUSALEM

In this respect it's conspicuous as well that even at the beginning of Jesus' actions in Jerusalem Luke brings up the future of Jerusalem. To that end he adds a scene with regard to Mark in which sadness and sorrow about the fate of the city prevail (Luke 19,41-44):

> 'Now as He drew near, He saw the city and wept over it, saying, "If you had known, even you, especially in this your day, *the things that make for your peace*! But now they are hidden from your eyes.'

Then the prospect of the destruction of the temple is put into words for the very first time, followed by Jesus' first action: the expulsion of the merchants from the temple with the object to restore the temple as a house of worship (Luke 19,45-46). Compared with Mark Luke has abridged this scene to a minimum, probably with a view to avoid the impression that Jesus as a Zealotic leader intended to seize power (cf. Mark 11,15-17). And this is immediately followed by the statement that Jesus 'was teaching daily in the temple' (Luke 19,47a).

Jesus' teachings weren't aimed at Jerusalem, neither at the way in which the city and the house of God were run by the priests and the scribes. This appears most clearly from the parable of the tenants (Luke 20,9-19, esp. v. 19). Also the other parts of Jesus' teachings in the temple are related to those Jewish factions that were in power in Jerusalem or that wanted to seize power. Chief priests, scribes, elders (Luke 20,1-8, 19-26, 45-47), Sadducees (Luke 20,27-38) and very probable Zealots (Luke 20,21-26, 39-44; 21,1-4) are discussion partners, subject or background in Jesus' teachings. However, it should be mentioned that in this part of the gospel of Luke the Pharisees are conspicuous by their absence. This will become clearer more and more, when we consider the fact that Luke doesn't include the text of Mark 12,28-34 about the first commandment in the temple-teachings of Jesus. The discussion described by Mark shows some points of view that were characteristic for those Pharisees who defined the face of later Judaism but who had only little influence yet in the days of Jesus.[206] And it is exactly in this Pharisaic tradition that we happen upon sayings and opinions on temple-management as critical as the sayings of Jesus and of his disciples in Luke. Yet these Pharisees didn't wash their hands of the temple and of Jerusalem. They'd sooner strive to influence positively the normal course of events in the temple by means of their teaching.[207] In this respect Jesus is very close to them in Luke's stories.

Rejection of the city and its sanctuary can't be deduced from Luke's description of Jesus' actions in the temple either. Jesus' actions present themselves sooner as a desperate attempt to save Jerusalem and the temple from destruction by cleansing, teaching and prophecies of doom. This attempt is expressed clearest by the opening words of his actions: 'If you had known, even you, especially in this your day, *the things that make for your peace*'. However, his prophecy on the destruction of the temple has a very mild character compared with the prophecy of Jeremiah (e.g. Jeremiah 25,1-11). Such prophecies were inspired by the motive to save Jerusalem instead of allowing it to perish. And as with the prophets in Tanakh, Luke paints another, distant picture of the future *behind* this gloomy one: 'And Jerusalem will be trampled by gentiles *until the times of the gentiles are fulfilled*' (Luke 21,24b, c.f. also Jeremiah 33,1-11). Does Luke hope to restore the position of Jerusalem in his days or in the near future via the road he describes in the Acts, the road that leads from Jerusalem to the ends of the earth? As happened in the days of Ezra and Nehemiah under the Persian kings? Is that the reason why the Acts end in Rome like the book 2 Kings ends in Babylon? We already found some clues for this[a]. Be that as it may, nothing else can be concluded from the overwhelming part Jerusalem and the temple play in the gospel of Luke and the Acts than that Luke looked

---

[a] See section 6.7.

at them as all other Jews: the house of God in the city of God, destroyed or not, for years to come.

7.3 Emmaus

This chapter on the geography of the Gospel of Luke wouldn't be complete without some observations devoted to the mention of Emmaus in Luke 24,13. The 'exact' location, sixty stadia from Jerusalem, is highly conspicuous. This notification caused the commentators some embarrassment as the Emmaus of the map was at least twenty miles from Jerusalem.[208] There are also some difficulties with another place possibly called Emmaus. Flavius Josephus mentions an Emmaus at a distance of thirty stadia from Jerusalem.[209] Some people even suppose that once there were three villages of that name.[210] In my opinion there is no reason for this supposition, for we shouldn't read this geographical note of Luke's topographically, but as a midrash. Because what is the matter?

There is no Emmaus in Tanakh. However, from the days of the Maccabees Emmaus plays an important part in Israel's struggles against the gentile oppression. It's mentioned for the first time as the place of encampment of the Seleucidic army led by the general Georgias. This army was defeated and put to flight by Judas Maccabeus in 166 BCE (1 Maccabees 3,40 f.). later Emmaus was turned into a fortified stronghold by the Seleucidic governor of Jerusalem Bakchides (2 Maccabees 9,50). A century later in 43 BCE the Roman general Cassius enslaves the people of Emmaus because they refused to pay taxes.[211] In the year 4 BCE Emmaus was burned to the ground by the Roman proconsul of Syria, Varus, because of the increasing actions of Zealotic groups immediately after Herod's death.[212] Also in the Jewish War (66-70 CE) Emmaus plays a part that looks like the one it played in the days of the Maccabees. Vespasian, the Roman general who had to suppress the revolt, established a fortified camp in this place in 68 CE. The Fifth, i.e. the Macedonian Legion[213] encamped there, a rather important fact, given the central part Macedonia appears to play in the second half of the Acts.[a]

Quite in line with this part of Emmaus in Israel's fight with the pagan occupier, is a parallel in the rabbis' midrashim for the distance of sixty stadia to Jerusalem. The midrash tells us that the distance from the tabernacle in Siloh to the camp of Goliath in the days of Saul was sixty miles,[214] the same kind of indication for the distance between the place of the sanctuary and the place of the enemy's encampment. Therefore it's probable that in Luke's view Emmaus has been the place from which the pagan occupier had tried to subdue the country and its people in the days of revolt and war. And it's exactly here, in Emmaus, in Luke's gospel, that Jesus appears to his disciples for the first time. In the middle of the potentially hostile encampment the eyes of Cleopas and his fellow-traveller are opened for the way of Jesus (Luke 24,31). Several passages from the story are clarified when read against this background.

The messiah-expectation pronounced by both men of Emmaus doesn't differ at all with the one many Jews cherished in those days: the messiah will deliver Israel from the yoke of the Romans (Luke 24,21). He will begin the revolt against the Roman authority in Jerusalem and with the help of heaven he will chase the enemy away from the country. In this Zealotic messiah-expectation there is no place for a leader who dies because of his persistent nonviolence. Even the rumour that Jesus was alive (Luke 24,22-24) didn't stop Cleopas and his friend from leaving Jerusalem. They were blind to another, longer road to the deliverance of Israel. Only after the scriptures with regard to this issue were explained to them (Luke 24,25-27), and Jesus had broken the bread at the place where Israel's enemies appear to encamp preferably, they recognize him (Luke 24,30-31a). Only then Jesus will be able to disappear

---

[a] See sections 3.4, 5.2 and 8.3 – 8.5

from among their midst (Luke 24,31b), because it's no longer about the person of Jesus, and certainly not about his physical presence, but about the way he showed.

Reading the Gospel of Luke as midrash its geography provides us with a consistent argument in favour of a nonviolent pursuit of the deliverance of Israel from the power of the Romans. How does Luke, the Jew, writing for a Jewish public continue this line of thought in his second book? In the next chapter I'll pursue this question in greater depth.

8. He decided to return through Macedonia
The geography of the Acts of the Apostles

In both preceeding chapters I concluded from the geography of Luke's gospel that certain anti-Zealotic polemics can be discerned. We've also found some clues that Luke considered the conversion of the nations and the conversion of Rome in particular as alternatives for the Zealotic violence, to restore Jerusalem in its function for Judaism by non-violent means and – in doing so – for the whole world. Discussing the geography of the Acts it's obvious to check to what extent these conclusions are supported by data in the text. However, I'll postpone this question for the greater part to chapter 10 on 'Israel and the nations'. In this chapter I'll concentrate the study of the geography of the Acts on a number of other aspects. Especially so because the geography of the Acts is more difficult to decipher than the geography of Luke's gospel. There are several causes. First of all there is no comparable source, as is the case with Mark's gospel for Luke's. In the second place the Acts occur for a large part at the northern side of the Mediterranean-basin and exactly about the Jewry in these regions little is known.[215] The only material of comparison at hand are Paul's letters. Since their character and contents differ a lot from the Acts, I'll restrict myself in this comparison to those cases that show a clear interface.

At the same time I won't aim at a comprehensive exposition on the geography of the Acts, but restrict myself to those regions outside the land of Israel that could be candidates for the origin of Luke and of his book, viz. Antioch in Syria, Macedonia and Rome. Before passing these three in review, I'll make a number of general remarks about how Luke deals with the geographical material in the Acts.

Map 7.1 *The map of the eastern part of the Roman Empire in the Acts of the Apostles.*

8.1 The map of the Acts

Right away two striking features of the geography of the Acts are clear. First the data on the land of Israel (Jerusalem, Judea, Galilee and Samaria) in the Acts are in agreement with the way Luke deals with these regions in his gospel.[a] In the second place the map Luke uses for the regions outside the land of Israel corresponds with our present map. Here a midrash-transformation of this map as Luke applies to the map of the land of Israel occurs nowhere.[b]

---

[a] See section 6.5 and 7.1
[b] See the previous note.

THE GEOGRAPHY OF THE ACTS OF THE APOSTLES

Another noticeable fact is that in the Acts Luke restricts himself almost entirely to the northern side of the Mediterranean-basin. In the story about an Ethiopian for example this man isn't followed any further on his way to the South (Acts 8,26-40). Likewise it's remarkable that the city of Alexandria in Egypt, one of the biggest in the Roman Empire, a city with a large Jewish community, is only mentioned twice in the Acts (27,6 and 28,11) in connection with a ship departing from that city. Apollos, an 'Alexandrian', had to be informed in more detail about the 'way' (Acts 18,24-26). And some other Alexandrians are mentioned who possess a synagogue in Jerusalem. The rest of Africa hardly ever occurs. We learn about Cyrenians in Jerusalem and in Antioch (Acts 6,9; 11,20), about Simeon Niger and Lucius of Cyrene (Acts 13,1).

Luke doesn't pay any attention as well to all regions east of Israel and Syria. And he even doesn't divide his geographical attention equally within the place of action of the Acts. Map 8.1 shows that he had especially known the east- and northern side of the Aegean very well. He mentions a strikingly large number of places in Macedonia. On the other hand only three places play a part in the cultural centre of Achaia. Luke's geographical attention restricts itself almost entirely to the coastal regions of Macedonia and Asia Minor. This is a strong indication that Luke was from these regions. Conspicuously Paul's first journey via Pisidia to Lycaonia and back has – geographically seen – a strange 'cul-de-sac' end. Paul obviously travels the wrong way after Pisidia and has to retrace his steps (Acts 13,51 – 14,21). The course of the second journey, again after a visit to this region, is equally remarkable. Now Paul's attempts to travel from here to Asia and next to Bithynia even failed because of the resistance of 'the spirit of Jesus'. So Paul is sent by orders 'from above' to Macedonia via Mysia (Acts 16,6-10). This shows the special place of Macedonia in Luke's thoughts, which supports the supposition that he was from this region. Yet this shouldn't tempt us to consider the Acts as geographical history. Just as he does in his gospel, he subordinates the geography of the Acts to the teaching-aim of his midrash-story. The discussion about Antioch in Syria will show us a clear example.

Finally I'd like to point to a curious way of story-telling in the Acts. An elaborate and often dramatic story is told about many places, whereas later in the story these places and their regions are only called at casually. This again could point to the fact that Luke meant to tell stories with an educational end and not to write history in a geographical perspective.

8.2 Antioch in Syria

In the Acts two Syrian cities catch the eye: Damascus and Antioch. Damascus is primarily the place of Paul's conversion (Acts 9,1-25). This city doesn't play a part in the discussion about Paul's origin. But that is not the case with Antioch. There is a very old tradition handed down by the church-father Eusebius (267 – 340 CE), that Luke would be from this Syrian city.[216] This tradition was so strong that in one of the old manuscripts from the 5th or the 6th century in Acts 11,28 the phrase slipped in 'When we had come together …' (in Antioch)[217], and a new we-story was added to the other we-stories in the Acts.[a] Now what can be said about the part Antioch plays in the structure of the Acts? And what can be deduced from this about Luke's origin?

After Jerusalem Antioch is the first place the story returns to regularly. It was one of the biggest cities in the Roman Empire and had a large Jewish population that lived scattered all over the city.[218] The Jews of Antioch kept up frequent contacts with Jerusalem. So it's not surprising that Antioch functions in the Acts as the first stage in the spread of the gospel outside the land of Israel. What's more, Antioch is the first big city on the way from Jerusalem to Asia Minor. However, the part

---

[a] See section 5.2

THE GEOGRAPHY OF THE ACTS OF THE APOSTLES

Antioch plays in the structure of the Acts shows a number of peculiarities that asks for further explanation. I'd like to mention the following:

- In Antioch the disciples are, for the very first time, called 'Christians' (Acts 11,26). This Greek word *'christianous'* could also be translated with *'messianics'*. In general this is understood as a notification of a historical fact. Apart from the question whether Luke would have been able to determine a fact like that with certainty, one should ask oneself whether Luke could have meant something else with this notification. What is the relation between this notification and the story told about Antioch?
- Initially only the Jews are spoken to in Antioch. Only in second instance the Greek are spoken to (Acts 11,19-20). This now makes Antioch the first city in the diaspora where gentiles are addressed as well.
- There are regular and intensive contacts between Antioch and Jerusalem. People from Jerusalem arrive to prophesy in Antioch (Acts 11,28), to teach the brothers (Acts 15,1) or to instruct the community on behalf of the apostles (Acts 15,22) and to encourage them (Acts 15,32).
- There is also a regular contact the other way round. During a famine the communities in Judea (Acts 11,29) and in Jerusalem (Acts 12,25) are supported materially. When problems occur concerning the interpretation of the Torah a delegation is sent to the apostles in Jerusalem so as to reach the correct decision (Acts 15,2).
- Contrary to the stories about the other diaspora-cities, to begin with Damascus (Acts 9,19b-25), nothing is mentioned about conflicts with the Jews or with the gentiles from Antioch. The Antioch community lived in peace with its surroundings. Internal disputes were peacefully solved by allowing the apostles the last word (Act 15,1-2). In this connection it attracts the attention that

in the Acts Luke doesn't mention anything about the conflict between Peter and Paul that took place in Antioch, concerning eating with gentiles at one table (Galatians 2,14). Obviously a story about this conflict doesn't fit in Luke's description of the peaceful community of Antioch.
- In the community of Antioch Saul receives his assignments to go to Jerusalem, twice (Acts 11,30; 15,2) and once to make a missionary journey to Cyprus and Asia Minor (Acts 13,2-5).

Only one conclusion can be drawn from these data, I think: Luke paints the Antioch community as a *model* of the *messianic community* in the diaspora. His story about Antioch isn't a historical report about the real events in Antioch, but a midrash that indicates how a messianic community in the diaspora should function. This model implies a community:

- which is open to Jews as well as gentiles,
- which supports the communities in the land of Israel materially,
- which lives peacefully in its surroundings,
- which submits internal conflicts to the apostles in Jerusalem.

Now this is a community from which one will be able to make missionary journeys in order to spread Jesus' teachings all over the world.

This model-character of the Antioch community is without any doubt also the reason why Luke mentions the fact that here the disciples were called 'Christians' for the first time: here indeed we find for the first time how the messianic community in the diaspora should look like. Indeed, Luke is concerned about this model and not about the historical community of Antioch itself, as will appear from the last observation rendered here.

In all stories about Antioch not one single Antiochan is mentioned! Cypriotic and Cyrenian men were the first to preach to the Greek (Acts 11,20). Barnabas is a Cypriot (Acts 4,36; 11,22). Saul is from Tarsus (Acts

9,11; 11,25). Prophets from Jerusalem, among them Agabus, appeared in Antioch (Acts 11,27-28). John, also called Mark, arrives from Jerusalem as well (Acts 12,25). Barnabas from Cyprus, Simeon Niger ('the black')[a], Lucius from Cyrene in North Africa and Saul from Tarsus (Acts 13,1) act as prophets and teachers. 'Certain men from Judea' caused problems (Acts 15,1). Judas and Silas came from Jerusalem as representatives of the apostles (Acts 15,22). These are all specifically named persons who play their parts in Antioch. There is only one Antiochian in the Acts: Nicolas, a proselyte, someone who converted to Judaism. He, however, doesn't live in Antioch but in Jerusalem, and he doesn't play a part whatsoever in the Acts (Acts 6,5).

This observation now throws a remarkable light on the tradition that Luke was from Antioch: Luke appears to call hardly anyone in Antioch by his name. In this respect I'd like to observe that Antioch doesn't occur in the we-stories[b]. The only time the city is mentioned in the second half of the Acts is between the first and the second we-story. But no further events are mentioned there (Acts 18,22-23).

With regard to Luke's origin we can conclude from the preceding that the old tradition that he was from Antioch is not supported by any text in the Acts.

8.3 Macedonia

In the previous chapters I've come forward with various arguments for the supposition that Luke could be from Macedonia. We've seen that the first we-story in the Acts began with the vision of the *Macedonian man*.[c] I assumed that Luke painted a self-portrait in this vision. The series of six conflicts between Paul and the inhabitants of six cities that

---

[a] He will be an African (cf. today's Falashahs).
[b] See section 5.2.
[c] See section 5.2

follows this vision and results in the great conflict in Jerusalem, is opened with three Macedonian cities: Philippi, Thessalonica and Berea.[a] In Macedonia the theme of Paul's Roman citizenship turns up, that is going to play such an important part in the trial in Jerusalem and that in the end will lead to his voyage to Rome. Moreover we saw that the mention of places, isles and regions in the Acts, as far as they are outside the land of Israel, were centered on the route from Israel to Macedonia. The density of these mentions on the map grows as the fellowship approaches Macedonia.[b] Now what new facts could the 'geographical' examination of the Acts yield? To begin with we could examine the mention of the geographical details. In some cities we find them: 'the street called Straight' in Damascus (Acts 9,11), 'the riverside where prayer was customarily made' in Philippi (Acts 16,13) or 'the house of Titius Justus next door to the synagogue' in Corinth (Acts 18,7). But such details are rather scarce and are mentioned with regard to very different cities, so a conclusion can barely be made.

One geographical detail, however, is well worth mentioning here: the mention that Paul leaves Berea 'to go to the sea' (Acts 17,14). We already saw that Luke seldom used the word 'sea'.[c] The word is especially kept for the last voyage from Jerusalem to Rome. Does Luke, when leaving Macedonia, want to point ahead to the sea between Israel and Rome Paul has to sail after his trial in Jerusalem? The theme of Paul's Roman citizenship in the Philippi-story also points forward from Macedonia to the trial in Jerusalem. This curious, geographical detail in Acts 17,14 could be considered to underline the position of Macedonia in the Acts. Now what could be the link between Macedonia and Jerusalem?

We discovered two clear thematic connections between the Macedonia-stories on the one hand and the stories of Paul's last stay in Jeru-

---

[a] See section 3.4.
[b] See section 8.1 and map 8.1.
[c] Greek: *thalassa* (see section 6.4).

THE GEOGRAPHY OF THE ACTS OF THE APOSTLES

Table 8.1
Thematic parallels between the Macedonia-stories (Acts 16,10 – 17,14) and the Jerusalem-Caesarea-stories (Acts 21,17 f.)

Macedonia	**Jerusalem/Caesarea**
Paul visits a place of prayer (16,13 and 16)	Paul visits the temple (21,26)
Population in turmoil; Paul and Silas are seized and carried off (16,19)	Population in turmoil; Paul is seized and carried off (21,27 and 30).
Accusation of undermining the Roman mores (16,21)	Accusations of teaching against the people, the law and the Temple (21,28)
Paul and Silas are arrested by the Roman government (16,22-23)	Paul is arrested by the Roman government (21,31-33)
Conversion of the prison warder (16,25-34)	Paul attempts to convert the people (21,40 – 22,21)
Paul's Roman citizenship (16,37-39)	Paul's Roman citizenship (22,25-28)
The magistrates got apprehensive (16,38)	The commander got apprehensive (22,29)
Confrontation with the Jewish leaders of Thessalonica (17,1)	Confrontation with the Jewish Council (22,30)
Paul teaches the resurrection of the dead (17,3)	Paul says to be judged concerning the resurrection of the dead (23,6)
Internal conflicts between the Jews; Paul kept out of it (17,5-9)	Conflict between the Pharisees and the Sadducees with Paul between them (23:7-10)
Paul is taken to Berea in the night (17,10)	Paul is taken to Caesarea in the night (23,23 and 31)
The Jews of Berea are fair-minded and search the Scriptures with Paul (17,11)	Paul praises Agrippa and agrees with his (Agrippa's) research (26,2)

Macedonia	Jerusalem/Caesarea
The Jews of Thessalonica followed Paul to Berea to stir up the crowds against him (17,13)	A delegation from Jerusalem follows Paul to Caesarea to accuse him (24,1)
Paul leaves into the direction of the sea (17,14)	Paul voyages to Rome by sea (27,1 f., 38, 40 and 41)

salem and Caesarea on the other. So the question arises whether there could be more thematic similarities between both parts of the Acts, eventually. Comparing both series of stories yields an abundance of thematic parallels, even the order in which they occur is almost entirely equal. This material is represented in table 8.1. On the basis of these facts only one conclusion is possible: already in the Macedonia-stories Luke sketches the plan of the trial against Paul in Jerusalem and Caesarea. This position of Macedonia in the structure of the Acts is a strong argument in favour of Luke's origin from this area, unless, of course, quite another meaning should be attached to Macedonia. In table 8.1 there is also a fine example of an internal midrash within Luke's work: the second series of stories about Jerusalem is so to speak a further elaboration of the first series of stories about Macedonia.

8.4 The itinerary of Paul in the second half of the Acts

There are a number of conspicuous moments in the itinerary Paul follows in the second part of the Acts (Acts 16 - 28), and especially in the way that itinerary came about. We already saw how Paul was drawn towards Macedonia by the vision of the Macedonian man, after a crisis had come up determining the itinerary (Acts 16,6-10). During the following journeys through Macedonia, Greece, Asia (via Ephesus to Caesarea), Syria (Antioch), Galatia and Phrygia (Acts 16,11 - 18,23) no problems with regard to charting the course are mentioned. The journeys from town to town and from region to region are mentioned as something that goes without saying. The same applies to Paul's next journey to Ephesus (Acts 19,1). But in the following Ephesus-stories there are a couple of moments in which this casualness is interrupted again.

Here we see how Paul is engaged in developing itineraries consciously. Curiously enough, Macedonia is first destination. Curiously, because he intends to travel to Jerusalem (Acts 19,21). But travelling via Macedonia is a long way about! Here we also catch sight of the journey to Rome for the very first time.

Then the part of Macedonia is underlined once more, because in the mean time Paul sends two of his fellow workers there, before he goes there himself (Acts 19,22). And once having reached Greece via Macedonia (Acts 20,1-2), this region plays again a remarkable part by planning the itinerary. Paul is on the verge to sail for Syria, but yet decides – at the last moment – to travel via Macedonia again (Acts 20,3). A detour once more! And precisely during this journey the writer of the we-stories turns up again in his company, in the Macedonian town of Philippi, that is (Acts 20,6).

So Paul visits Macedonia three times and all these times are preceded by a conscious decision. This is indicated by the words 'concluding' (Acts 16,10), 'purposed' (Acts 19,21) and 'decided' (Acts 20,3). Such a conscious choice of the itinerary and the destination is only mentioned in the second part of the Acts with regard to Jerusalem and Rome. This too illustrates once more the unique position of Macedonia in the Acts.

8.5 Paul's travelling company

Mentioning the persons, even those who belong to Paul's travelling company, is possibly even stranger than the way in which Luke incorporated most places and towns in his story. Names suddenly turn up in the stories and disappear just as suddenly. Silas, who's travelling with Paul from Antioch in Syria (Acts 15,40), disappears all of a sudden after Corinth and is mentioned no more (Acts 18,5). Priscilla and Aquila travel from Rome via Corinth to Ephesus (Acts18,2 and 18-28), but when Paul arrives in Ephesus after some time and stays there for a longer period, these two people are no longer mentioned either (Acts18,21-23; 19,1-40). In spite of all this, Paul's travelling parties shows some aspects that again point into the direction of Macedonia.

Timothy was, without any doubt, one of the most important of Paul's fellow workers. Historically seen this is quite clear from Paul's own letters.[a] Luke's treatment of Timothy is linked to Macedonia in a slightly strange way. Timothy turns up for the first time in the Acts immediately before the vision of the Macedonian man. Paul had him circumcised because his mother was a Jewess and because Paul wanted to take him along on his journey (Acts 16,1-3). When later Paul is taken to Athens by the brothers of Berea, Timothy ánd Silas stay behind in Macedonia (Acts 17,13-14). When he, Timothy, joins Paul again in Corinth, he quietly disappears from the story (Acts 18,5). Only in Ephesus he turns up again in Paul's company, at the moment he is sent to Macedonia together with Erastus (Acts 19,22).

When Paul travels to Macedonia for the last time we again meet Timothy in his company (Acts 20,3-4). After that he's seen no more. So Timothy always appears in the story when Paul goes to Macedonia and disappears again from the story after Paul has left Macedonia. It goes without saying to associate Luke's treatment of Timothy with the story about his circumcision. So the question arises whether the preservation of the circumcision was an essential characteristic of Luke's 'Macedonian theology'. Once again we recall the parallel between the Macedonia-stories and the last Jerusalem-story. Also in Jerusalem the preservation of the circumcision plays an important part in the meeting with James and the elders (Acts 21,21-25). Here we discern a feature in

---

[a] Romans 16,21; 1 Corinthians 4,17; 16,10; 2 Corinthians 1,1 and 19; Philippians 1,1; 2,19. The mention in Colossians 1,1 is deutero-paulinic.

THE GEOGRAPHY OF THE ACTS OF THE APOSTLES

Luke's set-up of the Acts, that not only points at his possible origin from Macedonia, but also at his Jewish identity.

Elsewhere also notes appear on people who are important to our subject. In the long Ephesus-story (Acts 19,1-40) we read, in addition to Paul's intention to travel via Macedonia, also about 'Gaius and Aristarchus, Macedonian travel companions of Paul's' (v. 29). In this Ephesus-story they are the only fellow workers mentioned by name next to Timothy and Erastus. When Paul begins at his last journey to Jerusalem, Luke describes a travelling company of seven people and the first three mentioned are: Sopater from Berea, Aristarchus and Secundus from Thessalonica (Acts 20,4). Now, I dare say, this number of seven won't be based on coincidence, but it will probably refer to the seventy nations of the world that in the then Jewry were distinguished by virtue of the list of nations in Genesis 10. We know of only two of them that they were Jews, Aristarchus and Timothy (Acts 16,1-3), so the company could be considered as a representation of the diaspora-communities. Paul travels with these seven to Jerusalem as Jesus in the gospel of Luke travels to the same town with his twelve disciples – a representation of Israel. Again we are confronted with the central position of Jerusalem in Luke's ideas of the diaspora-communities as well. Obviously this journey of Paul's and the 'seven' is so important to Luke, that in Macedonia he makes the we-figure turn up again in the story (Acts 20,5). The orientation towards Jerusalem appears to be an essential part of Luke's 'Macedonian theology'.

My final observation is that the only fellow worker mentioned by name, who accompanies Paul to Rome, is Aristarchus, who is described accurately as 'a Macedonian from Thessalonica' (Acts 20,5). The we-figure accompanies Paul as well on this journey (Acts 27,1 f.). Could this be Luke himself who accompanies Paul as 'the bearer of the Macedonian program' via Jerusalem to Rome?

At the end of this section I conclude that Luke's report on the coming about of Paul's itinerary and the arrangement of his travelling companies, strongly supports the supposition that he was of Macedonian origin. As we'll see in section 10.3 there is, however, another possible explanation for the important part of Macedonia in the second half of the Acts. Eventually both explanations could go hand in hand.

8.6 Rome

The Acts end in Rome and do so in a way many scholars are not satisfied with.[219] In Jerusalem and Caesarea Paul was taken to the court of the Roman governor by a group of Jews from Jerusalem. During this trial he, as a Roman citizen, appealed to the emperor and was sent to Rome consequently. In Rome however, nothing is told about this trial, apart from his house arrest (Acts 28,16). The sueing party should have sent a deputation to Rome to file a complaint against Paul with the Emperor, but within the mandatory term of two years, nothing is heard from it (Acts 28,21 and 30).[220] Paul preaches the kingdom of God in the Jewish community of Rome and this ends the Acts.

For those who consider the Acts a life of Paul's, this is a rather incomplete end. Of course one is curious about what happened with Paul, and why Luke doesn't inform us about that anymore. Some believed that the Acts were written for the Christians of Rome and that the book ends here because they knew the further course of Paul's life.[221] However, this argument is – in my view - based too much on the supposition that Luke intended to write a historical-biographical report. However, if we're going to read the Acts as a form of midrash other reasons should be looked for and found to explain why this book ends in Rome in such a way. In the preceding chapters I already put forward some suppositions: Luke aims at the conversion of Rome in order to

THE GEOGRAPHY OF THE ACTS OF THE APOSTLES

have the temple and Jerusalem restored in their function to Judaism and to the nations.[a] What more can the Acts tell us in this respect?

That the Acts were written for a public living in Rome, is supported by some geographical material. For example, some scholars discovered that Luke, as soon as the story approaches Rome, treats some geographical details differently. From Acts 15 we find rather a lot of details, such as names of people, places, provinces and even buildings. At the end of the Acts however, this interest of Luke's in personal and geographical details dwindles.[222] Indeed, he does mention Syracuse, Rhegium, Puteoli, Appi Forum and Tres Tabernae (Acts 28), all not far from Rome, but he doesn't specify these places in more detail. Elsewhere in the gospel of Luke and the Acts such specifications occur regularly, but if Luke wrote for a public living in Rome they are presumably redundant. However, this doesn't tell us anything about his motive for the open end of the Rome-story and with it of the Acts.

Rome occurs for the first time in the Acts when Paul arrives in Corinth and encounters a Jew named Aquila, who with his wife Priscilla, has left Rome due to the command of Claudius that all Jews were to disappear from Rome (Acts 18.2). The first picture Luke paints for us from Rome is the picture of *a town that tries to expel its Jews*.[b] Besides, it's not unimportant to point out that it's about the expulsion of the Jews and not of the Christians! The latter hardly play a part in Acts 28, as we'll see.

After the introduction of Rome into the Corinth-story we come across Rome for the second time in the Ephesus-story. In it Paul is firmly resolved to travel to Rome (Acts 19,21). It so happened that Aquila and Priscilla are in Ephesus too (according to Acts 18,18-26), but aren't mentioned once in the whole story of Paul's stay in that town (Acts 19,1 – 20,1). One gets the impression that Paul didn't agree with

---

[a] See section 6.7 and 7.2.
[b] Here again a parallel with Gerasa (Luke 8,37; see section 6.7).

their leaving Rome. Here Paul shows clearly that instead of leaving Rome one should go to Rome. There should be a Jewish community in Rome. One shouldn't weaken this community by leaving it, but one should strengthen it by going to it. Paul goes to Rome and even the forces of the underworld, the Hades, symbolized by the storm at sea (Acts 27)[a] cannot stop him from going there. And when Paul finally arrives in Rome, Claudius' aim turned out to be a failure: there still is a Jewish community of some importance (Acts 28,17f).

It's imperative now to show that the Acts ends in the Jewish community of Rome and not in the Christian community, although there were Christians in Rome already before Paul's arrival (Acts 28,15 and 22). And yet no attention at all is paid to the Christians during Paul's stay in Rome. In the Rome-story we don't even come across the preaching to the God-fearing gentiles, so characteristic for other places in the Acts. The Rome-story is restricted to the Jews and shows Paul's attempt to convince the Jewish community there with regard to Jesus' mission (Acts 28,23). This attempt is only partially successful (Acts 28,24-25) and finally Paul appeals rather despairingly to the prophet Isaiah, but even this doesn't change the situation. And it is here exactly that Luke ends the Acts, in itself reason enough to suppose, that the book was written for readers in Rome, Jewish readers! Here, in the Jewish communities of Rome the discussions about and the study of the Scriptures (and this is midrash!) will have to continue (Acts 28,23). Luke stops at a point where his Jewish readers should go on and continue his work. Here again we find support for the proposition that Luke wrote for a Jewish public. This public is found in Rome the centre of the pagan world of those days, the centre of power.

---

[a] See section 6.4.

9. Zealous toward God as you all are today
Factions in Judaism

The structure of the first-century Judaism was rather more complicated than we can imagine today. The traditional division into three factions as given by Flavius Josephus is not only too rough but incomplete as well. He distinguishes Sadducees, Pharisees and Essenes, but within these movements a whole range of groupings, schools and denominations existed. This applies in particular to the Pharisees. The term *Pharisees* is comparable to a term like *Protestants*, also an all-embracing collective for many denominations. Besides, there were other groups that can't be placed in Josephus' tripartition. We meet Herodians (Mark 12,13). The disciples of John the Baptist made up a group (Mark 2,18). The Zealots, sometimes considered to be Pharisees by Flavius Josephus and sometimes considered to be a separate group, were a rather influential movement. Sometimes one formed groups merely according to the place of origin (Acts 6,9).

Of course, these groups or factions weren't well-organized groups or associations. Very often the boundaries between the various movements can't be drawn clearly. What's more, there were of course, as is always the case, more or less outspoken adherents to the various trends. Besides, most Jews didn't belong to one of these movements specifically, but they had their sympathies, obviously. Perhaps this large group of ordinary people even made up the majority of the Jewish people. In the gospels we rather often find words like 'the multitude', 'the crowd', 'the people', etc. These words allude to all those common Jews who didn't belong explicitly to a specific group. The question that is important to us runs as follows: how did Luke look at the major movements in the then Judaism and how was in his view the position of Jesus and his disciples within that complex of movements? Discussing this subject, I'll restrict myself to three movements within the land of Israel, the Pharisees, the Sadducees and the Zealots.

9.1 *The Pharisees*

a. The Pharisees in Luke in comparison with Mark and Matthew
Traditionally most Christians look upon the Pharisees as legalistic quibblers, hypocrites and enemies if not persecutors of Jesus and his disciples.[223] This image of the Pharisees is based mainly on the bitter anti-pharisaic polemics in the gospel of Matthew and to a lesser extent on those in the gospel of Mark. Notorious is Jesus' speech in Matthew 23, in which the words "Woe to you, scribes and Pharisees, hypocrites" occur no less than six times. It's quite remarkable that Luke as soon as the Pharisees come up, changes his tune. He leaves out many of the harsh words of Jesus' directed at the Pharisees, we come across in Mark and Matthew. One single remark of Jesus' protest against the pharisaic ideas of purity remains (compare Mark 7,1-23 and Matthew 15,1-20 with Luke 11,39). The story of the Pharisees who want a sign, doesn't occur in the gospel of Luke (Mark 8,11-13; Matthew 16,1-4). The question about divorce the Pharisees asked Jesus, according to Mark and Matthew, in order to test him, is not found in Luke (Mark 10,2-12; Matthew 19,3-12). Jesus' long answer to that question comes up briefly in Luke in another context and here the relation with the Pharisees is not clear (Luke 16,18). Jesus' fierce speech against the Pharisees in Matthew 23 is only found back in a very abridged form in the gospel of Luke and in much milder words and only a part of which concerns the Pharisees (Luke 11,39-44). This softening of the anti-pharisaic polemics by Luke has already attracted the attention of many commentators. Some concluded that Luke wrote for the Christians from the gentiles: presumably these anti-pharisaic traditions wouldn't be of interest to them.[224]

Factions in Judaism

However, there is, possibly, another explanation for Luke's milder attitude towards the Pharisees. To that end I'll have a closer look at his treatment of the Pharisees in his gospel and in the Acts.

Not only the milder tone in the polemics against the Pharisees ask for our attention, but also a number of other points that could give us some insight in Luke's ideas about this important movement in the then Judaism. Luke is the only evangelist who tells us that Jesus visited the Pharisees at home to have a meal with them, not once, but three times (Luke 7,36f; 11,37f; 14,1f). In Luke's view the contact between Jesus and the Pharisees wasn't limited to public occasions but he moved in their circles. Contrary to the gospels of Mark and Matthew, where the atmosphere is almost always angry as soon as some Pharisees turn up, in Luke hardly any hostilities can be perceived on the part of the Pharisees. Only two passages could be explained as less friendly (Luke 6,7 and 11,53-54). The only time the tension increases, is when Jesus himself adopted a hostile attitude towards the Pharisees (Luke 11, 37-54). A striking contrast to this fierce confrontation is a conspicuous alteration Luke made in a text of Mark's. Mark writes:

"Then the Pharisees went out and immediately plotted with the Herodians against him, how they might destroy him" (Mark 3,6).

Luke's version in his parallel-story reads:

"But they got completely confused, and discussed with one another what they might do to Jesus" (Luke 6,11).

This tendency to represent the Pharisees more sympathetic than the other evangelists also permeates Luke's impression of things with regard to the events in Jerusalem that precede Jesus' death. Then and there Luke severs any relation between the event and the Pharisees. In fact, this severance already begins in Luke 6,11. More distinct even is the note in the middle of the travel story, when some Pharisees warn Jesus that Herod wants to kill him (Luke13,31). During Jesus' stay in Jerusalem no Pharisees are found at all in Luke's gospel. They are mentioned for the last time in Luke 19,39. This also means that Luke removed the Pharisees from the story about paying taxes to the emperor (cf. Luke 20, 19-20 with Mark 12,13). Luke obviously wanted to prevent each suspicion of involvement of the Pharisees in the death of Jesus.

How much this mild attitude of Luke's towards the Pharisees contrasted with the negative view of Matthew on this group becomes clear when we discover how often Matthew adds the Pharisees as opponents of Jesus to the stories about his actions in Jerusalem (in five out of seven stories: see table 9.1). Matthew sees the Pharisees as the most important adversaries of Jesus, but Luke obviously doesn't. Of course it is possible that in his view the similarities between Jesus and the Pharisees had been more important than the differences. This idea is confirmed by Luke's description of the Pharisees in the Acts. In Acts 5,34 Gamaliel, the great scholar from the Pharisaic School of Hillel, appears as a defender of the apostles. He prevents them from being killed. In Acts 15,5 some Pharisees appear to belong to the Christian community. Once more we meet Gamaliel, but now as someone Paul can appeal to and who presumably educated him, says Paul (Acts 22,3). Paul even describes himself as "a Pharisee, a son of Pharisees" (Acts 23,6) and defends himself against Agrippa with the remark that "after the most strictest sect of our religion I lived a Pharisee" (Acts 26,5). There is no question at all of any hostility in the Acts between the Pharisees and the Christian community. Once again the Pharisees stand up in the Sanhedrin for a disciple of Jesus', for Paul (Acts 23,9), and precisely on this occasion Luke underscores the affinity of ideas. Both movements share the belief in the resurrection and in the existence of angels and spirits (Acts 23,6-8). Now all this evokes two questions:

FACTIONS IN JUDAISM

- How can Luke's friendly attitude towards the Pharisees be explained compared with Matthew's hostile attitude for instance?
- How can we explain that in spite of his friendly attitude Luke yet includes such a sharp attack of Jesus' on the Pharisees in his gospel? (Luke 11,39-44).

To answer these questions we'll have to work out first and foremost who in fact were the Pharisees.

Table 9.1

Survey of places in Mark, Matthew and Luke that mention or don't mention the Pharisees in the Jerusalem-stories.

Story/texts	Mark	Matthew	Luke
Entry into Jerusalem (Mark 11,10f; Matthew 21,9f; Luke 19,39)	no	no	yes
Parable of the wicked vinedressers (Mark 12,12; Matthew 21,45; Luke 20,19)	no	yes	no
Paying taxes to Caesar (Mark12,13; Matthew 22,15; Like 20,19)	yes	yes	no
Which is the first commandment of all? (Mark 12,28; Matthew 22,34; not found in Luke)	no	yes	---
The son of David (Mark 12,35; Matthew 22,41; Luke 20,39-41)	no	yes	No
Beware of the scribes and the Pharisees (Mark 12,38; Matthew 23,2f; Luke 20,45-47)	no	yes	No
The vigil at the tomb (Matthew 27,62; not found in Mark and Luke)	---	yes	---

FACTIONS IN JUDAISM

b. The character of the Pharisaic movement

In the days of Jesus' the Pharisaic movement already existed for more than a century. In all probability they were the successors of the so-called *chassidim*. This was a movement of pious, law-abiding Jews in the second century BCE, that offered resistance to the Hellenistic policy of the Syrian tyrant Antioch IV Epiphanes (175-164 BCE). The Pharisees saw themselves as successors of Ezra and Nehemiah, who inspired the Torah-abiding Judaism enormously. As all Jewish movements did, the Pharisees accepted the Torah, the first five books of the bible as the most authoritative Holy Scriptures. In its written form the Torah was recorded during or just after the Babylonian Exile. This means that in the centuries around the beginning of the Common Era many rules of the law could no longer be applied literally, because obviously the historical circumstances had changed. In the new historical situation of Jesus' days the Jews ran into questions and problems that couldn't be solved immediately by the Torah. In those days all Jewish movements found their own solutions to this problem. It was the Pharisees' ambition, the progress of history notwithstanding, to keep on involving the Torah in all fields of life. To reach that aim they developed an interpretative method that provide the link between the text of the Torah and the life of every day. Three elements in this interpretative method played an important part:

- The other books of Tanakh: the Prophets and the Writings were seen as interpretations of the Torah one could fall back on, establishing the correct explanation of the text of the Torah.
- The Oral Torah. This is a complex of orally passed down rules of life (*halachah*) and stories (*aggadah*), that was refined and extended by every generation of rabbis in its turn. One took the view that both the Written and the Oral Torah were given by Moses at Mount Sinai. What the rabbis did over the centuries was nothing

else but developing what had essentially been given at Mount Sinai.
- A number of explanatory rules were formulated in this Oral Torah with the help of which the Written Torah was interpreted and adapted to all kinds of situations in life. The first rabbi who explicitly formulated a number of these rules was Hillel the Elder (beginning of the 1st century CE). Other rabbis after him extended the number of rules.[225]

In this way the Pharisees were able to adapt the exegesis of the Torah to the changing circumstances. Likewise, in certain cases, it was possible as well not to apply the Torah literally. In these cases one explained its rules according to the spirit instead of to the letter. A clear example is the rule 'eye for eye, tooth for tooth' (Exodus 21,24). This was interpreted as 'the *value* of an eye for an eye and the *value* of a tooth for a tooth'. Corporal retaliation was replaced by financial compensation. In this way the pharisaic rabbis attempted to lessen physical violence in society. Thus, as a matter of fact, the Pharisees constituted a progressive movement in the then Judaism.[226]

Now the fact is that the Pharisees developed a large number of ideas we also meet in the gospels. From this we can deduce that there must have been a clear relationship between the Pharisees on the one hand and Jesus and his followers on the other. This makes Luke's mild attitude towards these group easier to understand. But on the other hand it causes Matthew's hostile attitude towards the Pharisees to become more problematic . Before going into that I'll first mention four remarkable points of similarity with the Pharisees. As far as the gospels are concerned I'll only refer to Luke although it would have been equally possible to refer to the other gospels as well.

- In the Acts the resurrection of the dead as the common faith of the Pharisees and the devotees of Jesus is explicitly mentioned (Acts

FACTIONS IN JUDAISM

23,6). This faith expresses that God acts justly, in spite of the great injustice in the world.[227]

- The second point mentioned in the Acts is the belief in the existence of angels (Acts 23,8). The Hebrew word for angel, *malach*, simply means 'messenger'. So the belief in the existence of angels means and expresses that God goes on taking care of the world even after the Creation and that he goes on revealing himself to Israel even after the gift of Torah on Mount Sinai.
- A third point of agreement is the idea that good behaviour will be rewarded and bad behaviour will be punished[228] (Luke 13,27; 16,19-31; 18,7-8,14,30; 20,16 and others). The distinction that is made between the righteous ones and the sinners is closely connected with this concept[229] (Luke 15,7; Acts 24,14-15). All the same, the possibility for the sinner to repent plays an important part both with the Pharisees and with Jesus and his followers[230] (Luke 15,7 and others).
- The possibility of man to serve God outside the temple in Jerusalem is a point of agreement as well. The Pharisees see the study of Torah, prayer and practising charity as service to God next to participating in the sacrificial service.[231] When the sacrificial service is eliminated in 70 CE, the study of Torah, prayer and practising charity even becomes an alternative for the sacrificial service.[232, a] The tenor of all gospels is that God is not only served inside the temple. Luke doesn't look upon this outside-the-temple service to

---

[a] Nothing of this can be found yet in Mark, Matthew and Luke, because they were still under the impression that the disappearance of the temple would turn out to be a temporary affair. In my opinion, with regard to this question, the fourth gospel takes up a position comparable to the one of rabbis like Rabban Jochanan Ben Zakkai, the great Jewish leader after the destruction of the temple in 70 CE (see the previous endnote). In my book *Het evangelie uit het leerhuis van Lazarus/The Gospel from the study-house of Lazarus* (Dutch edition: Van 't Riet, 1996) I explained and substantiated this point of view.

Factions in Judaism

God as the replacement of the sacrificial service. This appears from the fact that neither in his gospel, nor in the Acts it's a subject under discussion. On the contrary, the temple service is very much taken for granted (Luke 1,9; 2,24 and 41; 5,14; 6,4; 13,1; 21,1-4; 22,7-8; Acts 21,26; 24,17).

The existence of these similarities doesn't alter the fact that there were – of course – some differences between the ideas of the Pharisees and the ideas of Jesus and his followers. That was the case for instance with the application of the laws of purity. On the strength of the rule "And you shall be to me a kingdom of priests and a holy nation"(Exodus 19, 6), the Pharisees held the view that every Jew should obey these rules, even outside the temple. Other Jewish groupings were of the opinion that these laws should only be turned into practice by common Jews when they were really and actually in the temple precincts.[233] That's the reason why we find a good many discussions about this matter between Jesus and the Pharisees (e.g. in Luke 11, 39-41). In order to reach a correct appreciation of the differences of opinion, we'll first have to discuss an important issue which is overlooked by many commentators (more often than not).

The Pharisaic method that offers the possibility to interpret the Torah time and again, if required by new circumstances, didn't result in a uniform arrangement of the *"halachah"* (the collection of Jewish laws and rules for life). As a consequence there were within the Pharisaic movement schools and groups that thought differently about all kinds of issues in Jesus' days. And exactly because the Pharisaic method of Torah-exegesis offered the possibility to adapt the halachah to the circumstances one lived in, progressive and conservative wings came into being within this movement. The Talmud mentions seven kinds of Pharisees. This is of course not a historical number of seven, but it indicates that there were Pharisees of all sorts. After all, the number seven means completeness.[234] We are rather well informed about two schools within the pharisaic movement: the strict, conservative

School of Shammai and the more enlightened, progressive School of Hillel.[235]

The School of Shammai was the dominant group in Pharisaism until the destruction of the temple in 70 CE.[236] This situation changes drastically after 70. The School of Shammai disappears from the scene in some decades and the rabbis from the School of Hillel take charge. Other Jewish groups like the Sadducees and the Zealots are wiped off the map and from then on the School of Hillel even fulfils an executive function in the entire Judaism and not only in the movement of the Pharisees. From then on the Pharisees as a specific movement in Judaism disappear completely. The Talmud, compiled by the successors of the School of Hillel does no longer speak about 'Pharisees' when the own rabbis are meant, but about the 'Sages'.[a, 237] The word 'Pharisees' gets another often negative function and sound. I'll return to this later.

c. **The evangelists' attitude towards the Pharisees**
The evangelists' way of writing about the Pharisees can be explained against the above-mentioned background. Matthew's negative attitude towards the Pharisees was probably a reaction to the strict Pharisaic School of Shammai that was dominant in the days of Jesus. And perhaps there were even more conservative groups within the Pharisaism of those days which further defined Matthew's image of the Pharisees. Matthew probably wrote his gospel in Galilee not long after 70 CE. Without any doubt the influence of the School of Shammai was still very well noticeable at that time.[238] For Luke things were different. He wrote his gospel a decade later and – what's more – not in the land of Israel itself. In those days the School of Hillel came up as the new authoritative school of Judaism. In the diaspora in the years after 70 CE one had to deal more with the School of Hillel than with the disappearing School of Shammai, which perhaps had never had a lot of influence

---

[a]   In Hebrew: *chachamim*.

outside the land of Israel anyway. Moreover, the School of Hillel constituted for the followers of Jesus a lesser threat than the School of Shammai had ever done. This appears clearly from the defence Gamaliel conducted in the Supreme Court in favour of the apostles (Acts 5,34-40). Gamaliel was a grandson of Hillel and one of the most important representatives of the School of Hillel. The controversies that may have existed between Jesus, albeit in Matthew's eyes, and the strict Pharisees, were no longer of much importance to Luke. It was more interesting for him to indicate the relation with the enlightened Pharisees from the School of Hillel. At the end of the first century CE, when Luke wrote his books, they directed the recovery of Judaism after the 70's catastrophe. To a great extent they aimed at the same targets Luke had in mind with his gospel and the Acts. The fact is that there are a lot of points of agreement between the ideas of the School of Hillel and Luke's ideas. I'll pass a number of the similarities in review, but in doing so I make no claim to be exhaustive.

d. Luke and the School of Hillel

There is no evangelist who pays more attention to the issue of poor and rich than Luke.[239] It goes without saying that Luke is sympathetic to the poor (e.g. Luke 4,28; 7,22). Who compares the intent of the Sermon in the Field (Luke 6,20) with the purpose of the Sermon on the Mount (Matthew 5,3) understands he refers to material poverty. The 'blessed are you poor' in the Sermon in the Field faces the 'woe to you who are rich' (Luke 6,20 and 24). The same benevolent attitude to the poor occurs in the School of Hillel. In a number of cases Hillel himself replaced the literary explanation of the text of the Torah by an interpretation more favourable to the poor. An important example is the so-called 'prosbul'. The Torah requires that every seven years, during the sabbatical year, 'you shall grant a release of debts' (Deuteronomy 15, 1-6). The rich in the days of Hillel were little inclined to lend money to the poor because of the bad economical situation. This especially was the case in the years before a sabbatical year. In that case they ran the risk of not getting back their money of course. The situation of the less fortunate got worse, since they were dependent on borrowed money for their economical possibilities. The prosbul now made it possible to call in a loan even after a sabbatical year. Borrowing and lending became easier and the poor got more financial headroom.[240] Hillel took other measures as well in favour of the poor and the impoverished.[241] In his youth he had lived in dire poverty. In the Talmud he's seen as an outstanding example of a poor man who engages in the study of Torah in spite of his bad financial situation.[242]

Another point of agreement between Luke and the School of Hillel concerns the attitude towards the gentiles. It's true, Jesus' actions were directed towards Israel[a], but it is clear that in his view the gentiles would, in the end, participate in the salvation of Israel. This kind attitude towards the gentiles is found with Hillel as well. The Talmud describes how three gentiles independent of each other first go to Shammai and then to Hillel with the request to become proselytes, but they make rather strange demands. One of them demands for example that he's taught the Torah, standing on one leg. Shammai, the strict Pharisee, gets awfully angry and chases him off. Then he turns to Hillel who turns him into a proselyte immediately and teaches him: "Do unto others as you would them to do unto you. That is the entire Torah, the rest is interpretation. Go and learn!" The other two gentiles make similar demands and are chased off as well by Shammai. But Hillel turns them into proselytes and shows them the correct understanding about their demands. When, after some time these three proselytes meet, they say: "Shammai's impatience wanted to expel us from this world, Hillel's kindheartedness took us under the wings of God's presence.[243]

---

[a] See chapters 5, 6 and 7.

FACTIONS IN JUDAISM

Some other details in the Talmud are important in this respect as well. Forced by the School of Shammai eighteen *halachot*[a] were proclaimed that should prevent any contact between Jews and gentiles. The resistance of the School of Hillel must have been so fierce that the students of the School of Shammai decided the argument to their advantage by means of bloodbath. The later rabbis condemned this event with the words: "This day was for Israel as grievous as the day they made the gold calf!" Another tradition: "That day Hillel sat in front of Shammai with his head bowed as a mere student."[244]

Luke saw Jesus as a peaceful and non-violent messianic man. This attitude aimed at peace is found with Hillel as well. In the *Sayings of the Fathers*, one of the most important and well-known chapters in the Talmud, the first reported saying of Hillel is: "Be among the disciples of Aaron, loving peace and pursuing peace, loving people and bringing them closer to the Torah".[245] The first description this Talmud-tract gives of Hillel, is defined by his pursuit of peace. This attitude was not only characteristic for Hillel, but also for the rabbis from the School of Hillel after him. From this peace-centred attitude stems a fourth similarity between Luke and the School of Hillel.

We already saw that the Gospel of Luke could especially be read as an anti-zealotic argument.[b] And it is precisely this rejection of the zealotism that Luke connects in the Acts with the School of Hillel. Gamaliel, Hillel's grandson, defends the apostles with words that express his disapproval of the actions of the zealotic rebel-leaders Theudas and Judas the Galilean (Acts 5, 36-37). However, Gamaliel's speech is rather dubious, in view of the history, because for one thing Judas the Galilean didn't appear after but before Theudas[c], and for

---

[a] Plural of *halachah*, the Jewish religious system of rules of life.
[b] See chapters 6 and 7.
[c] According to Jos. Ant. 20,97f. Theudas appeared under the procurator Cuspius Fadus (ca 44 CE). Judas the Galilean on the other hand appeared in the days of the registration (6 CE).

another thing Theudas only appeared around 44 CE whereas, from the course of actions in the Acts, this speech of Gamaliel's should be dated a lot.[246] So it's obvious: Luke tries very hard to show the essence of his relation with the School of Hillel: his rejection of the violent character of the zealotic movement. A fifth similarity is connected with this conclusion.

Luke's attitude towards the Roman Empire could be called peaceful at least, as is the case with most rabbis of the School of Hillel. During the revolt of 66 to 70 CE Jochanan ben Zakkai, one of the most important rabbis of the School of Hillel, belongs to the peace party in Jerusalem. When the town runs the risk of starvation by the Roman siege he decides to leave Jerusalem by means of a ruse. Once outside the town he has himself taken to the Roman general Vespasian. He asks his permission to be allowed to found a House of Learning in Javne.[247] Rabban Gamaliel II, who succeeded him as the leader of the House of Learning around 80 CE, even tried to persuade the Roman government to acknowledge him as the leader of the Jews. He also travelled to Rome to intercede for his people at the imperial court.[248] For many Jews in the diaspora maintaining contacts with the Roman government or with the local rulers was customary as well. Some examples of Luke's in the Acts are certainly not exceptional (Acts 18,12; 19,33-34). However, this doesn't mean at all that the Jews were well-disposed towards the Roman empire or the local pagan authority. They were prepared to keep in touch with them and to make use of their services as long as they didn't come into conflict with the essence of their own Jewish tradition. In this respect Luke's attitude is also very much cognate to that of the rabbis from the School of Hillel. Did Luke recognize in the Pharisees from this school a movement within Judaism that supported the same ideas and objectives to a large extent? This is, I think, the most plausible explanation for the fact that Luke treats the Pharisees in his gospel and in the Acts so well.

FACTIONS IN JUDAISM

e. The conflict with the strictest Pharisees

A last question remains: why do we still find such a sharp attack on the Pharisees in Luke 11,39-44, in spite of his kindness? To answer this question I'd like to say first of all that the Pharisees in the writings of the rabbis are often attacked as strongly as in the gospels and for the same reasons usually.[249] This is strange, the more so as the rabbis who edited the Talmud and the collections of midrashim, were the successors of the Pharisees. But we should realize that the word *Pharisees* had another meaning in the first centuries CE than the meaning Christians later on put on to the word. The view many had on the Pharisees for ages on end, was especially determined by the gospels and by the work of the Jewish historian Flavius Josephus. Due to the study of both kinds of writings the image came into being of the Pharisees as a carefully defined group in the Judaism of those days. A Jew was either a 'member' of this grouping, or he wasn't. This view 'sees' the Pharisees as more or less comparable to a sect or a denomination one can be a member of, whether or not. This impression of things however, is not correct as far as the Pharisees are concerned.

The word *Pharisees*, in Greek *pharisaioi*, is derived from the Hebrew stem PaRaSh. This verb-stem means 'to separate'. So the word 'Pharisees' could be translated with the 'separatists', better still: 'those who separate themselves from'. The imperfect tense in this last translation is essential. The point is that the Pharisees didn't belong to a group that once, long ago, had broken away from another group and that now lived a life of its own. Separating oneself was a daily reality for the Pharisees. It belonged to the essence of their existence! By virtue of the commandment "And you shall be to Me a kingdom of priests and a holy nation" (Exodus 19,6) they aimed at a way of life that in all respects was permeated by the Torah. Consequently, associating with other people who didn't live entirely according to the Torah became impossible in a number of occasions. In these cases they separated from that part of the people that didn't live according to the pharisaic *halachah* (rules of life). Within the pharisaic movement, however, the Torah was interpreted differently. The stricter its explanation, the more difficult the contact with the other Jews was rendered or was lost even. The milder the interpretation of the Torah the more the relation with the rest of the Jews remained upheld. This means that one could be a Pharisee, more or less, and that the word *Pharisee* didn't have a fixed meaning, similar to all adherents of this movement.

Depending on the kind of Pharisees we're actually dealing with, the word *Pharisees* has a more or a less powerful meaning and a more or less favourable ring to it. To a certain extent this situation can be compared with a word like 'Calvinists'. There are all kinds of Calvinists, too. The more serious they are within the Reformation, the more 'calvinistic' their reputation is. That's why one can hear the word 'Calvinists' used off and on favourably and on and off unfavourably. And within Calvinistic circles at that! Of course it depends very much who uses the word and for which group. This is altogether true for the Pharisees as well.

This now implies that the words "Woe betide you Pharisees" needn't refer to the entire movement of the Pharisees. The violent attacks on them in the gospels and in the writings of the rabbis were always intended for certain groups of Pharisees which had alienated themselves unnecessarily much from the majority of the people by their behaviour, mentality or their strict Torah-explanation. In Luke 18,9-14 a mentality of self-justification is exposed that no doubt occurred with certain Pharisees.[250] This mentality was simply part of their Pharisaism. It separated them from "this crowd that doesn't know the law" (John 7,49). But other Pharisees condemned such an attitude of self-justification as vigorously as Jesus did in this story of Luke's. Hillel says for instance: "Do not separate yourself from the community; do not believe in yourself until the day you die".[251] The expression 'do not separate yourself' (in Hebrew the verb-stem PaRaSh is used) is a clear polemic and possibly aimed against a certain form of Pharisaism. Again a similarity between the ideas of Luke and the School of Hillel in their resistance against extreme pharisaic notions.

Luke 11,37-44 isn't a polemic against all Pharisees either, but only against those Pharisees who alienated themselves from their surroundings by means of an extreme interpretation of the Torah. The best way to make this clear is found in the words of Jesus: "But woe to you, Pharisees! For you tithe mint and rue and all manner of herbs, and pass by justice and the love of God". On the basis of the Torah (Numbers 18,21f; Deuteronomy 14,22f; 26,12f) the tithes of the harvest should be handed over to the Levites. The Torah doesn't specify however, which crops do or don't fall under this commandment. It is beyond doubt that some Pharisees out of respect for and obedience to the Torah applied this commandment to everything that was grown for the purpose of consumption, including garden herbs. Although mint isn't mentioned anywhere in the Talmud, meadow rue together with a number of other garden herbs is explicitly exempted from paying tithes.[252] This shows that there was a difference of opinion in those days. The rabbis from the School of Hillel who edited the Talmud chose for the mild interpretation of the Torah here as well. Milder even than Jesus who concluded his pronouncement with the words: "These (paying tithes of garden herbs) you ought to have done, without leaving the others undone (the judgement and the love of God)".

f. Summary and conclusion

Summarizing we can argue that by and large Luke treats the Pharisees friendly in his gospel and in the Acts, because the Pharisees from the School of Hillel, who gained the upper hand in Luke's days (after 70 BC), had largely the same intentions and strove for the same aims. The few times Luke approaches the Pharisees critically even illustrate this relationship with the hillellite school that was also critical of the strictest Pharisees. The conclusion can be drawn that Luke was nearer to the then rabbinical Judaism, than many presumed until recently.

9.2 The Sadducees and the chief priests

The Sadducees were a group in Judaism that existed from about 200 BCE to 70 CE. They were mainly found in and around Jerusalem. They were an aristocratic party that consisted of rich merchants and distinguished families as well as well-to-do families of priests that governed the temple. These priests are called the 'chief priests' in the New Testament. The Greek text however, uses the same word for 'chief priests' and 'high priests' (*archiereus*). These families of priests descended from Zadok, who was high priest in the days of Solomon. Zadok's descent from Aaron and his loyalty to David and Solomon are mentioned regularly in Tanakh (2 Samuel 8,17; 15,24f; 1 Kings 1,32f; 1 Chronicles 12,29). His descendants, the sons of Zadok, were charged with the responsibility for the temple after the Babylonian Exile (Ezekiel 40,46; 43,19; 44,15-16). It's highly probable that the name *Sadducees* was derived from the name of this Zadok.[253]

As 'sons of Zadok' the sadducean families of priests were not only in charge of the temple. Since the government of Herod the Great (37-4 CE) they supplied the temple in turns with a high priest. Their dominant position in Jerusalem and in the temple existed until about 50 CE. Only during the last twenty years of the existence of the temple they had to relinquish their dominant position to the Pharisees.[254] After the destruction of the temple in 70 CE the Sadducees disappeared from the stage of history once and for all. In the days of the gospels and the Acts the Sadducees also dominated the Sanhedrin (the Supreme Court), the highest council of state in the then Judaism. This court had its seat in Jerusalem. The ideas and the actions of the Sadducees and the chief priests who belonged to their ranks, are very important for the good understanding of the gospels and the Acts of the Apostles. Everything described in these books took place in the time the Sadducees supervised Judaism. That doesn't mean that they could do what they wanted. They really had to reckon with the wishes of others like the common people, the Pharisees, the Herodians, the zealotic resistance movement and the Romans in particular. They played their parts in an elaborate process that eventually would lead to their ruin. But in the days of Jesus and the apostles they still played an important part as one of the major groups. That's why we meet the Sadducees regularly in the gospels and the Acts, albeit less frequently than the Pharisees, who were more numerous, lived scattered across the land of Israel and who were closer to Jesus and his disciples as for their ideas.

In both Luke's books the name *Sadducees* is mentioned in four stories (Luke 20,27f; Acts 4,1f; 5,17f; 23,6f). Three out of these four stories are about the belief in the resurrection of the dead. This theme plays an important part in the first, the second and the fourth story. Twice Luke observes that the Sadducees denied the resurrection (Luke 20,27; Acts 23,8). The question arises why exactly Luke links this point of faith up with the Sadducees. There must have been more differences of opinion between this Jerusalem aristocracy and the followers of Jesus, mustn't there? To answer this question we'll have to go more deeply into the ideas of the Sadducees.

The Sadducees were not only a party of leaders. They also formed a conservative group both in political and in religious respect. The Sadducees would have nothing to do with the innovations introduced by the Pharisees interpreting and using the Torah. They only accepted the written Torah (Genesis to Deuteronomy) as authoritative. They didn't attach any value to the Prophets and to the Oral Torah of the Pharisees. Their explanation of the Torah was as simple and literary as possible. "An eye for an eye, a tooth for a tooth", explained by the Pharisees as financial compensation for damage suffered[a], was implemented literary by the Saddusees.[255] Accordingly the interpretation of the Torah wasn't a matter of extensive study or great scholarship in their eyes. The Sadducee scribe Eleazar ben Po'era reflected his point of view as follows: 'The Torah has been written and lies in a corner; who wants to study should come and study'.[256] In other words, this is not a matter of many years' study and months-long discussions.

For no other reason than that the Sadducees only accepted the written Torah, they rejected a great number of ideas of other groups of Jews that attributed authority to the Prophets as well. They didn't want to have anything to do with the resurrection of the dead, the existence of angels, the coming of a messiah and the like. For all these religious notions can't be based directly or indirectly upon the Torah. They were derived from the books of the Prophets, but the Sadducees considered these books as inferior writings. After all, they, the Sadducees, had other ideas!

In their opinion God had created the world and had revealed himself to Israel via the Written Torah only. That should be enough for the Israelites to live with. They very probably didn't believe that God actively maintained and governed the world after the Creation as well.[b,] [257] As a group of priests around the high priest they were now God's representatives on earth and the appointed leaders of Israel who governed the people and administered justice on the basis of the Written Torah in the name of God. This Sadducean notion is found in the parable of the wicked vinedressers (Luke 20,9-19), that begins with: 'a certain man ... went into a far country for a long time'. It's very appropriate that this parable in the Gospel of Luke is only directed towards the chief priests and their scribes (v. 19), and not towards the Pharisees as is the

---

[a] See section 9.1.

[b] Josephus description of the Sadducees shows a lot of similarities with the Greek movement of the Epicureans (see endnote).

case in Matthew 21,45.[a] There was, in the eyes of the Sadducees, no place for a revelation completing the Torah. That's the reason why the wicked vinedressers in the parable kill or send back the messengers who were sent to them. That's why the Sadducees didn't believe in the existence of angles either, that is to say in the existence of messengers who directly showed Israel God's will.

The Sadducees saw the meaning of the existence of man as restricted to the life here and now. They rejected the idea of life after death in any form. During his life man was free to act well or badly. Good deeds were rewarded during this life, and wrong actions were punished during this life. "Is it possible that a day labourer should toil all day long and not receive his wages in the evening?" This was the sadducean point of view on the basis of Deuteronomy 24,14-15.[258] God lived in the temple in Jerusalem and should be worshipped there, as one honoured a king in his palace. The individual worshipper should contribute to it. And death comes as the end. No other task was granted to him. His raison d'être was begetting offspring to preserve the tradition and the temple service. One derived one's authority especially from one's lineage and one's position of power.[259] Within this "immanent" outlook on life the Sadducees saw their well-being and their power undoubtedly as proof of their being in the right. After all, acting well was rewarded in this life! Their wealth and position were the reward for their service to God in and around the temple. So the principal effort of the Sadducees was to allow the temple service to proceed in peace. They were even prepared to collaborate with the Romans to a considerable extent. They also rejected the idea of the coming of a messiah, who would liberate Israel from the Roman yoke. They were fiercely

---

[a] Preceding this parable Matthew has another parable of two sons, not found in Luke and Mark. Now it is quite possible that the first parable was meant for the Pharisees, the second one of the wicked vinedressers for the Sadducees and the chief priest. After all Matthew 21,45 mentions 'parables' (plural).

opposed to the messianic pretentions of the Zealots, who endangered peace and order in Jerusalem with their violent resistance to the Romans. As after the Babylonian Exile Ezra and Nehemiah accepted the authority of the Persian kings in order to be able to build a new society around the temple, so the Sadducees accepted the authority of Rome in order to be able to maintain the temple and the sacrificial service. Against the background of all these notions the faith in the resurrection of the dead posed a threat to them. And that in dual respect.

In the first place the faith in the resurrection expresses the idea that God is righteous in spite of the injustice of this world. Adversity in life isn't seen by the adherents of this faith as proof of wrong behaviour, prosperity in itself not as a reward for acting well. Already the prophet Isaiah observes that in this life justice is not always rewarded. His discussion about the 'man of sorrows' (Isaiah 53) is not a prophecy put in the future tense, but an observation written in the past tense. The belief in the resurrection expresses that the value of a life can't be judged from the prosperity one acquires in life. The value of someone's individual life is chiefly decided by the meaning someone has in the eyes of God and one's fellow man. From this stems the meaning man has for the future of the kingdom of God. This in itself hasn't anything to do yet with a corporeal resurrection from the dead. Jesus' answer to the Sadducees in Luke 20,37-38 shows this clearly. Abraham, Isaac and Jacob were not really, physically alive in the days of Moses. However, their significance for the cause of God and with it for later generations is such that they are considered as "those being alive among the living". In the stories of Israel they are alive as if resurrected from the dead. In this way they are still a daily inspiration for the faithful Jew. The faith in the resurrection implies the possibility that someone only after his death receives a "reward", for instance in the form of recognition by the community of faith and also that someone's life goes on and grows within the circle of his adherents. Jesus is the perfect example Peter argues towards the Sadducees (Acts 4,10).

FACTIONS IN JUDAISM

That's why the faith in the resurrection of the dead undermined the sadducean notion that good works will be rewarded in this life. Their wealth, their ancestry and their position of power were no reason for those Jews who believed in the resurrection of the dead, to stand in awe of them. Exactly this theme plays a part in the confrontation between the apostles and the Sadducees (Acts 4,19; 5,29). Their position and their power are no guarantee for large groups of Jews for the justice of the sadducean cause. That is the reason why Luke made the theme of the resurrection play such an important part in his stories about the Sadducees.

Secondly, the resurrection of the dead has always been closely connected in Judaism with the faith in the final deliverance of Israel. It's hardly an individual matter, but a matter of a whole people and, in the end, of the whole world.[260] The prophet Ezekiel in the famous vision of the 'Dry Bones' connects the resurrection of the dead directly with the liberation of Israel from the exile (Ezekiel 37,1-14). In the ancient Jewish Eighteen Prayer, the Amidah, the resurrection of the dead and deliverance are connected as well.[261] It's obvious that this aspect of the faith in the resurrection of the dead could also pose a threat for the Sadducees. Israel was not in exile in their view. After all, they served God in his temple in Jerusalem! They needn't be liberated from the Romans. The deliverance from the Roman yoke would sooner affect than improve their position. In the eyes of many Jews there was no place for the Sadducees in a liberated Israel. They collaborated too much with the Romans.

Now it is this specific element of captivity and deliverance that plays a part in all four sadducean stories of Luke's. In the first story God calls Moses from the burning bush to get the deliverance of Israel going (Luke 20,37). In the second and the third story the apostles are arrested twice by the Sadducees (Acts 4,1-3; 5,17-18). In the last of these two stories the Sadducees very clearly appear to be at the wrong side (Acts 5,19-20). And also in the fourth story it's the Sadducees who want to

FACTIONS IN JUDAISM

Table 9.2
Jews and Jewish groups in Jerusalem, as mentioned by Luke, that fought Jesus and his disciples (with the exception of the Herodians).

Opponents of	People and groups described by Luke	Texts in which they are mentioned
Jesus	Chief priests	Luke 19,47; 20,1 and 19; 22,2, 4, 52 and 66; 23,10 and 13.
	Scribes	Luke 19,47; 20,1 and 19; 22,2 and 66
	The elders	Luke 19,47
	The captains of the people	Luke 20,1; 22,52 and 66
	Officers (in the temple)	Luke 22,4 and 52
	The High Priest's slave	Luke 20,50
	The Rulers	Luke 23,13 and 35
	The people	Luke 23,13
	One of the crucified criminals	Luke 23,39
Peter and the apostles	Chief priests	Acts 4,1[262]; 5,24
	The captain (of the temple)	Acts 4,1; 5,24 and 26
	Sadducees	Acts 4,1; 5,17
	Their rulers, elders and scribes	Acts 4,5
	The high priest	Acts 4,6; 5,17, 21 and 27
	Caiaphas, John, Alexander and all those who were of the family of the high priest	Acts 4,6
	All those who were with him (the high priest	Acts 5,17 and 21
	The captain's servants	Acts 5,26

FACTIONS IN JUDAISM

Opponents of	People and groups described by Luke	Texts in which they are mentioned
Stephen	Some of the so-called synagogue of the Freedmen, the Cyrenians, the Alexandrians, and those from Cilicia and Asia	Acts 6,9
	The people, the elders and the scribes	Acts 6,12
	The high priest	Acts 7,1
	Saul	Acts 7,58; 8,1
Paul	Jews from Asia	Acts 21,27; 24,19
	Jews	Acts 22,30; 23,12, 20 and 27; 24,9, 27; 25,9-10; 26,7 and 21
	Chief priests	Acts 22,30; 23,14; 25,2
	The high priest	Acts 23,2; 24,1
	Sadducees	Acts 23,6-8
	More than forty (men)	Acts 23,13 and 21
	The Elders	Acts 23,14; 24,1
	Tertullus (a certain orator)	Acts 24, 1-2
	The chief men of the Jews	Acts 25,2
	The Jews who had come down from Jerusalem	Acts 25,7

keep Paul in confinement, this in contrast with the Pharisees (Acts 23,9-10). It's also this aspect of the resurrection of the dead, that is to say Israel's ultimate deliverance in which there would be no place at all for the Sadducees, why the faith in the resurrection was a dangerous factor for this Jerusalem aristocracy. Luke was very much aware of this and used the name "Sadducees" to aggravate his story on that point. For not only in these stories they play a part of significance.

Factions in Judaism

In table 9.2 I've mentioned the adversaries of Jesus and his disciples as Luke gives them on different occasions. This information shows that the central position among them is taken by the chief priests, the high priest, the Sadducees and the captains of the temple. Luke even adds these captains to the story of the last days of Jesus (compare Luke 22,4 and 52 to Mark 14,10 and 43). A clearly less central position is for the scribes, the elders and the rulers. Very probably these officials partly belong to the Sadducees like the chief priests. This is clearest in Acts 4,5 where Luke links them explicitly to the Sadducees. The Jews in the Diaspora who'd set their faces against Stephen and Paul (Acts 6,9; 21,27; 24,19), could very possibly have been Jews who sympathized with the Sadducees.[a]

That Luke saw the Sadducees especially as adversaries and antagonists of Jesus and his disciples, is obvious as well from the way in which he deals with the Pharisees. In the previous section I already discussed the fact that no Pharisees are found in the stories about the last days of Jesus in Jerusalem. There is here a remarkable parallel with the story of Stephen. That story too finishes with an execution. And again, there are no Pharisees in this story. There is a similar parallel between the trial of Peter and the apostles and the trial of Paul. Neither of these trials end in an execution. In both cases the Pharisees are present indeed as defenders of Jesus' adherents. All this points at a remarkable structure in the Gospel of Luke and the Acts. The stories of the trials of Stephen and Paul can be understood as a midrash-in-a-midrash to the stories of the trial of Jesus and of the trial of Peter and the apostles. This parallelism can further be substantiated thematically and linguistically[b]. In table 9.3 this parallelism is summarized as far as our subject is concerned.

---

[a] Just like Paul (then Saul) before his conversion (e.g. Acts 9,1).
[b] I'll leave this to the reader.

FACTIONS IN JUDAISM

Table 9.3

Parallelism between the trials of Jesus and Stephen on the one hand and those of Peter and the apostles and Paul on the other.

	Luke 22 and 23 / Acts 5	Acts 7 / Acts 23
Absence of the Pharisees – execution	1. Jesus	3. Stephen
Defence by the Pharisees – no execution	2. Peter and the apostles	4. Paul

Also remarkable in table 9.2 is the frequent use of the word 'Jews' in the stories of the trial of Paul. In the stories about the other three trials the opponents are never referred to with this word. In section 10.1 we'll take a closer look at Luke's use of this word. It will become clear that in his stories he almost always makes a distinction between Jews and non-Jews with this word whereas it only indicates those Jews who play a part in the story in question. Luke hardly anywhere refers to the Jewish people as a whole with the word 'Jews', unless in sayings of some gentiles (see e.g. Luke 23,3, 37 and 38). The Jewish people as a whole is called 'Israel' by Luke in agreement with the Jewish usage of those days.[263] This means that one can't conclude from the usage of the word 'Jews' in the stories about the trial of Paul that it concerns the Jewish people as a whole.

The image Luke draws of the opponents of Jesus and his disciples basically shows the aristocratic, managerial circles in Jerusalem: Sadducees and chief priests. Although we have to take into account that, in the Gospel of Luke and the Acts, we are dealing with midrash and not with exact historiography, it is very well possible that with it Luke had his stories dovetail with the historical reality. The Jewish historian Flavius Josephus describes an event that took place in 62 CE, that shows a striking resemblance to a story of Luke's.[264] The Roman governor was not present in Jerusalem. The high priest, a Sadducee, convened the Sanhedrin for a trial against James the brother of Jesus (mentioned in Acts 12,17; 15,13; 21,18). He was sentenced to death by stoning and the sentence was carried out. The high priest had managed to bring together at least 23 members of the Sanhedrin, all of them Sadducees. This minimum number of members was needed for a legal session according to the Jewish law in which a death sentence could be demanded. All the same, the Pharisees protested against this course of events and declared this session illegal. They appealed to Rome and to king Agrippa. The result being that the high priest was removed from his post. Here we see the same course of events again: the Pharisees taking a stand against the Sadducees for the followers of Jesus. Obviously Luke was very well informed about the relations between the various Jewish groups in Jerusalem and about the aims they pursued.

Various stories in the gospel of Luke and in the Acts should be explained against this sadducean background. To demonstrate this I'll briefly consider the stories about the trial against Jesus. After being captured, we read how the temple guards, after blindfolding him beat him and ask: 'Prophesy, who is the one who struck you?' (Luke 22,63-65). Sadducean circles didn't attach any value to prophecy. The Sadducees held the view that the books of the Prophets were dangerous reading, because they almost permanently oppose the actions of the managerial circles in Israel. This mockery of Jesus as told by Luke can be considered as typically sadducean.

The question, too, of the chief priests in the Council whether Jesus was the messiah (Luke 22,67), shows the sadducean interest. Messiah-pretenders were dangerous men in their eyes who made the people revolt and risked the existence of the temple. Jesus answered: 'If I tell you, you will by no means believe'. This answer is based not so much on their unbelief in Jesus' messianic task as on their rejection of any form of messiah-expectation. When finally Jesus speaks about 'the son of man' who will sit on the right hand of the power of God (Luke 22,69),

FACTIONS IN JUDAISM

it was the last straw. This image was borrowed from the book of Daniel and from Psalm 110 and it expresses the belief that God shares his power with those who lead Israel according to his will and his intention. Daniel 7,13 and the next verses foretell Israel's deliverance from pagan suppression and announce the restoration of the kingship in Israel. But the Sadducees rejected the book of Daniel. In Jesus' answer the image of the 'son of man' is linked to 'sit on the right hand of God'. Daniel 7,13 and Psalm 110,1 are combined. Psalm 110 is a so-called royal psalm and played a part in ancient Israel in the liturgy on the occasion of the king's accession to the throne.[265] No doubt the Sadducees will have accepted many psalms as part of the temple-liturgy. Psalm 110 had however, fallen into disuse in the absence of a king from the house of David. For them this psalm had no longer an actual meaning. But this was not the case for many other Jews. In those days this Psalm 110 played an important part in the expectation of the messiah, as is clear from Luke 20,42. Psalm 110 must have been a very popular psalm indeed in zealotic circles. It only needs reading to be convinced. So it's not surprising that the Sadducees concluded from Jesus' words that he considered himself king of Israel, anointed by God. They were outraged and shouted: 'In that case you are the son of God!' (Luke 22,70). Most translations render this phrase, erroneously in my view, as a question (even the NKJV). But the Greek text allows for a conclusion. The title 'son of God' is one of the titles of the kings of Israel (Psalm 2,7). Jesus' interrogators give their final verdict with these words in this case. Jesus' answer: 'You say that I am' (Luke 22,70), only means: that is your conclusion. For the saducean chief priests and scribes it's a foregone conclusion. They need no further testimony (Luke 22,71). Jesus must be handed over to the Romans as a messiah-pretender (Luke 23,1). He should suffer the fate of a zealot, arch-enemy of the Sadducees.

Conspicuously, in this story about Jesus at the Council, Luke only includes those questions which concern any presumed messiah-pretentions of Jesus'. In Luke's eyes this trial has a strong political character.

Luke completely leaves out the question of the destruction of the temple and its building up again in three days (Mark 14,58; Matthew 26,61). Probably because this issue has no function with regard to the zealotic background against which Luke writes. The Zealots didn't intend to destroy the temple, on the contrary, they wanted to liberate the temple from the hands of the Sadducees and wipe out the stains. Here, clearly, a problem arises.

In the previous chapters I argued that Luke is engaged in a certain polemic aimed at the Zealots. How then to explain that he makes Jesus suffer the fate of a zealotic messiah-figure? Part of an answer is that the Sadducees didn't care whether Jesus was a violent or a non-violent messiah-pretender. They approached every form of active messianism with quite a lot of distrust. A non-violent messianic figure must have even been impossible in their eyes. Sooner or later these pretenders undermined the established order in the country. Exactly with this accusation they take Jesus to Pilate: he forbids the people to pay taxes to Caesar (Luke 23,2), he claims to be a messiah (Luke 23,2) and he stirs up the people (Luke 23,5). These supposed actions make the Sadducees consider Jesus an arch-Zealot. Comparison with Mark and Matthew (15,1-5 and 27,11-14 respectively) shows that Luke even aggravates the story in this respect. Because of this we'll further examine the zealotic background of the Gospel of Luke and the Acts in the next section.

9.3 *The Zealots*

The Jewish-religious movement of freedom fighters from the first century CE is usually referred to with the collective 'Zealots'. Although Flavius Josephus sometimes allocates the name 'Zealots' for a specific group within this movement, I'll use this word for the whole movement in the next sections. It will turn out, that it won't be significant for our argument to explicitly distinguish the various zealotic groups. And this is caused mainly by a first notable feature that not only characterizes the Gospel of Luke and the Acts, but also the other gospels.

a. The Zealots are only mentioned sporadically

The Zealots are mentioned openly in the New Testament very rarely. Pharisees, Sadducees and chief priests are frequently mentioned, often as direct adversaries of Jesus and his disciples. Not so the Zealots. Only a handful people are mentioned, who presumably belonged to or had belonged to the zealotic movement, and they're only found in Luke: Simon the Zealot, a disciple of Jesus' (Luke 6,15; Acts 1,13), Barabbas (Luke 23,18), Theudas (Acts 5,36), Judas of Galilee (Acts 5,37) and the 'Egyptian' (Acts 21,38). None of them is represented as a direct adversary of Jesus and his disciples. When, in other cases, Zealots do turn up, the text gives too little to go by to determine positively and without further analysis whether they are indeed Zealots or not.

The word 'Zealot' too, doesn't play a part of any significance at all in the gospels and the Acts. It's a Greek word and it means 'devotee'. In Mark and Matthew we only meet this word with regard to Simon the Zealot. In that case – in Mark 3,19 and Matthew 10,4 – both evangelists use the Aramaic word *Kananites* . Twice the Greek word *zelootès*, meaning 'devotee', is found in the Acts 21,20 and 22,3. It's clear that here the word doesn't allude to members of the zealotic movement, but really has some polemic overtones directed towards the Zealots. This means that the Zealots are mentioned sporadically in the books of Luke as well, but more frequent in this work than in the other three gospels. This is remarkable for more than one reason.[a]

- In the first place the zealotic movement had a lot of influence in the first century Judaism. The teachings of Judas of Galilee, usually considered the founder of the zealotic movement, stirred the

---

[a] I restrict myself to Luke in the following.

land of Israel more than any other Jewish teachings.[266] Judas made his appearance around the year 6 CE. The zealotic movement gathered more and more strenght till the outbreak of the Jewish War in 66 CE. In the end the Zealots managed to press on with the revolt against the Romans and to maintain this attempt for four years (from 66 to70 CE). The last zealotic stronghold, the Herodian fortress of Masada, even fell three years later in Roman hands.

- In the second place the zealotic movement had its adherents from all sections of the population.[267] In numerous groups they gained approval or met with opposition. We learn about Pharisees and Essenes who supported the Zealots, but also about adversaries of this zealotic pursuit from these movements. The movement's structure was very heterogeneous and it suffered very much from internal division in the end.

Because of these two characteristics of the movement of the Zealots, it's the most obvious conclusion that Jesus and his followers would certainly have met them. The sporadic mention of the Zealots in Luke's work is however, remarkable for another two reasons.

- One could suppose that Luke was largely silent about the Zealots, because he wrote after 70. After the fall of Jerusalem the zealotic movement should have become less important. However, this is not correct from a historical point of view. After the catastrophe of 70 the spirit of Zealotism continued to exist among the Jewish people and drove it slowly but surely to new revolts. The first was in 115 CE when large groups of diaspora-Jews rose against the Roman emperor Trajan. This revolt ended in 117 CE. Fifteen years later the land of Israel rose in revolt again led by Bar Kochba (132-135 CE). Even in the days of Luke, the end of the 1st century, the zealotic ambition must still have been powerful among the Jews.

FACTIONS IN JUDAISM

- Moreover, Luke was very much interested in political affairs.[a] The zealotic movement must have occupied his mind very much. More specifically, his interests in Roman affairs must surely have confronted him regularly with zealotic ideas.

It would have been very strange against this background if especially Luke had ignored the Zealots rather completely in his gospel and the Acts. So there must be quite another explanation for the fact that Luke mentions the Zealots so sporadically. And this explanation is, how strange it may sound on first hearing: *he mentions them so little because they are his most important opponents against whom the polemics of his gospel and the Acts are directed.* He hardly mentions them because his entire argument is directed against their way of action. Not mentioning one's opponent in a polemic is not strange at all in Judaism. Very often the real opponent isn't mentioned at all. Examples of this phenomenon within Jewish literature can be found for ages on end. It already begins in the first chapter of the book of Genesis. The stories about the creation and the flood contain a clear polemic against the pagan views with regard to man and his relation with the gods.[268] The authors of the Bible incorporated images and concepts of many surrounding nations in their stories. Their narrative however, had a content of its own, in all respects straight across from the pagan views. Yet these pagan views are not mentioned at all.

The rabbis from the first centuries do not often mention their opponents by their names too, when telling midrashim with a polemic content.[269] Sometimes these opponents are referred to vaguely. Then they're called *minim*, usually translated with 'heretics'. We'll just have to gather from the midrash which group it is directed to. For example, there is a midrash that tells about a Galilean *min* (heretic) who lodged a complaint against the Pharisees because they entered the name of the

---

[a] See section 3.4

Roman emperor together with the name of Moses in a bill of divorcement in order to date it. The pharisean reaction is to lodge a complaint against this Galilean *min* because he (like all other Jews anyway) writes the name of the Pharaoh, a pagan ruler too, and the name of God in one and the same column of the Torah-scroll. Worse, he writes the name of Pharaoh *at the top* of the column and the name of God *underneath*! For it is written: 'And Pharaoh said, "Who *is* the LORD, that I should obey His voice to let Israel go?" (Exodus 5,2). The Pharisees' argument is a so-called 'a minore ad maius'. It boils down to the fact that if an unsure practice like writing the name of the Pharaoh, the pagan ruler, above the name of God, is permitted in the major case of the Torah, it is certainly permitted to do so in the minor case of the bill of divorcement.

Now there are three clear clues assuming that the Galilean *min* against whom this midrash is directed, was a Zealot:[270]

- His point of view agrees completely with the point of view we may expect from a Zealot in a case like this. The Zealots took the view that one was not allowed to acknowledge any power except the God of Israel. The mention of the Roman emperor in a bill of divorcement with the purpose to date it, would have been – without any doubt – an unacceptable practice for them. In their view one showed submission to Roman authority in doing so.
- The choice of the text from Torah can be considered a second clue for Zealotism. This text from Exodus 5,2 very much accentuates the contents of the conversation to the submission of Israel to a pagan power. Moreover, the text confronts the opponent with the fact that he – in case of revolt – could expect a fierce response on the part of the Pharaoh c.q. the Romans.
- The *min* (heretic) is from Galilee and that is the third clue. As seen above, the founder of the zealotic movement was from Galilee, he was even called Judas of Galilee. Many other zealotic leader were from Galilee as well. In certain circumstances the name 'Galileans'

could be more or less identical with the name 'Zealots'.[271] This was not always so, of course, but often the terms 'Galilean' and 'Galilee' will have evoked associations with and suspicion of zealotic sympathies.

So this is a clear example of how one should try and deduce from the contents of a midrash who was the opponent of the polemic.

Even today there are examples of the Jewish custom not to mention one's opponent directly. For instance, in 1905 the Jewish scholar Leo Back wrote the book *Das Wesen des Judentums*. It's a clear polemic against the writing *Das Wesen des Christentums* by the protestant theologian Adolf von Harnack.[272] But his name isn't mentioned in Leo Back's book at all.

Luke's almost complete silence about the Zealots may now be explained by the same polemic tradition. But it is also clear that this theory needs further support from data in the text. I'll look for them into two directions. First I'll put the zealotic movement and the movement around Jesus, at least as Luke describes them, next to and facing each other. Next I'll throw more light on a number of stories from the Gospel of Luke and the Act, in which the anti-zealotic polemic can be recognized clearly.

b. Analogies and differences between Luke and the Zealots.
There is a large number of analogies between the Zealots and the movement around Jesus as described by Luke. There are also some differences that play a central part in Luke's polemics. These similarities are:

- Both movements are closely associated with the establishment of God being king in Israel and in the world. The central theme of Judas of Galilee's doctrine was the absolute power of God. That's why they and their followers didn't acknowledge the authority of

FACTIONS IN JUDAISM

the Roman emperor.[273] The coming of God's kingdom plays an important part in the Gospel of Luke as well.[a]

- Consequently both movements showed strong messianic features. There were rather a lot of characters among the Zealots with royal or messianic pretentions.[274] Anyway, whether Jesus has ever considered himself a messiah can't be concluded from Luke's gospel. There is no text indicating as much. However, it goes without saying that Jesus' followers and Luke among them saw him as a messianic figure.
- Both Judas of Galilee and Jesus, as Luke describes him, preached their doctrine openly. Judas preached in public and not in the seclusion of the house of study.[275] We already saw in Luke, more than in Matthew, that Jesus taught the crowd openly.[b]
- Both movements didn't shrink from martyrdom.[276] Jesus too died a martyr. Luke doesn't present his death as a concurrence of circumstances, but as the ultimate consequence of all his actions (Luke 9,18-22 and 43b-45; 18,31-33). Jesus' followers too, should be prepared to suffer the same fate (Luke 9,23-24).
- In both movements social motives played an important part.[277] I already pointed out Luke's interest in and sympathy for the poor.[c] Although there are hardly any reports about the Zealots as far as this is concerned, it is certain that an important part of their struggle was directed at a revolution in the social order in the land of Israel. As well as great wealth one came across a lot of poverty. The Zealots robbed the rich to divide their possession among the poor.[278] They burned municipal archives to destroy the records of debts, an overt fight against the leaders of the social order.[279] One

---

[a] See section 7.1.
[b] See section 5.1.c.
[c] See section 9.1.

of the zealotic leaders, Simeon bar Giora, fought for the emancipation of the slaves. He fought the rich fiercely. He became a leader of the lower classes in the entire land of Israel.[280] With Luke as well as with the Zealots we find the same social tendency, although they tried to reach their targets by quite different means.

- Originally both movements were strongly connected to Galilee. I already said so with regard to the Zealots.[a] This requires no explanation for Jesus and his disciples. But both movements had the whole Jewish country as their field of activity. This is, where Jesus is concerned, clearer in Luke than in Mark.[b] The ultimate aim was Jerusalem. Once that aim was reached, a return to Galilee didn't come up anywhere in Luke.[c] The Zealots too, aimed at the liberation of Jerusalem. And once in Jerusalem in 66 CE, they fought to the last ditch.
- Both movements enjoyed a great popularity with the people. As fighters for the liberation of Israel the Zealots could count upon the sympathy of many.[281] Luke mentions regularly that Jesus and the apostles were in favour with the people.[d]
- Both movements had followers from all kinds of different Jewish groups. I already mentioned this with regard to the Zealots.[e] The followers of Jesus too, belonged to a variety of Jewish groups, at least in Luke's books. We encounter a Zealot (Luke 6,15), a Samaritan (Luke 17,16), a publican (Luke 19,1-10), an Ethiopian Jew (Act 8,27 and 38), Pharisees (Acts 15,5) and followers of John the Baptist (Acts 19,1-3).

---

[a] See section 9.3.a.
[b] See section 6.5.
[c] See section 7.2.
[d] See Luke 4,42; 8,4; 9,37; 11,19; 12,1; 13,17; 14,25; 19,48; 20,19; 21,38; 22,2, 6; Acts 2,47; 5,13, 26.
[e] See section 9.3.a.

FACTIONS IN JUDAISM

- That doesn't alter the fact that both movements have been related most with the Pharisees. With regard to the Zealots we know this among other things from an observation by Flavius Josephus.[282] For Luke's description of Jesus and his followers I already mentioned this before.[a]
- The Zealots clearly aimed at the liberation and the cleansing of the temple in Jerusalem.[283] We also saw in Luke that the temple played a central and positive part in the stories about the last days of Jesus.[b]
- Both the Zealots and Jesus and his followers referred to Tanakh to motivate their ideas and their acts.[284]
- There are clear indications that the Zealots not only aimed at the national liberation of Israel. Their idea was in all likelihood that after Israel's liberation the nations of the world would be judged. The kingship of God would be established worldwide.[285] The blueprint of this course of events can be found in the small prophetical book of Joel. So it's not surprising that Peter quotes precisely this Prophet in his first speech in Jerusalem before the people (Acts 2,14-36, especially the verses 17-21). The kingship of God not only in Israel but in the end in the entire world played an important part both in the zealotic movement and in the movement around Jesus.

After all these similarities it has become clear that there must have been a fertile soil for polemics between both movements. The more so since two most essential differences between Luke and the Zealots can be pointed out.

---

[a] See section 9.1.
[b] See section 7.2.

FACTIONS IN JUDAISM

- I already discussed the non-violent character of Jesus' actions.[a] Neither were his followers guilty of violence, at least according to Luke in the Acts. This contrasts sharply with the actions of the Zealots who didn't stop at anything if they thought that Israel's cause was at stake. They fought not only the Romans by fire and sword, fellow Jews who stood in their way weren't spared either. They looked upon Jews who paid taxes to the Romans, as gentiles. Jews who conformed to the Roman measures were seized roughly by Judas of Galilee.[286]
- Luke's attitude towards the non-Jews, the Romans in particular, also contrasted sharply with the attitude of the Zealots. As for Luke, I'll return to it in chapter 10. The Zealots saw themselves involved in a holy war against the Romans and derived their inspiration from the war of the Maccabees against the Seleucid kings of Syria.[287] Gentiles taken prisoner were only spared when they had themselves be circumcised. Other non-Jews too, who wanted to support them, had to be circumcised to join them completely.[288] In this they agreed with the strict Pharisees of the School of Shammai.

The above makes two conclusions possible. First Luke had every reason to engage in a polemic with the Zealots. Perhaps he didn't polemize directly with the Zealots but he did so anyhow with the zealotic spirit that moved without any doubt many Jews in the Diaspora. In the second place, Jesus and his followers shouldn't reckon on any sympathy on the part of the Zealots. They should sooner expect reprisals and violence from the Zealots, than discussion and reply.

---

[a]   See section 7.1.c.

Factions in Judaism

c. The polemic against the Zealots

The first indication that Luke engages in a polemic with the Zealots is found in his story about the birth of Jesus. He "dates" this event during the census, that 'first took place while Quirinius was governing Syria' (Luke 2,1-3). This was in the year 6 CE. This census was the basis for the Roman levying of taxes. Both the census and the taxation were the immediate cause for the origin of the zealotic movement led by Judas of Galilee.

This now appears to be a huge problem for almost all exegetes. Because Matthew maintains that Jesus was born during the reign of Herod the Great (Matthew 2). But Herod had been dead for ten years in 6 CE! He died in 4 BCE. According to Matthew (2,16) Jesus must have been two years old already, so there is a difference of as much as twelve years between Matthew's dating of Jesus' birth and Luke's!

Not surprisingly, many attempts were made to 'clear up' these contradictions. However, there's no going back on Matthew's dating. All these attempts amount to the fact that the census Luke tells us about should have taken place about fourteen years earlier than the census we know from history.[289] These explications are extremely feeble, historically. First, nothing is known about a government of Quirinius over Syria earlier than the year 6 CE, the year of his commission.[290] Secondly, till 6 CE Judea was a more or less autonomous province, not directly governed by the Romans, but by the princes from the Herodian royal family. Only in the year 6 CE Archelaos, son of Herod the Great, was deposed by the Romans and did the district of Judea come under direct Roman rule. Until that time the Jews of Judea didn't pay taxes to the emperor but to the Herodian prince. Exactly *because* Judea became a Roman province in 6 CE a census must be held as a basis for the levying of taxes. Consequently, dating such a census fourteen years earlier is highly unlikely, at least historically seen. After all it's inexplicable why a census for the benefit of the Roman levying of taxes in 6 CE did evoke resistance among the Jews but not so fourteen years earlier. The more so since pockets of resistance already existed under Herod the Great.[291]

There is, however, no need at all to try and harmonize Matthew and Luke historically. If we read the gospels as midrashim, these attempts to harmonize the gospels are sooner impeding than stimulating the understanding of the stories of Jesus' birth. Luke "dated" the birth of Jesus during the census of 6 CE, not because Jesus was really born in that year, but because the zealotic movement, led by Judas of Galilee, began to manifest itself from then on. Collaborating on a Roman census and levying of taxes was to the Zealots entirely contrary to God ruling Israel. Flavius Josephus, a contemporary of Luke's, emphasizes time and again that the zealotic actions started in 6 CE owing to these Roman measures.[a, 292] The violent advance of Judas of Galilee to Judea contrasts sharply with Joseph's and Mary's journey (Luke 2,4-5). Not a single Jewish reader of the gospel of Luke will have failed to notice this at the end of the first century CE. Acts 5,37 really proves that Luke has had Judas' actions in mind. In this text these actions are associated with the census as something very obvious. Both in Luke 2,2 and in the Acts 5,37 Luke uses the same Greek word *apografè* (census). From the outset Luke very clearly informs his readers with his birth-story that he sees Jesus as the alternative for the movement of the Zealots.

So it's not surprising that the same theme returns in the story of the trial of Jesus. Contrary to Mark and Matthew Luke reports that Jesus before Pilate was accused of the fact that he had forbidden the people to pay taxes to the emperor (Luke 32,2). In this way Luke combines the stories of Jesus' birth and death.[b] It's the well-known transformation of

---

[a] The zealotic actions during the Jewish War (66-70 CE) are traced back repeatedly by Flavius Josephus to the actions of Judas of Galilee during the census of 6 CE.

[b] We should keep in mind that there are more links between Luke's story of Jesus' birth and the stories about his death.

history Luke applies here[a], to emphasize the polemic with the zealotic movement. And so Jesus becomes the prototype of the anti-zealotic, messianic man in the gospel of Luke.

Also Luke's staging of the second session in the trial before Pilate (Luke 23,13-25) can be explained through the anti-zealotic polemic. Pilate calls together the chief priests, the elders and the people and repeats the accusation they brought against Jesus. He should have 'misled'[b] the people. This translation rather disguises what it is really about. This word should better be translated with 'someone who incites the people to rise in revolt'.[293] Once again Jesus is depicted in this accusation as a leader of the zealotic rebels. Strange enough Luke ascribes quite another part to the chief priest, the people and Pilate in the sequel of the story than Mark does. It's not difficult to point at some inconsistencies in Mark's story. Luke removed them all apparently. In Mark Pilate faced the people with a choice to free either Jesus or Barabbas on the occasion of the feast (Mark 15,9-10). He evidently does so in the hope that the people will choose in favour of Jesus. But who knows the zealotic sympathies of the people will be able to predict the outcome. In Luke such "tactics" can't be found. Barabbas enters his story even without announcement. As soon as Pilate proposes to release Jesus (Luke 23,16), the people begin to cry for the release of Barabbas. Then Barabbas is twice described as the prototype of a Zealot (Luke 23,19 and 25). This order in the staging, first the people ask for the release of Barabbas and then the reader is informed about Barabbas' identity, can only have one meaning: the people know Barabbas and are bent on his release. Barabbas is someone who has won his spurs in the zealotic movement, and that's why he can count on the sympathy of the people in advance. It's not necessary either that the people, as in Mark 15,11, are incited by the chief priests to ask for the release of Barabbas. This

---

[a] See section 4.6.b.
[b] In Greek *apostréphonta*.

Table 9.4

Thematic and structural similarities between 2 Kings 2,1-18 and Acts 1,1-11.

2 Kings 2,1-18	Acts 1,1-11
- by the Jordan (v. 7)	- John baptized at the river Jordan (v. 5; see also Luke 3,3)
- struck the water (v. 8)	- baptized with water (v. 5)
- a double portion of your spirit (v. 9)	- baptism with the holy spirit (twice; v. 5 and 8)
- course of the last conversation: - Elia (v. 9a) - Elisa (v. 9b) - Elia (v. 10)	- course of the last conversation: - Jesus (v. 4 and 5) - his disciples (v. 6) - Jesus (v. 7)
- a difficult matter (v. 10)	- it is not for you (v. 7)
- walking and talking (v. 11)	- now when he had spoken these things (v. 9)
- and separated the two of them (v. 11)	- he was taken up (v. 9)
- if you see me; and Elisha saw (v. 10 and 12)	- while they watched (v. 9)
- so he saw him no more (v. 12)	- a cloud received him out of their sight (v. 9)
- went up .... into heaven (v. 11)	- went up (v. 10)
- clothes (v. 12)	- white apparel (v. 10)
- who were [opposite][294], and saw (v. 15)	- stand gazing up (v. 11)
- has taken him up (v. 16)	- who was taken up (v. 11)
- you shall not send anyone (to search) (v. 16)	- don't stand gazing up into heaven (to see Jesus return) (v. 11)
- went up to Bethel (i.e. the House of the Lord) (v. 23)	- returned to Jerusalem (v. 12)

FACTIONS IN JUDAISM

'incitement' in Mark can be seen as an inconsistency in his story. The Sadducees too won't have had any interest in the release of Barabbas. So in Luke the Sadducean chief priests play no part at all in the release of Barabbas.

Now the question is whether Luke was of the opinion that the entire Jewish people was guilty of the death of Jesus. This doesn't seem relevant but Christianity has answered this question in the affirmative for centuries on end, not only with regard to Luke but with regard to the gospels in general.[295] As for Luke we saw that the Pharisees were left out of the final chapters of his gospel[a]. In many discussions 'the people'[b] are too easily identified with the entire Jewish people, even though there are enough examples in the gospels when this word only denotes a group of people present then and there.[296] Also the zealotic context of the evangelists' stories about the trial of Jesus is overlooked by virtually all researchers.[297] In Luke 23,13 'the people' doesn't mean anything else than what we usually call 'the common people'. And it was exactly among this common people – not necessarily a negative term – that the spirit of Zealotism was widely spread, influential and deeply rooted. The choice in favour of Barabbas and against Jesus was, in Luke's eyes, a logical consequence of the sympathy for the zealotic movement cherished by a larger part of the people.

I'll mention briefly another aspect of the polemics against the Zealots in the Gospel of Luke and the Acts: the identification with Elijah. We already saw that Matthew identified John the Baptist with Elijah.[c] I also discussed the fact that Luke removed everything from his gospel that pointed at this identification.[d] Quite understandable, considering that Luke regularly paints Jesus as a Elijah-figure. I'll pass in review four of Luke's stories which show this phenomenon most clearly.

---

[a] See section 9.1.
[b] In Greek *laos*.
[c] See section 4.3.
[d] See section 4.4.

FACTIONS IN JUDAISM

- The story about the raising of the only son of the widow of Nain (Luke 7,11-17) was written against the background of the story about the raising of the only son of the widow of Zarephath (1 Kings 17,7-24).[a] Jesus' part matches the one of Elijah in the Tanakh-story.
- The same applies to the story about the rejection of Jesus by a Samaritan village (Luke 9,51-56) and the Tanakh-story about Elijah's actions against the soldiers of Ahaziah (2 Kings 1,1-18).[b]
- A third example of this identification of Jesus' with Elijah is the short story about following Jesus (Luke 9,57-62). Its Tanakh-background is the story about the calling of Elisha, the son of Shaphat, by Elijah (1 Kings 19,19-21). The same themes are found in both stories:
  - Following Elijah and Jesus respectively.
  - The wish to bid farewell to one's family.
  - Elijah's and Jesus' refusal to grant this wish.
  - The ploughing-motive.
  - The radical breach with their present lives.
- Nowhere else however is the identification of Jesus with Elijah clearer than in the story about Jesus' ascension (Acts 1,1-11). There is only one story in Tanakh that describes an ascension explicitly: Elijah's (2 Kings 2,1-18). In table 9.4 I put both stories side by side. It is beyond doubt that Luke wrote his story about Jesus' ascension with Elijah's ascension in mind.

The part Elijah played in the ideas of the Zealots is especially now important for our subject.[c] In Tanakh and the Apocrypha Elijah is

---

[a] See section 6.8.c.
[b] See section 7.1.c.
[c] I already explained this part in section 7.1.c.

described as 'zealous' (1 Kings 19,10 and 14; 1 Maccabees 2,58; Jesus Sirah 48,2). In the eyes of the Zealots he was 'a hero of the faith' as such, because their name 'Zealots' means 'the zealous ones' after all. They had undoubtedly found support for their zealous and violent actions in the age-old thought that Elijah had to come first 'before the coming of the great and dreadful day of the LORD'(Malachi 4,5; see also Matthew 17,10). As Zealots they followed in the footsteps of Elijah and so prepared the coming of the messianic kingdom.

But Luke takes the sting out of their appeal to Elijah by painting Jesus as an Elijah-figure. He shows that Elijah's actions can be translated quite differently towards his own days, instead of following the Zealots' way. The high eschatological expectations the Zealots cherished, and many early Christians with them, are put, in this way, into another perspective by Luke. The final deliverance of Israel has not yet begun with Jesus' actions, it's only being prepared. The high hopes that lay hidden behind the question of the disciples: 'Will you at this time restore the kingdom to Israel?', are pushed aside by Luke via this identification of Jesus with Elijah (see Acts 1,7).

We've now reached the final aspect of Luke's polemic with the Zealots. The spokesmen of the zealotic messiah-expectation in both Luke's books are not the Zealots themselves but Jesus' own disciples. The above-mentioned text (Acts 1,6) is a clear example. We've come across another example of this zealotic mentality in James' and John's attitude towards the Samaritans (Luke 9,51-56). In the story of the men of Emmaus we saw how the zealotic messiah-expectation was worded by Kleopas and his companion.[a] In this respect the last of the travel-stories in Luke's gospel is of relevance as well (Luke 19,11-27). There Jesus tells the parable of the ten minas, because he was near Jerusalem and they *thought that the kingdom of God would appear immediately* (Luke 19,11). This parable was written against the historical background of the

---

[a] See section 7.3.

actions of Archelaos, son of Herod the Great.[298] When Herod died in 4 BCE, he left his realm to his sons. Archelaos would get Judea, Samaria and Idumea, and the title of king. But Herod's testament needed the emperor's assent. That's why Archelaos travelled to Rome as soon as possible where he hoped to obtain this emperial approval (compare Luke 19,12). The Judeans had him followed by a delegation to plead with the emperor for his deposition. They knew his cruelty to be greater than his father Herod's (compare Luke 19,14, 21-22 and 27). Jesus' argument in this parable amounts to this: who thinks to hasten the coming of the messiah by violent actions, as the Zealots did, will only get a tyrant like Archelaos.

Other stories too, in the Gospel of Luke and the Acts can be explained as polemics against the zealotic movement. However, I've shown ample examples of these polemics in this section. And, as far as I am concerned, the fact that Luke wrote for a Jewish public has been demonstrated sufficiently. Now it only remains for me to expound, in the next chapter, Luke's view on Israel's relation to the nations.

10. For the hope of Israel
Israel and the nations

It's a rather perilous undertaking to end this book with a short chapter on 'Israel and the nations'. In fact, Luke's view on this subject deserves a full study. That's why I'll confine myself to three issues important for the winding up of my discourse. The anti-zealotic polemic in Luke's gospel, in which he preaches the non-violent way of Jesus, has obviously some implications for the exegesis of the Acts of the Apostles. That's why I'd like to make some brief observations about: Jews, gentiles and Romans.

10.1 The Jews

In no other book of the so-called New Testament does the word 'Jew' (Hebrew *jehudi* ; Greek *Ioudaios*) and its derivations occur more often than in the Acts: about 80 times. These words are regularly used in the Tanakh as well. We have to consider however, that the English word 'Jew' is only one possible translation of the word *jehudi*. Originally only the members of the tribe of Judah were meant with it. Later the inhabitants of the southern realm of Judea, including the tribe of Benjamin. After the destruction of the northern realm of Israel the term *jehudi* became the name of all Israelites left and with it of everyone belonging to Judaism. However, the word 'Jew' was mainly used outside the land of Israel, by Jews as well as non-Jews and usually not in Hebrew.

In Tanakh the word *jehudi* occurs especially in those stories that play in pagan surroundings or in which pagans play an important part, for example in Esther, Ezra and Nehemiah. But as soon as the story describes an internal Jewish situation in the land of Israel, one prefers the word 'Israel' to refer to the Jewish people. In addition to this, the word *jehudi* (and consequently its Greek equivalent *Ioudaios*) can be a

ISRAEL AND THE NATIONS

designation of the inhabitants of Judea, in which case it had better be translated by 'Judeans'.[299] Now it is exactly this characteristic use of words that one finds reflected to a large extent in the gospel of Luke and the Acts.

Four times does the word 'Jews' occur in the Gospel of Luke. Once as distinct from the non-Jews that play a part in the story (Luke 7,3). Three times it's used by the Romans (Luke 32,3 and 37 and 38). In the Acts too, the word 'Jew' is mainly used in stories in which the pagan element plays an important part. It is said of some people in a pagan environment that they are Jews (Acts 13,6; 16,1; 19,14 and 34; 24,24). The word 'Jews' occurs regularly in everyday life between Jews and non-Jews (Acts 10,39; 18,14; 23,20; 24,5 and 18; 25,8, 10, 15 and 24). The word occurs also in the letter of the Roman ruler Claudius Lysias to the governor Felix (Acts 23,27). In the Diaspora-stories a group of Jews is distinguished from the non-Jews by the word 'Jews'. In that case the word refers to a local Jewish community or to the active, usually managerial part of it. Sometimes the local restriction is present explicitly (Acts 9,22; 14,19; 16,3; 17,13; 19,13 and 17; 22,12). However, more often the word 'Jews' is not provided with a specification of place. But in that case we'll be able to gather from the context which local group of Jews is meant (Acts 9,23; 11,19; 13,5, 45 and 50; 14,1, 2, 4 and 5; 17,1, 5, 10 and 17; 18,2, 4, 5, 12, 19 and 28; 19,10 and 33; 20,3; 28,17). The word is also used for the Diaspora-Jews living in Jerusalem (Acts 2,5 and 14; 9,29; 21,27). Once or twice Jews are distinguished from devout gentiles, that is from proselytes (Acts 2,10; 13,43). Paul, too, is talking to Agrippa about 'Jews' in the presence of the Roman governor Festus (Acts 26,2, 3, 4, 7 and 21), whereas he conspicuously avoids the word 'Israel' (compare Acts 26,7 with 28,20). The word 'Jews' occurs only a few times in a meaning not bound to a local group. In that case it's about a kind of summary of everything Paul was subjected to by local groups of Jews (Acts 20,19), or about the Diaspora-Jews in general (Acts 20,21; 21,21).

The word *ioudaios* is not only used for groups of Jews in the Diaspora but also for Jews from Judea and especially from Jerusalem. Then the word especially means 'Judeans' (Acts 12,3 and 11; 21,11 and 20; 22,30; 23,12; 24,9 and 27; 25,2, 7 and 9; 28,19). Here also the word *ioudaios* has the function to describe a certain, small group of Jews. I'd like to point out that Luke doesn't call the Jews from Galilee 'Jews' anywhere. For them he uses the term 'Galileans' or cognate expressions (Luke 13,1 and 2; 22,59; 23,6; Acts 1,11; 2,7; 5,37). Only once all inhabitants of the land of Israel are indicated with the expression 'all the nation of the Jews'. This is not by Jews however, but by gentiles (Acts 10,22).

In a number of situations the word 'Jews' is not used but the word 'Israel'. That is for instance the case when Jews address each other with the words 'men of Israel' (Acts 2,22; 3,12; 5,35; 13,16; 21,28). Or when the subject dealt with surpasses the importance of a small group of Jews (Acts 1,6; 2,36; 4,10, 27; 5,31; 9,15; 10,36; 13,23, 24; 28,20). The Sanhedrin is also described in its representative function for all Israel (Acts 5,21). And finally there are the references to Tanakh in which the word 'Israel' plays a part (Acts 7,23, 42; 13,17). It's clear that this usage of words of Luke's fits in closely with our knowledge on this point of the then Judaism.[300]

The question that should be asked now, is whether or to what extent Luke's usage of the word 'Jews' has a negative undertone. Today the question after any anti-Judaism in the gospels is asked more than once. With regard to Luke it's out of the question, at least in my view. Paul is not only explicitly counted as a Jew when he is put in a bad light by pagans (Acts 16,20), but he also describes himself twice as a Jew (Acts 21,39; 22,3). Other prominent members of the Christian movement are also explicitly described as Jews (Acts 18,2 and 24). Paul even circumcises Timothy, the son of a certain Jewish woman, admitting him to Judaism (Acts 16,1-3).

Quite another matter than the anti-Judaism is the large opposition the apostles and Paul encounter of various Jewish groups in the Acts.

It's not about the fight of an old religion against a rising new religion. It's about an internal Jewish fight for the explanation and the practice of Torah and Tanakh. Wherever Paul arrives, he first gets in touch with the Jews who live there (Acts 9,19-20; 13,5, 14; 14,1; 16,13; 17,1, 17; 18,4; 19,8; 28,17). Only when they reject his teachings, he turns demonstratively to non-Jews in a limited number of cases (Acts 13,46; 18,6). In most cases he leaves for another place (Acts 9,25; 13,6; 17,10, 14; 18,1; 20,1). And once there, he turns again to the Jews initially. The book of the Acts ends in Rome when the discussion among the Jews was still well under way. Luke broke off his story in Rome when in many other places the decisive opposition against Paul got into its stride. So the Acts are an appeal to Judaism and especially the Judaism in the diaspora, to pursue the deliverance of Israel according to the way begun by Jesus. But why did this doctrine meet with so much opposition in large sections of the then Judaism?

I can only go into this matter briefly. Two aspects are important enough to bear in mind. In the first place we saw in the previous chapters that the way of Jesus was a non-violent way. Both the Jews who wanted to maintain the existing power relations and those who wanted to overthrow these relations by violence, wouldn't have regarded Jesus and his followers favourably. But a second issue is at least as important. To free Israel from the Roman yoke one shouldn't fight the pagans, one should convert them, at least that's Luke's point of view. In that way, through their conversion they should play a key role in the deliverance of Israel. Was it this thought that turned out to be unbearable for many Jews?

By way of conclusion I'd like to observe that not all Jews are represented as Paul's adversaries (Acts 14,1; 17,4, 11; 18,8, 20; 19,33; 28,22; cf. also 21,20). In the next section we'll discover that according to Luke there was, among the gentiles too, a strong resistance against the first Christians.

10.2 The Gentiles

The word 'gentiles' is the translation of the Hebrew word *goyim* and the Greek word *ethnos*. Another less emotionally charged translation is 'the nations'. This word refers to the seventy nations that populate the world according to Genesis 10. In Tanakh Israel is usually called in Hebrew: *am*, and in Greek: *laos*.

Who now supposes that Luke had an in essence positive view on the gentiles, is greatly mistaken. The number of statements in Luke's gospel that put the gentiles in bad light is not exactly small. They are presented to the disciples as negative examples (Luke 12,30; 22,25). Jesus will be handed over to them and they will treat him horribly (Luke 18,32). And Jerusalem 'will be trampled by the gentiles' (Luke 21,24). The gentiles are mentioned as adversaries of God and his anointed (Acts 4,25-27). In the days of Joshua it was God who drove them out of the land of Israel (Acts 7,45; 13,19). And all these gentile nations went their own way without taking the slightest notice of the living God (Acts 14,16).

Not only are these statements as clear as anything, but also the gentiles' attitude towards Paul is often a hostile one. In Iconium gentiles and Jews together try to beat up and kill Paul and Barnabas (Acts 14,5). In Lystra Paul and Barnabas hardly manage to dissuade a gentile crowd from worshipping them as gods (Acts 14,14, 18). In Philippi Paul is flogged and imprisoned by the Roman population (Acts 16,22-23). The Athenians reject Paul's teachings (Acts 17,32). And in Ephesus the whole city, led by Demetrius a silversmith, 'rushed into the theatre with one accord' to deal with Paul and his fellow worker (Acts 19, 29-31). And finally Paul will be turned over into the hands of the gentiles (Acts 21,11). So it's not surprising that in Luke's view the gentiles, living in darkness, need a light to bring revelation from Israel (Luke 2,32; Acts 13,47; 26,17-18).

ISRAEL AND THE NATIONS

We should now realize that the intensive contacts between the first Christian Jews and the gentiles were not exactly something new in those days. Especially in the Diaspora the contacts between the Jews and their pagan surroundings had always been numerous. The enormous numbers of Jews in those days can only be explained by the many conversions of gentiles.[a] Besides, around the Jewish communities circles of God-fearing people existed, consisting of gentiles who had not or not yet been converted to Judaism, but who were taught a more Jewish attitude in life and faith in the synagogue. They were not part of the covenant God had made with Israel at Mount Sinai (Exodus 19 f.), but were considered to belong to the so-called Noahide covenant God had made with Noah and his offspring (Genesis 9). So they needn't fulfil all commandments and interdictions of the Torah. They were expected however, to observe a limited number of them: the so-called Noahide laws, rules that belonged to the covenant of Noah. This number of laws was still under discussion in the first century CE. The commandment not to use the name of God in vain was undoubtedly one of them (Exodus 20,7), as well as the commandment not to shed blood (Exodus 20,13). And it is particularly conspicuous that it is Luke who presents us with the oldest list of some of these Noahide laws, about which there was no consensus yet among the rabbis halfway through the first century (Acts 15,20). This enumeration however, agrees largely with the list that will be decided upon later by the rabbis as the 'final result' of a age-long discussion.[301]

Exactly these God-fearing people or those 'who feared God', were the first gentiles who met the followers of Jesus and were impressed by their actions and their teachings (Acts 10,2, 22; 13,16, 26, 43). The first Jewish Christians could build on the already existing relations between Jews and the God-fearing gentiles for their contacts with the gentiles.

---

[a] See section 2.2.

In one respect apparently they went one step further than usual in most Jewish circles.

The gentile God-fearing people attended the synagogue. But the situation was more difficult the other way round. Observing the dietary laws, the laws on purity and many other rules of Torah made it impossible for the Jews to use the hospitality of the God-fearing people. This was especially the case in the land of Israel because here the Torah was observed more strictly than in the Diaspora. In this situation joining Judaism through circumcision could be an obvious solution. Many Jews urged them to do so (Acts 15,1, 5). Many Christian Jews however, took another view in this matter. They not only admitted the God-fearing gentiles in their homes, but they also visited them and ate with them (Acts 11,3). This created a problem with regard to the observance of the Torah. In his letter to the Galatians one can read the radical stand Paul took up in this matter. Luke didn't agree with Paul. In the Acts he makes Peter, the apostles and James, the brother of Jesus, solve the problem differently. In Acts 10 Luke explains that a Jew for the sake of contacts with God-fearing gentiles needn't observe the strict dietary laws when visiting these people. Finally, these God-fearing gentiles were asked to observe a number of basic dietary laws (Acts 15,19-20). It's important however, to stress the point that a Jew is not allowed to neglect the dietary laws at home.

Also the attempt to proselytize the converted gentiles through circumcision (Acts 15,1, 5) is mitigated by Luke (Acts 15,19-20). It was altogether wrong to urge them to be circumcised. But nowhere in the Acts a ban on circumcision of gentiles is found.[a] Again explicitly it is stated that circumcision remains obligatory for Jews (Acts 16,3; 21,21-24). Acts 15 and 21,17-26 show clearly Luke's view on the Christian community. It should consist of a Jewish core living according to Torah, surrounded by a circle of God-fearing gentiles living according to the

---

[a] In Galatians 5,2 Paul doesn't ban circumcision as well, but advises against it urgently.

Israel and the Nations

Noahide Laws. They are allowed to have themselves circumcised and become proselytes, but they needn't do this. That's why the Jewish Christians will be allowed to observe certain Jewish customs less strictly in certain specific circumstances because of their contacts with God-fearing, non-Jewish, fellow-believers (Acts 10).[a] And all important decisions with regard to these issues are made in Jerusalem, in Luke's eyes the centre of the Christian community.

10.3 The Romans

When Luke wrote his gospel and the Acts Jerusalem lay in ruins. The triumphal procession of the Roman general Titus was still fresh in the memory of the Jewish community of Rome. They could have watched the holy temple vessels. In the hands of pagans! Even today one can watch on the triumphal arch of Titus Roman soldiers carrying the menorah, the seven-branched candlestand, triumphantly into Rome as spoils of war. The light that always burned in the temple, for Israel by day and for the seventy nations of the world by night, appeared to be extinguished definitively. What other place could be more suitable to pursue the restoration of the temple of Jerusalem than Rome, the centre of the power in the world?

Many Roman names are mentioned in Luke and the Acts. Many more than names of people of other pagan nations. And they are always the names of soldiers or high administrative officers. Luke writes about them in a way that differs completely with the images the book of Revelation uses for the Roman Empire: the harlot of Babylon and the beast

---

[a] One should be careful however and make no mistakes when interpreting Acts 10. Cornelius is emphatically painted as a pious God-fearing man. The voice in Peter's vision needn't be a divine voice, but can also be a seductive voice. Three times Peter refuses to obey the 'order' to eat unclean animals. And when he visits Cornelius' house Luke avoids mentioning that he uses the meal there.

from the sea.[302] Many commentators think that Luke treats the Romans so friendly in the Acts to show them clearly that the Christian preaching didn't involve any danger for the Roman Empire.[303] But I think that this doesn't do justice to Luke's intentions with regard to the Roman Empire. True, he doesn't emphasize the evil sides of the Roman administration too much, yet his description can't be considered impartial or positive in every respect.

For example, Pilate is shown indeed in all his cruelty (Luke 13,1) and opportunism. He acknowledges Jesus' innocence (Luke 23,22), yet he hands him over to be crucified for opportunistic reasons. The emperor Claudius too, is represented as a persecutor of the Jews (Acts 18,2). The same opportunism that characterizes Pilate, characterizes also the two other governors of Judea described by Luke. Felix keeps Paul imprisoned as a favour to the Judeans, although the term of custody has expired (Acts 24,27). Festus will have him transferred from Caesarea to Jerusalem as a favour to the Judeans again (Acts 25,9), under the pretext towards Agrippa that the Romans are not in the habit of handing over someone by way of a favour (Acts 25,16). Luke demonstrates his critical attitude to the Romans most clearly in the Philippi-story. The Jewish Christians are dangerous for the Roman Empire indeed, exactly because they are Jews: 'and they teach customs which are not lawful for us, being Romans, to receive or observe' (Acts 16,21).

Yet the conclusion should be that Luke's treatment of the Romans is mild in many respects. Perhaps this has something to do with his legal interest in the law.[a] Did he value certain principles of the Roman Law and did he see some starting points for the Jews to bring about the conversion of the Romans? The care for a good progress of a process (Acts 25,16), the possibility of appeal (Acts 25,11), the protection of the suspect against maltreatment (Acts 16,37) are some principles of Roman

---

[a] See section 3.3.

Law – it's true, valid only among Romans – , that are pointedly presented. Although the legal practice of Pilate, the governors of Philippi, Felix and Festus, is corrupt, yet a correct progress of a process is essentially possible. Gallio is an example of this. The Roman principle that the Jews were expected to arrange their own affairs, is maintained by him without any opportunism (Acts 18,12-17). But there is just another thread that runs through the stories of Luke about the Romans.

It's conspicuous that the first gentile that is converted to the way of Jesus is a Roman, a Roman soldier no less! The story of this conversion is even one of the longest in the Acts and takes up one and a half chapter (Acts 10,1 – 11,18). As he often does, Luke describes his final purpose in this first case too: eventually the conversion of the gentiles will result in the disappearance of the militarism that kept the Roman Empire going. A second story worth mentioning in this respect is the story of Paul's meeting with the proconsul of Cyprus, Sergius Paulus, and his conversion (Acts 13,4-12). So the first gentile converted by Paul is a Roman and a Roman governor as well! From the middle of this story on Saul is called Paul, a Latin, Roman name. Now in Tanakh a change of name has always something to do with the need to define someone's part in life more accurately. Here in this story Paul's part is defined by Luke as the part of someone who's got the assignment to try and win the Romans for the way of Jesus. From this need and assignment the theme of his Roman citizenship comes forward (Acts 16, 37-38; 22,25-29) as well as the theme of 'being brought before Caesar' (Acts 27,24). But this part of Paul's is especially meant as an example for his fellow-Jews, because there is no confrontation at all with Caesar or an imperial court in Acts 28. And in this Jewish community of Rome he exclaims: *'because for the hope of Israel* I am bound with these chains' (Acts 28,20). The hope he's talking about is, I think, no other hope for the Jews in those days than the hope of the deliverance of Israel and more especially the deliverance of Jerusalem from the 'dungeon' of Roman rule.

This theme of hope turns up in particular in the story the second part of the Acts begins with.

Immediately after the vision of the Macedonian man (Acts 16,9) Paul does leave for Macedonia. In three days he travels from Troas in Asia Minor to Philippi, named after Philippus, the father of Alexander the Great. Luke describes Philippi as the first town in this part of Macedonia and as a Roman colony. A curious description, because both Troas and Antioch, where Paul had been before (Acts 13,14), were Roman colonies as well but without this mention by Luke.[304] The fact that here Philippi gets the addition 'a Roman colony' must have a special meaning. I think it's because the *Romans* are the leading figures in the Philippi-story. Paul and Silas are being flogged and imprisoned not because they are Christians, but because they are Jews (Acts 16,20-23)! Here as well the essence of the story is not the relation between Christians and Romans, but the relation between the Jews and the Romans. Paul and Silas serve as models for Judaism, not for Christianity! The prison they were put in, is nothing else but the 'dungeon' of the Roman Empire, the same prison Israel was in. Once surrounded by the darkness of their captivity they turn to the essence of their Jewish existence: praising God in their prayers, and then 'the foundations of the prison were shaken; and immediately all the doors were opened'.

In this story Luke tells us, at the beginning of the second part of the Acts, his final purpose: the deliverance of Judaism from the dungeon of the Roman Empire. Perhaps this is the reason too, why he situated this story in the Macedonian town of Philippi. Two and a half centuries ago Israel had been liberated by the Maccabees from the oppression by the Seleucides, the Syrian rulers who were from Macedonia originally. The first book of the Maccabees begins explicitly with the origin of Antioch Epiphanes from Macedonia (1 Maccabees 1,10). Does Luke want to evoke this memory of this deliverance with this story?

The Maccabees' struggle undoubtedly inspired the Zealots of the first century CE very much.[305] Luke pursued the same target as the zealotic movement: the deliverance of Israel from the Roman yoke. But the means he wants to apply to reach this target are essentially different. Here we find in the Acts the continuation of the anti-zealotic polemic, he started in his gospel: the non-violent way is not a way of subordination to Rome. Nonviolence doesn't leave the oppression of Israel alone. Jesus' way to Jerusalem does indicate the ultimate goal, but for the time being it's pursued in the Diaspora. Through the conversion of the gentiles and especially the Romans Israel and Jerusalem will be delivered in the end. In the Acts Luke tries, contrary to the spirit of Zealotism, to persuade the Jews that this way is the way God wants them to follow. History's tragedy is that when the Christian church had conquered Rome, there was no Jewish core left, and it had already long ago removed the liberation of Israel and Jerusalem from its list of principles. How then could we ever return to Luke the Jew?

Notes

1 Ben-Chorin, 1978, p. 91; Den Heyer, 1998, p. 22 f.
2 Adv. Haer. III.1.1.
3 Klijn, 1974, p. 54, 237 f.
4 Geldenhuys, 1950, p. 17.
5 Cf. Thompson, 1972, p. 4-5.
6 Mulder, 1942, p. 186.
7 Mulder, 1942, p. 193.
8 Den Heyer, 1981, p. 16.
9 Mulder, 1942, p. 187.
10 Thompson, 1972, p. 5.
11 Klijn, 1974, p. 155.
12 Klijn, 1974, p. 217 f.
13 E.g.: Klijn, 1974, p. 55; B.H.W., Lucas, Evangelie van.
14 E.g.: Lindijer, 1981, p. 7 f.
15 E.g. Veldhuizen, 1926, p. 24 f.; Caird, 1963, p. 15; Rengstorf, 1969, p. 11.
16 Millgram, 1971, p. 113 f.
17 Rabin, 1976, p. 1032.
18 Green, 1979, p. 13.
19 E.J., Alexandria; Antioch.
20 Safrai, 1978, p. 21.
21 Stern, 1974, p. 122 note 4.
22 Stern, 1974, p. 122.
23 E.J., Rome, The Classical Period.
24 Simon, 1965, p. 98.
25 bT Megillah 8b f.
26 bT Megillah 9a.
27 A New English Translation of the Septuagint, OUD New York 2007, p. 715.
28 Caird, 1963, p. 31. See for the interpretative character of the Septuagint e.g.: Hemelsoet, 1969, p. 9. See also: E.J., Bible, Translations, Greek.
29 E.J., Bible, column 855.
30 jT Megillah 1.71a; M. Megillah 1:8.
31 jT Megillah 1.71a.
32 Smith, 1972, p. 9.
33 Pirke Avot 1,3; E.J., Antigonos.
34 Mussies, 1976, p. 1044.
35 Mussies, 1976, p. 1057.
36 Mussies, 1976, p. 1053; Hengel, 1976, p. 325.
37 Mussies, 1976, p. 1058.

NOTES

38 Mussies, 1976, p. 1054.
39 M. Sotah 9,14.
40 Hengel, 1976, p. 205 f.
41 Mussies, 1976, p. 1054.
42 jT. Megillah 1.71c; Mussies, 1976, p. 1055.
43 bT. Sotah 49b.
44 Mussies, 1976, p. 1045.
45 Where the ratio between the number of Greek and Latin words is 100 to 1 (see: E.J., Greek, column 885).
46 An overview of the most important Semitisms in the Greek tongue can be found in: Mussies, 1976, p. 1048.
47 Mussies, 1976, p. 1049, 1053.
48 Mussies, 1976, p. 1052.
49 Mussies, 1976, p. 1050, 1053.
50 Mussies, 1976, p. 1050.
51 Jos. Apion 1.50.
52 Mussies, 1976, p. 1049 f. counts four groups that form a subdivision of the following groups.
53 Van 't Riet, 1996.
54 Mussies, 1976, p. 1050.
55 Liber Hebr. M.P.L. 23, p. 1002.
56 Schlatter, 1975, p. 27.
57 Barclay, 1975, p. 3; B.H.W., Lucas, Evangelie van.
58 Sparks, J.T.S., XLIV, p. 129-138; Sparks, 1950, p. 16-28; Haencken, 1968, p. 149.
59 Turner, 1955, p. 107.
60 Turner, 1955, p. 103 f.
61 Turner, 1955, p. 106.
62 Winter, 1954, p. 112.
63 Klijn, 1974, p. 54.
64 Schweizer, 1950, p. 1-25. This is the case in the periscopes Luke 1 – 2; 5,1-11; 7,11-17, 36-50; 8,1-3; 9,51-56; 11,27-28; 13,10-17; 14,1-6; 17,11-19; 19,1-10; 23,50 – 24,53.
65 According to Winter (1954) the following scholars are of this opinion: Dalman, Moulton, Harnack, Burkitt, Cadbury and the majority of the English Bible scholars.
66 Winter (1954) gives seven examples.
67 Van 't Riet, 2005, p. 230 f.
68 Sparks, 1950, p. 21. See also: Drury, 1976, p. 82 f.
69 Three quotations from one of the most Semitic oriented publications in this area, written by the Jewish scholar Paul Winter (1954), may serve here to illustrate this: "… the Greek author … was not freely composing his story …"

NOTES

(p. 111); "The First Gospel was written for Jews ... This was not so in the case of the Third Gospel which, like the Second, never had any noticeable distribution amongst Judaeo-Christians ..." (p. 120); "Readers of the Third Gospel, being Gentiles by descend and using the Greek language as a medium of their thought and expression ..." (p. 121). An exception on this general accepted opinion can be found in: Thompson, 1972, p. 10 f.

70 A glance in the Greek edition of the New Testament by Nestle can quickly show this.
71 The same conclusion, although formulated a bit differently, can also be found in: Sparks, 1950, p. 27-28.
72 Jos. Apion 1.1. See also the Letter of Aristeas.
73 Like the so-called Attisists and Asianists before and in the time of Luke.
74 Hanson, 1967, p. 53.
75 Veldhoen, 1924, p. 48.
76 In Greek: rhetor.
77 Hanson, 1967, p. 52.
78 James Hope Moulton, quoted in: Winter, 1956, p. 242.
79 Jos. Apion 1.50.
80 E.g.: Veldhuizen, 1926, p. 106; Geldenhuys, 1950, p. 19-20. Both authors give further references.
81 Cadbury, 1969, p. 39 f.
82 Veldhuizen, 1926, p. 106.
83 E.J.: Medicine, Psychiatry, Psychology.
84 Hanson, 1967, p. 22.
85 Veldhuizen, 1926, p. 75.
86 Van der Kwaak, 1969, p. 127 f.
87 Veldhoen, 1924.
88 Veldhoen, 1924, p. 56-57.
89 Veldhoen, 1924, p. 40-41.
90 Veldhoen, 1924, p. 43, 120-121.
91 Veldhoen, 1924, p. 103.
92 Veldhoen, 1924, p. 104.
93 Veldhoen, 1924, p. 46, 123.
94 Hanson, 1967, p. 6.
95 Veldhuizen, 1926, p. 142.
96 E.g.: Veldhuizen, 1926, p. 141.
97 Hanson, 1967, p. 3-4.
98 Veldhoen, 1924, p. 121-122.
99 Deissmann, 1923, p. 299 f.
100 Veldhoen, 1924, p. 12 f.
101 Hanson, 1967, p. 3.

NOTES

102 Hanson, 1967, p. 2.
103 Hanson, 1967, p. 2.
104 Hanson, 1967, p. 2.
105 Hanson, 1967, p. 7.
106 Veldhoen, 1924, p. 56-57.
107 In section 8.3 the link between Macedonia and Jerusalem will be elaborated once more.
108 Zie bijv.: Veldhuizen, 1926, p. 45; Geldenhuys, 1950, p. 41; Grundmann, 1971, p. 1; Schuman, 1981, p. 11, 12.
109 Zie bijv.: Flusser, 1968, passim; Vermes, 1973, passim.
110 Zie bijv.: Drury, 1977, p. 40.
111 A comprehensible explanation about all these approaches can be found in: De Jonge & Van Duyne, 1982.
112 E.J. onder: Midrash.
113 Drury, 1977, p. 44; Van der Sluis, 1979, p. 380; Van der Sluis, 1980, p. 76 e.v.
114 In later publications as well I paid extensive attention to the midrash-character of the gospels. See e.g. Van 't Riet, 2009, chapter 4; Van 't Riet, 1996, p. 15 f.; Van 't Riet, 2005, passim.
115 Jos. Ant. 18, 116-119.
116 Dodd, 1968, p. 119 f.; De Beus, 1973, p. 85
117 De Beus, 1973, p. 86.
118 The Hebrew text of 2 Kings 1,8 reads: ba'al se'ar, i.e. 'a hairy man'. The Septuagint translates: aner dasus, i.e. 'a man with a full head of hair'. This means that Matthew doesn't quote 2 Kings 1,8 directly in 3,4. He uses Zechariah 13,4 however as a stopover. There the Hebrew text reads: adderet se'ar, i.e. 'a robe of hair'. Furthermore, the expression 'a leather belt' isn't completely in accord with the Hebrew text of 2 Kings 1,8. It is in accord however with the translation the Septuagint renders of this text. The opinion that John the Baptist didn't want to reveal himself as "Elijah redivivus" by means of his clothing (Vielhauer, 1965; see: De Beus, 1973, p. 94), is based on the incorrect supposition that the story of Matthew contains a historical note about the clothing of John. Matthew, however, tells a midrash-story about John in which he identifies him with Elijah. Therefore, Matthew accommodates the description of John's clothing to Zechariah 13,4. In the exegesis of Matthew 3,4 we should involve not only 2 Kings 1,8, but Zechariah 13,4 as well. Then we'll see also the connection between Matthew 3,5-6 and Zechariah 13,1. Zechariah 13 is closely related with Matthew's argumentation about John the Baptist.
119 E.J., Elijah; Ginzberg, 1968, Vol. IV, p. 233 f.
120 E.J., Abraham, col. 116.

121 See: E.J., Zechariah, col. 952. There it is stated that both Zechariahs are sometimes confused in the midrashim. In my opinion these cases are based on identification. In Van 't Riet, 2009, section 2.3.b, I've explained this identifications in Matthew 23,25 more extensively.
122 E.J., Aggada, Historical Aggada.
123 E.J., Jochanan Ben Zakkai.
124 E.J., Aggada, col. 361.
125 See e.g.: Bouhuijs & Deurloo, 1967, p. 23. Recently I've written my book "The Philosophy of the Creation-story" (Dutch title: "De filosofie van het scheppingsverhaal", Kampen 2008) about this issue.
126 E.J., Polemics.
127 For the midrashim of the Ammora'im (the rabbis between 200 and 600 CE) this process of implicit polemics is clearly described in: Urbach, 1979, Vol. 1 p. 184 f.
128 See e.g. the polemic against the Sadducees in Tosefta Nidd. 5,3.
129 E.J., Conflict of Opinion.
130 E.J., Elijah; Ginzberg, 1968, Vol. IV, p. 233 f.
131 See also: Sandmel, 1974, p. 169 f.
132 In: Van 't Riet, 2005, I've discussed these differences in opinion between both evangelists extensively.
133 E.J., Agency.
134 Klijn, 1966, p. 61.
135 Between the stories about the baptism and the death of Jesus Matthew has 975 verses where as Luke has 965. Stories and speeches only in the circle of the disciples or the apostles have 359 verses in Matthew, where as 201 in Luke. This is 36,8% and 20,8% respectively. Stories and lectures in public but with a special position of the disciples or apostles have 110 verses in Matthew and 77 in Luke. This is 11,3% and 8% respectively. These counts are based on the translation of the Dutch Bible Society from 1951, inclusive possible glosses. The first group of verses consists of Matthew 8,14-15, 18-27; 9,37-11,1; 13,10-23, 36-52; 14,22-33; 15,12-20; 16,5-17,13; 17,19-23; 17,25-19,1; 19.10-12; 19,23-20,28; 24,1-26,2; 26,17-47 and Luke 5,4-11, 14-16; 6,12-16; 8,9-18, 22-25; 9,1-6, 10, 18-22, 28-36, 43b-50; 10,2-24; 11,1-13; 16,1-17,10; 17,22-18,8; 18,28-34; 22,14-47. The second group consists of Matthew 5,1-7,28 and Lukas 6,20-49; 12,1-13, 22-53.
136 E.g.. Nielsen, 1979, p. 19; Schmid, 1963, p. 35.
137 Drury, 1976, p. 6 f.; Sandmel, 1974, p. 170.
138 Lapide, 1983, p. 27.
139 Conzelmann, 1963, p. 5-6. In the literature on this subject one can find a division into four we-stories as well (e.g. in Hanson, 1967, p. 21). Defining these stories by coastal areas however is an argument for a division into three

NOTES

parts. The possible break in the second we-story in Acts 20,17-38 takes place explicitly at the coast (see Acts 20,16-17).

140 Hanson, 1967, p. 23. This is a second argument for a division into three we-stories.
141 E.g.. Wikenhauser, 1961, p. 9-10.
142 See also: Hanson, 1967, p. 21 f.
143 Williams, 1964, p. 193; Hanson, 1967, p. 168.
144 Hanson, 1967, p. 23.
145 Jos. Ant. 17,78; 18,123.
146 Tcherikover, 1975, p. 346.
147 Tcherikover, 1975, p. 523 note 5.
148 Mulder, 1980, p. 48.
149 More examples can be found in: Hegermann2, 1973, p. 353.
150 Jos. Apion 2,49-53.
151 Hegermann1, 1973, p. 330.
152 Jos. Ant. 13,285-287, 349-351.
153 E.J., Tiberius Julius Alexander.
154 Tcherikover, 1975, p. 302-303.
155 E.g. Schlatter, 1975, p. 16.
156 E.g. Geldenhuys, 1950, p. 41.
157 E.g. Caird, 1963, p. 14.
158 E.g. Streeter; see also: Geldenhuys, 1950, p. 41, note 3.
159 Thompson, 1972, p. 12.
160 C.f. Dalman; see: Van Veldhuizen, 1926, p. 78.
161 Conzelmann, 1964, p. 23 f.
162 The accuracy of the limitations of these periods is a source of discussion (see for example: Conzelmann, 1964, p. 55 f.). Here I abide by the partition of Conzelmann except that I've put the end of the second period on Luke 19,28 instead of 19,27.
163 The first three were also brought forward by Conzelmann (1964, p. 56) as parallels between period 1 en 2. Remarkably all three have a parallel also in period 3.
164 See section 4.1.
165 See section 7.3.
166 B.H.W., onder: Bethlehem.
167 PRE 10 (Friedlander, p. 66).
168 Noth, 1966, p. 378.
169 E.J., onder: Israel, names.
170 In chapter 7 I'll return to this subject in the context of the travel-story.

Notes

171 Conzelmann, 1964, p. 45.
172 See also: Conzelmann, 1964, p. 46 f.
173 E.J., Pig.
174 E.g. Grundmann, 1971, p. 123; Schuman, 1981, p. 45; even Ginzberg, 1968, Vol. VI, p. 318 note 9 under the influence of the dominant Christian exegeses.
175 Ginzberg, 1968, Vol. IV, p. 197; Vol. VI, p. 318, note 9.
176 Grundmann, 1971, p. 123.
177 E.g.: Grundmann, 1971, p. 123.
178 Conzelmann, 1964, p. 28.
179 E.g. Conzelmann, 1964, p. 24.
180 B.H.W., Naïn.
181 Lapide, 1983, p. 10.
182 Safrai, 1976, p. 747.
183 B.H.W., Bethsaïda.
184 Conzelmann, 1964, p. 61.
185 E.J., Geography.
186 E.J., Geography.
187 E.J., Geography.
188 E.J., Huleh.
189 Daniel-Rops, 1965, p. 362.
190 See also: Daniel-Rops, 1965, p. 362.
191 E.J., Geography.
192 E.J., Gerizim.
193 Conzelmann, 1964, p. 53.
194 E.J., onder: Messiah.
195 Daniel-Rops, 1965, p. 508. See for Jerusalem as the center of the salvation process: Elke Morgen Nieuw, 1978, p. 287 e.v.
196 B.H.W., Samaritanen; Daniel-Rops, 1965, p. 59; Hengel, 1976, p. 353 f.; E.J., Eleazar ben Dinai; Keller, p. 71.
197 Hengel, 1976, p. 167.
198 Hengel, 1976, p. 151 f.; E.J., Zealots.
199 Ginzberg, 1968, Vol. IV, p. 196; Hengel, 1976, p. 172 f.
200 Hengel, 1976, p. 168.
201 Hengel, 1976, p. 172 f.
202 Farmer, 1973, p. 181.

NOTES

203 Like an annotation at Luke 19,11 in the Dutch Petrus Canisius Translation of the Bible suggests. Such an unearthly and a national opinion about the kingdom of God is often connected with a wrong interpretation of the parable of the ten minas.
204 Only the Fourth Gospel can compete with Luke-Acts in this respect (see e.g. Van 't Riet, 1996, p. 145 f., 281 f.).
205 C.f. Klijn, 1974, p. 77.
206 Flusser, 1968, p. 69.
207 E.J., Sages, 640-641. See for Luke 19:45-48 also: Flusser, 1968, p. 109-110.
208 Strack & Billerbeck, Vol. II, 1969, p. 270; Grundmann, 1971, p. 444.
209 Jos. Bell. VII, 6:6.
210 B.H.W., Emmaüs.
211 E.J., Emmaus.
212 E.J., Emmaus.
213 E.J., Emmaus.
214 Ginzberg, Vol. IV, 1968, p. 65.
215 Simon, 1965, p. 98.
216 Hist. Eccl. III 4 6 (see also: Klijn, 1974, p. 54).
217 Klijn, 1974, p. 54, 55.
218 E.J.: Antioch.
219 See c.f. Hanson, 1967, p. 28 f.
220 See also: Veldhoen, 1924, p. 118 f.
221 Hanson, 1967, p. 34, 35.
222 Hanson, 1967, p. 35.
223 Herford, 1962, p. 12. A one-sided and negative image of the Pharisees is found in many Christian commentaries (e.g.: Barclay, 1975, p. 57 f.).
224 Kümmel, 1973, p. 118.
225 See Aschkenasy and Whitlau, 1981, p. 25f.
226 E.J., Pharisees.
227 E.J., Pharisees.
228 E.J., Pharisees.
229 E.J., Righteousness; E.J., Zaddik.
230 E.J., Repentance; E.J., Righteousness.
231 E.J., Pharisees.
232 Neusner, 1973, p. 22.
233 Neusner, 1973, p. 20 f.

NOTES

234 bT Sotah 22a,b; jT Berakhoth IX.5.
235 For the differences between both schools, see: E.J., Bet Hillel and Bet Shammai.
236 Hengel, 1976, p. 340; Mayer, 1980 p. 19.
237 Bowker, 1973, passim.
238 E.J., Bet Hillel and Bet Shammai.
239 Lindijer, 1981, passim.
240 E.J., Prosbul; Mayer, 1980, p. 317, nt. 397.
241 E.J., Hillel.
242 bT Joma 35b; Mayer, 1980, p. 420.
243 bT Shabat 31a. The passage is rather freely translated from the German translation in: Mayer, 1980, p. 227 f.
244 Hengel, 1976, p. 205 f.
245 Pikei Avos 1:12. Dasberg, 1977, p. 193.
246 Conzelmann, 1963, p. 42.
247 bT Gittin 55b-56b.
248 E.J., Gamaliel, column 298.
249 Bowker, 1973, p. 1 f.
250 The saying of Hillel in Pirke Avot 2,5, which will be quoted below in this paragraph, brings forward a "better" prove of the existence of this habit than the examples given in Strack-Billerbeck, 1969, p. 240-241.
251 Pirkei Avos 2,5.
252 Strack-Billerbeck, 1969, p. 189.
253 E.J., Sadducees; Mulder, 1973, p. 21 f.
254 E.J., Sadducees.
255 E.J., Sadducees.
256 bT Kidd. 66a; Mulder, 1973, p. 67.
257 Mulder, 1973, p. 10.
258 E.J., Antigonus of Sokho.
259 E.J., Sadducees.
260 Elke Morgen Nieuw, 1978, p. 159. See also: E.J., Resurrection.
261 Elke Morgen Nieuw, 1978, p. 147 f.
262 Here some manuscripts render 'priests', others render 'chief priests'. Considering Luke's description of the struggle against Jesus and his followers, 'chief priests' is the most probable text variant.
263 E.J., Jew.

NOTES

264 Flusser, 1983, p. 65.
265 Drijver, 1964, p. 152.
266 Hengel, 1976, p. 95; Brandon, 1967, p. 47.
267 Urbach, 1979, p. 595 and p. 958, nt. 20.
268 In my book *De filosofie van het scheppingsverhaal / The philosophy of the Creation narrative* (2008) I showed many examples. See also: Bouhuijs & Deurloo, 1967, p. 23; Beek, 1969, p. 27.
269 Hengel, 1976, p. 345, 346.
270 Hengel, 1976, p. 58, 59.
271 Hengel, 1976, p. 61.
272 E.J., Baeck, Leo.
273 Hengel, 1976, p. 93, 94.
274 Hengel, 1976, p. 296 f.; Brandon, 1967, p. 29, 59.
275 Hengel, 1976, p. 94.
276 See for the Zealots: Brandon, 1967, p. 34, 40, 52, 57.
277 See for the Zealots: Brandon, 1967, p. 56.
278 Hengel, 1976, p. 45.
279 Stern, 1976, p. 577.
280 Stern, 1976, p. 579.
281 Brandon, 1967, p. 33.
282 Brandon, 1967, p. 34, 37, 38, 54.
283 Brandon, 1967, p. 58.
284 See for the Zealots: Brandon, 1967, p. 59 f.
285 Brandon, 1967, p. 60.
286 Hengel, 1976, p. 133, 144.
287 Farmer, 1973, passim.
288 Hengel, 1976, p. 148.
289 See e.g.: B.H.W., Inschrijving.
290 E.J., Quirinius, P. Sulpicius.
291 Brandon, 1967, p. 47, 53.
292 Brandon, 1967, p. 31-40, 52.
293 C.f. the New World Translation.
294 The NKJV has skipped the Hebrew word *minnègèd*, which indicates that they stood there, maybe on the other side of the river Jordan, and watched Elisha at a distance.

NOTES

[295] See for the Dutch discussion about this issue in Matthew: Schoon, 1983, passim.
[296] Schoon, 1983, p. 20. Compare also the use of the Hebrew word *am* ('people') in the expression *am ha-arets* ('people of the country') by the rabbis.
[297] Schoon, 1983, too doesn't refer to the zealotic background of the gospels at all.
[298] E.J., Archelaus; Dijk, 1980, p. 65-66.
[299] For all these data, see: E.J.: Jew.
[300] See: E.J.: Jew.
[301] E.J.: Noachide laws.
[302] E.g.: Kroon, Undated, p. 105 f., 133 f.
[303] Conzelmann, 1963, p. 10; Hanson, 1967, p. 8, 9.
[304] B.H.W.: Antiochië2 and Troas.
[305] Farmer, 1973, passim.

Literature

English literature

E.J.	Encyclopaedia Judaica, Jeruzalem, 1972.
J.P.	The Jewish People in the First Century, Vol. 1 en 2, S. Safrai, M. Stern (Ed.), Assen/Amsterdam, 1974 en 1976.
J.T.S.	The Journal of Theological Studies.
N.T.S.	New Testament Studies.
PRE	Pirke de Rabbi Eliezer, G. Friedlander, New York, 1970.

Barclay, W., *The Gospel of Luke*, Edinburgh, 1975.
Bowker, J., *Jesus and the Pharisees*, Cambridge, 1973.
Brandon, S.G.F., *Jesus and the Zealots*, Manchester, 1967.
Cadbury, H.J., *Style and literary method of Luke*, New York, 1969.
Caird, G.B., *Saint Luke*, Harmondsworth, 1963.
Dodd, C.H., *The interpretation of the fourth gospel*, Cambridge, 1968.
Drury, J., *Tradition and Design in Luke's Gospel*, Atlanta, 1976.
Efird, J.M. (Ed.), *The Use of the Old Testament in the New and other Essays*, Durham, 1972.
Farmer, W.R., *Maccabees, Zealots and Josephus*, Westport, 1973.
Geldenhuys, N., *Commentary on the Gospel of Luke*, London/Edinburgh, 1950.
Ginzberg, L., *The legends of the Jews*, Deel I t/m VII, Philadelphia, 1968.
Hanson, R.P.C., The Acts, Oxford, 1967.
Herford, R.T., *The Pharisees*, Boston, 1962.
Hertz, J.H., *The Authorized Daily Prayer Book*, London, 1976.
Millgram, A., *Jewish Worship*, Philadelphia, 1971.
Mussies, G., Greek in Palestine and the Diaspora, in: *J.P.*, Vol. 2, 1976.
Neusner, J., *Invitation to the Talmud*, New York, 1973.
Rabin, Ch., Hebrew and Aramaic in the First Century, in: *J.P.*, Vol. 2, 1976.
Riet, P. van 't, *Reading Torah, The Key to the Gospels*, E-book, Folianti, Zwolle, 2012.
Safrai, S., Home and Family, in: *J.P.*, Vol. 2, 1976.
Sandmel, S., *A Jewish Understanding of the New Testament*, New York, 1974.
Smith, D.M., The Use of the Old Testament in the New, in: *Efird, 1972*, p. 3 e.v.
Sparks, H.F.D., The Semitisms of St. Luke's Gospel, *J.T.S. XLIV*, no. 175-6, p. 129-138.
Sparks, H.F.D., The Semitisms of the Acts, *J.T.S. n.s. 1*, 1950, p. 16-28.
Stern, M., The Jewish Diaspora, in: *J.P.*, Vol. 1, 1974.

LITERATURE

Stern, M., Aspects of Jewish Society: The Priesthood and other Classes, in: *J.P.*, Vol. 2, 1976.
Tcherikover, V., *Hellenistic Civilization and the Jews*, New York, 1975.
Thompson, G.H.P., *The Gospel according to Luke*, Oxford, 1972.
Turner, N., The Relation of Luke 1 and 2 to Hebraic Sources and to the Rest of Luke-Acts, *N.T.S.*, Vol. 2, No. 2, 1955, p. 100-109.
Urbach, E.E., *The sages*, Deel I en II, Jeruzalem, 1979.
Vermes, G., *Jesus the Jew*, Londen, 1973.
Williams, C.S.C., *The Acts of the Apostles*, London, 1964.
Winter, P., Some Observations on the Language in the Birth and Infancy Stories of the Third Gospel, *N.T.S.*, Vol. 1, No. 2, 1954, p. 111-121.
Winter, P., On Luke and Lucan Sources, *Zeitschrift für die Neutestamentische Wissenschaft*, 47. Band, 1956, p. 217-242.

German literature

Ben-Chorin, Sch., Paulus : *Der Völkerapostel in jüdischer Sicht*, 1978, Jerusalem/München.
Conzelmann, H., *Die Apostelgeschichte*, Tübingen, 1963.
Conzelmann, H., *Die Mitte der Zeit*, Tübingen, 1964.
Deissmann, A., *Licht vom Osten*, Tübingen, 1923.
Flusser, D., *Jesus*, Reinbek, 1968.
Grundmann, W., *Das Evangelium nach Lukas*, Evangelische Verlagsanstalt, Berlijn, 1971.
Hegermann[1], H., Das Griechischsprechende Judentum, in: *Literatur und Religion*, p. 328-352, Würzburg, 1973.
Hegermann[2], Philon von Alexandria, in: *Literatur und Religion*, p. 353-369, Würzburg, 1973.
Hengel, M., *Die zeloten*, Leiden/Köln, 1976.
Kümmel, W.G., *Einleitung in das Neue Testament*, Heidelberg, 1973.
Mayer, R., *Der Talmud*, München, 1980.
Noth, M., Geschichte Israels, Göttingen, 1966.
Rengstorf, K.H., *Das Evangelium nach Lukas*, Göttingen, 1969.
Safrai, S., *Das Jüdische Volk im Zeitalter des Zweiten Tempels*, Neukirchen, 1978.
Schlatter, A., *Das Evangelium des Lukas*, Stuttgart, 1975.
Schweizer, E., Eine hebraisierende Sonderquelle des Lukas?, *Theologische Zeitschrift*, Vol. 6, No. 3, 1950, p. 1-25.
Strack, H.L., Billerbeck, P., *Kommentar zum Neuen Testament aus Talmud und Midrasch*, 2. Band, München, 1969.
Vielhauer, Ph., *Aufsätze zum Neuen Testament*, München, 1965.
Wikenhauser, A., *Die Apostelgeschichte*, Regensburg, 1961.

LITERATURE

Dutch literature

B.H.W.   Bijbels-Historisch Woordenboek, Deel 1 t/m 6, B. Reicke, L. Rost (Red.), Utrecht/Antwerpen, 1969.

Aschkenasy, Y., Whitlau, W.A.C., Joodse Hermeneutiek, in: *Geliefd is de mens*, B. Folkertsma Stichting voor Talmudica, Hilversum, 1981.

Barnard, W.J., Riet, P. van 't, *Zonder Tora leest niemand wel*, Bouwstenen voor een leeswijze van de evangeliën gebaseerd op Tenach en joodse traditie, Kampen, 1986.

Barnard, W.J., Riet, P. van 't Riet, *Als een duif naar het land Assur*, Het boek Jona verklaard vanuit Tenach en rabbijnse traditie tegen de achtergrond van de tijd, Kampen, 1986.

Beek, M.A., *Wegen en voetsporen van het Oude Testament*, Amsterdam, 1969.

Beus, Ch. de, *Johannes' getuigenis van het woord*, Nijkerk, 1973.

Bouhuijs, K., Deurloo, K.A., *Dichter bij Genesis*, Amsterdam, 1967.

Daniel-Rops, H., *Het dagelijks leven in Palestina ten tijde van Jezus*, Utrecht/Antwerpen, 1965.

Dijk, J., *Het begon in Jeruzalem*, Ede, 1980.

Drijver, P., *Over de Psalmen*, Utrecht/Antwerpen, 1964.

Elke morgen nieuw, Inleiding tot de Joodse gedachtenwereld aan de hand van het Achttiengebed, samengesteld door D.J. van der Sluis e.a., B. Folkertsma Stichting voor Talmudica, 1978.

Flusser, D., *De laatste dagen in Jeruzalem*, Kampen, 1983.

Green, M., *Evangelieverkondiging in de Eerste Eeuwen*, Goes, 1979.

Hemelsoet, B., Talen en Vertalen, in: *De Bijbel, Zoals er gezegd is over*, Deel 30, Bussum/Antwerpen, 1969.

Heyer, C.J. den, 'Oude wijn is voortreffelijk', *Verkenning en Bezinning 14*, nr. 4, Kampen, 1981.

Heyer, C.J. den, *Paulus : Man van twee werelden*, Zoetermeer, 1998.

Jonge, M. de, Duyne, H.M.J. van, *Van tekst tot uitleg*, 's-Gravenhage, 1982.

Keller, W., *En zij werden verstrooid onder alle volken*, Zwolle, z.j.

Klijn, A.F.J., Discipel en Apostel, in: *De kring der Leerlingen, Zoals er gezegd is over*, Deel 20, p. 61-65, Bussum/Antwerpen, 1966.

Klijn, A.F.J., *De Wordingsgeschiedenis van het Nieuwe Testament*, Utrecht, 1974.

Kroon, K.H., *Openbaring, Verklaring van een bijbelgedeelte*, 2 Delen, Kampen, z.j.

Kwaak, H. van der, *Het proces van Jezus*, Assen, 1969.

Lapide, P., *Hij leerde in hun synagogen*, Een joodse uitleg van de evangeliën, Baarn, 1983.

Lindijer, C.H., *De armen en rijken bij Lucas*, 's-Gravenhage, 1981.

LITERATURE

Mulder, H., *Lukas, Zijn taak en plaats in de heilsgeschiedenis*, Baarn, 1942.
Mulder, H., *De sadduceeën*, Amsterdam, 1973.
Mulder, H., *Proselieten tussen Ja en Nee*, Kampen, 1980.
Nielsen, J.T., *Het Evangelie naar Lukas I*, De Prediking van het Nieuwe Testament, Nijkerk, 1979.
Riet, P. van 't, *Het evangelie uit het leerhuis van Lazarus*, Een speurtocht naar de joodse herkomst van het vierde evangelie, Baarn, 1996.
Riet, P. van 't, *Lukas versus Matteüs, De terugkeer van de midrasj bij de uitleg van de evangeliën*, Kampen, 2005.
Riet, P. van 't, *De filosofie van het scheppingsverhaal, Genesis 1 opnieuw belicht*, Kampen, 2008.
Schmid, J., *Het Evangelie volgens Lucas*, Het Nieuwe Testament met Commentaar, Bilthoven, 1963.
Schoon, S., 'Zijn bloed over ons en over onze kinderen', Een tekst en zijn uitwerking, *Verkenning en Bezinning 16*, nr. 4, Kampen, 1983.
Schuman, N.A., *Een reisverhaal, Leesoefeningen in Lucas*, 's-Gravenhage, 1981.
Simon, M., *De Joodse Sekten ten tijde van Jezus*, Amsterdam, 1965.
Sluis, D.J. van der, Jesus is the Messiah...and the Jews be damned, *Wending*, 1979, no. 6.
Sluis, D.J. van der, 'Daarmee help je de openbaringsgeschiedenis om zeep', *Wending*, 1980, no. 1.
Tussen Oud en Nieuw, Deuterokanonieke of Apokriefe Boeken, Amsterdam, 1975.
Veldhoen, N.G., *Het Proces van den Apostel Paulus*, Alphen aan de Rijn, 1924.
Veldhuizen, A. van, *Lukas de Medicijnmeester*, Kampen, 1926.

About the author

Dr. S.P. (Peter) van 't Riet (1948) studied mathematics and psychology at the Free University of Amsterdam and wrote his thesis on an educational-psychological subject. He was successively a teacher of mathematics at a school for secundary education, teacher of the didactics of mathematics at the Technical University of Delft, manager at the Teacher Training Centre of Zwolle, director and professor at the Windesheim University of Zwolle.

Since the seventies he has studied the Judaism of the first centuries as well as the Jewish exegesis of the Bible, especially the Jewish character of the New Testament. He published the following titles in Dutch (the first four together with his fellow-author Will J. Barnard):

- Luke, the Jew (1984)
- Reading Tora, the Key to the Gospels (1986)
- As a Dove to the Land of Assur (1988)
- Catching the Coat-tail of a Jewish Man (1989)
- The Gospel from the Study-house of Lazarus (1996)
- Luke, the Jew (2e revised edition, 1997)
- Christianity à la Jesus (2001)
- Luke versus Matthew (2005)
- The Image of Man in the Torah (2006)
- The Philosophy of the Creation-story (2008)
- Luke, the Jew (3e revised edition, 2009)
- Reading Tora, the Key to the Gospels (2e revised edition, 2010)

In 2012 two English translation were published as e-books: *Reading Tora, the Key to the Gospels* and *Luke, the Jew,* in 2014 followed by *The Image of Man in the Tora* and in 2018 by *A Dove to the Land of War*. More information about these and other publications of the author can be found on his website: www.petervantriet.nl.

www.ingramcontent.com/pod-product-compliance
Lightning Source LLC
Chambersburg PA
CBHW060509090426
42735CB00011B/2150